ALBAN BERG

ALBAN BERG

A biography by
KAREN MONSON

M&J

MACDONALD GENERAL BOOKS
Macdonald and Jane's – London and Sydney

© 1979 Karen Monson

First published in the United States of America in 1979 by
Houghton Mifflin Company, Boston

First published in Great Britain in 1980 by
Macdonald General Books
Macdonald and Jane's Publishers Limited
Paulton House
8 Shepherdess Walk
London N1 7LW

ISBN 0 354 04464 8

Printed in Great Britain by
Richard Clay (The Chaucer Press) Ltd

Acknowledgments

MUCH OF THE RESEARCH for this book was done for a radio series broadcast on WFMT in Chicago in April and May of 1977. My thanks go to Lois Baum, Norman Pellegrini, Ray Nordstrand, and others at the station for their help and encouragement, and to Bob Crawford, who first suggested the book.

Thanks for help in my research go to the staffs of the Austrian National Library and the City Library of Vienna, to Mrs. Egon Wellesz, Mrs. Charles Kessler, Erich Alban Berg, Ernst Krenek, Paul Pisk, and the others in Vienna, Los Angeles, Palm Springs, Chicago, and New York who shared their memories and their own discoveries with me. And, most of all, to the friends who, even when they had doubts, kept saying the book could be done.

— Karen Monson

Contents

Illustrations

FOLLOWING PAGE 174

Alban Berg in 1904. Courtesy of the Portrait Collection, Austrian National Library, Vienna.

Arnold Schoenberg, about 1910. Courtesy of the Arnold Schoenberg Institute, Los Angeles.

Helene Berg in 1916. Courtesy of the Portrait Collection, Austrian National Library.

Smaragda Berg, by Edith Stengel. Courtesy of the Portrait Collection, Austrian National Library.

Alma Mahler by Oskar Kokoschka. Private collection, Chicago. Photograph by Michael J. Pado.

Helene Berg's family home in Hietzing. Photograph by Robert M. Lightfoot III.

The Bergs' home at Trauttmansdorffgasse, Hietzing. Photograph by Robert M. Lightfoot III.

Berg as drawn by F. A. Doblin. Courtesy of the Portrait Collection, Austrian National Library.

Berg with a portrait of Mahler in the background. Courtesy of the Portrait Collection, Austrian National Library.

Hanna Fuchs-Robettin. Photograph courtesy of the *New York Times.*

Evelyn Lear and Andrew Foldi in *Lulu,* as produced by the San Francisco Opera, 1965.

Anja Silja as Lulu, San Francisco. 1971. Photograph by Ken Howard.

Geraint Evans as Wozzeck in the Royal Opera House, Covent Garden production. Photograph by Reg Wilson.

Scenes from the Royal Opera House, Covent Garden production of *Wozzeck,* starring Geraint Evans. Photographs by Reg Wilson.

Alban Berg, about 1935. Courtesy of the Portrait Collection, Austrian National Library.

Introduction

THEY WERE beautiful people — Alban Berg; his wife, Helene; his sister, Smaragda — walking arm in arm into the concert halls of the Musikverein building, the Opera, theaters, cafés, galleries, all of Vienna's best places. They were the kind of people the Viennese loved to talk about: on the surface, they satisfied the precious, conservative values of *alt Wien;* underneath, they suggested mystery, even scandal.

Everyone who remembers them recalls the beauty of the tableau. The Bergs were young and fashionable — the tall, aristocratic, delicately featured man in well-tailored suits; his softly blond wife, with a curl of hair peeking out from under a black cloche; the chic sister, her sharp, dark eyes gleaming defiantly. Their air of haughtiness inspired curiosity. And they were members of the circle envied even by members of the Austrian high society, the cultural elite.

They were cultivated but vulnerable. On one level or another, they all practiced the art closest to the souls of the Viennese: music. Helene Nahowski Berg had studied

voice and piano before she gave up thoughts of a career
on the operatic stage to act the role of a wife. Smaragda
was an exceptional pianist and chamber musician in her
youth, before she married, divorced, and lived quietly
but openly as a lesbian.

And Alban Berg was one of the most successful composers in the world. The Viennese loved his success —
though they did not much like his music. It was hard for
the city's music lovers to admit that they had to rely on
Berg to maintain the cultural supremacy they had as-
serted for more than a century, back through the reigns
of Gustav Mahler, Hugo Wolf, Anton Bruckner, Johannes Brahms, Franz Schubert, Ludwig van Beethoven,
Josef Haydn, and Wolfgang Amadeus Mozart. Not all of
these composers had spent significant periods of time in
Vienna, but all of them lived there long enough for the
Viennese to claim to have had a nurturing role in their careers. Berg, however, made his principal home in Vienna
for all of his fifty years, only to hear from National So-
cialist politicians, toward the end of his life, that his
works were not those of an "indigenous" composer and
would, therefore, not be performed in the German-
speaking world.

The Austrians were caught unprepared when their political system, their currency, and their cultural values
crumbled with the Hapsburg empire as the nineteenth
century died and the twentieth century began. The last
thing conservative Viennese audiences wanted to admit
was that the pretty, peaceful music that had served them
so well for so long was being displaced by other, less
well-mannered and pleasant sounds that better mirrored
the tumult of the era. But music was changing, and Berg
was the one who could lead his countrymen, most sym-
pathetically and most provocatively, in this new aesthetic

direction. Although his friends and colleagues often had
to explain their links with the musical past in words and
theories, Berg unabashedly wrote his ties with history
into his scores for all to hear. He shared with his compa-
triots a nostalgia for the good old days. His was music
that linked the present to the past, instead of charging
boldly into the future. If the Viennese preferred their
composers dead, at least they had to admit that Berg's
music let them remember past glories. There was something almost soothing about a musician whose work implied that new challenges could be faced without the denial of old accomplishments.

What was no less significant, Berg's music had flair.
His gift for drama did more than make him the man who
brought opera into the twentieth century; it permeated
even the smallest and most potentially abstract of his
works. Musical theories and systems never supplanted an
essential humanism in Berg, a conviction that tones were
sounded not from a vague, airy unknown, but by men
and women with hands and brains. Berg's music seemed
to communicate on such a personal level that some people speculated whether the composer might have been
writing old-fashioned "program" music, works with
stories implied in them, though it was unlikely anyone so
modern would have resorted to such gimmicky devices.
In fact, Berg *was* writing program music, but it took fifty
years for listeners to find the program. An uncovered
love affair that lasted through the final decade of the composer's life helped explain what listeners had sensed all
along: passion ran deep in Berg's music, just as it ran
deeper in the man himself than anyone knew.

Berg was the romantic of the New Viennese School,
which was headed by the controversial and dictatorial Arnold Schoenberg. The fact that Berg was not merely a

student, but a staunch disciple and surrogate son of Schoenberg both helped and hurt him. Without his teacher's authoritarian direction, Berg might never have become a musician at all. But as a member of Schoenberg's inner circle, the younger composer was immediately — and, in general, unfairly — classified as a radical, a revolutionary, a slave to the master's techniques. Olin Downes wrote the inevitable pun into a review of Berg's works in the *New York Times* of October 29, 1926: "The music of Alban Berg . . . is tenuous stuff, brain-spun, labored and self-conscious, diluted with Schoenberg, who, in spite of his name, is no more beautiful than his pupil."

Even Downes's turn on the German *schoen* (beautiful) carried with it the implication that something about Berg set him off — for better or for worse — from his master and his fellow students in Schoenberg's school. Berg's romanticism, his sense of drama and his theatricality distinguished him in the musical triumvirate he formed with Schoenberg and Anton von Webern. Berg was the one of the three who would receive the applause of an international public. He did so by giving new life to an art form so impractical, so unrealistic, and so apparently anti-modern, that it had been proclaimed dead.

The plaque on the wall of the apartment building where Berg lived in the Vienna suburb of Hietzing describes him as the composer of *Wozzeck,* the opera that brought him fame, and even a small fortune, after its first performance, in 1925. The Viennese city fathers singled out *Wozzeck;* much of the rest of the world would have also mentioned *Lulu,* Berg's controversial and mysterious second opera, which he was completing at the time of his death, in December 1935. For forty-four years, *Lulu* was known to the public only as a fragment. Its reputation rested on its first two acts; the third, with notes still to be filled in and finishing touches to be added, lay under lock and key, the subject of a wild array of extrasensory perceptions, legal battles, and musicological arguments. *Wozzeck* made Berg a star; *Lulu* became a cause célèbre. *Lulu* is the masterpiece, yet a cast of characters colorful enough to form an opera plot of their own kept Berg's final and most fascinating work from being performed in its entirety until 1979.

There are still people in Vienna who cannot believe that such a kind, reserved, gentlemanly person as Alban Berg could have written the sexy, lurid *Lulu*. They are like the people who listened to the conservative romantic idealists and not to Karl Kraus; who refused to admit that Gustav Klimt painstakingly painted genitalia underneath the heavily decorated skirts of his society models; who saw none of the relationships between Klimt's golden ornamentation, which they liked, and Egon Schiele's bleeding nudes, which they did not. These were the people who wanted to believe that Alban and Helene Berg had a perfect marriage, and who were unwilling to recognize the truth about the composer's illegitimate daughter and his secret love affair.

There are composers whose lives seem entirely detached from their works. Alban Berg is not among them. When a Bach chorale turns up in the taut, virtuoso Violin Concerto; when a cabaret song cuts through the densely woven twelve-tone fabric of an opera, the personality of the creator makes itself felt. Imagination is the key not only to high art, but also to high entertainment. Hoelderlin said, "To live is to defend a form." Kraus wrote, "One should grind one's heel into the faces of all rationalistic helpers of 'normal men,' who give reassurance to people unable to appreciate the works of wit and fantasy."

Very little in this book is imagined. I have occasionally

surmised how Berg may have felt, but never what he did or said. I have filled in some details, but the outline was all there. By knowing more about the man, it is possible for us to come closer to the music, even though, in Berg's case, it was the music itself that hid the secrets of the man.

Alban Berg

Chapter 1

Early Life

IN 1885, Johannes Brahms was writing his Fourth Symphony, Grover Cleveland became the twenty-second President of the United States, the American Telephone & Telegraph Company was organized, Gilbert and Sullivan introduced *The Mikado,* and Dr. Chichester A. Bell and Charles S. Tainter invented the wax-cylinder Graphophone, the sire of the phonograph. Lilli Lehmann made her American debut singing Carmen at the Metropolitan Opera, while, also in New York, Richard Genée's comic opera *Nanon, the Hostess of the Golden Lamb* was enjoying long runs in both German and English. Civil War heroes Ulysses S. Grant and George B. McClellan died; so did William Henry ("The public be damned") Vanderbilt. Conductor Otto Klemperer was born in Breslau, Germany; composer Edgar Varèse was born in Paris.

Also born, on February 9, 1885, in Vienna, was Albano Maria Johannes Berg, son of Conrad Berg, aged thirty-nine, and Johanna Maria Anna Braun Berg, aged thirty-four. The *o* appears to have been dropped from

"Albano" almost immediately, and forever; it appears on
the birth register but on no subsequent documents. The
baby boy's unusual Christian name was suggested by a
friend of Conrad Berg's, the Greek consul in Vienna,
who also came up with the name "Smaragda" for the
Bergs' only daughter.

Alban Maria Johannes spent his early years in a flat at
Tuchlauben 8, in an elegant old building called the
Schoenbrunner House because of its distinguished past
and its clear but modest resemblance to the 1441-room
summer residence of the ruling Hapsburgs on the outskirts of Vienna, Schloss Schoenbrunn. The Bergs lived
on what they counted as the third floor and Americans
count as the fourth. Below them was a music store, as
well as the home of the Vienna Society for the Arts,
where the Secession movement began. The birthplace of
the Vienna Philharmonic Orchestra and the old Haslinger
establishment, where music by both Beethoven and
Schubert was published, were across the street, neighbors
to businesses that still number among Vienna's most
prestigious. Mozart had met his future wife, Constanze
Weber, in a house nearby. And only a few steps separated
Tuchlauben 8 from the pure Baroque St. Peter's Church,
the avenue called the Graben, which was the city moat in
medieval times, and the Gothic tower of St. Stephen's
Cathedral, the center point of a city that grew out in con-
centric rings.

Alban's paternal grandfather, Josef Sebastian Berg, was
born in Munich and moved to the old university town of
Nuremberg. A veteran, he was able to obtain a license
from King Maximilian I of Bavaria to open a beer hall. In
a suburb of Nuremberg called Woehrd, Conrad Berg was
born, on August 30, 1846. At twenty-one, he left Bavaria
for Vienna, where he found work at the export house of
Edward Kanitz. He also opened a shop where he sold the

books and icons that are still so much a part of Viennese Catholicism.

In 1871, the son of the beer-hall keeper married up in the world. Johanna Braun's family had been in Vienna for more than a century; her father, Franz Xaver Melchior Braun, had achieved the rank of court jeweler. His intricate and ornate creations in gold and precious stones were perfectly suited to Viennese tastes. Franz Braun was also a regular concertgoer, with enough training to be able to re-create on his parlor piano what he had heard at a performance. It was Johanna, then, who brought appreciation of music and art to the Berg household, though her tastes were distinctly bourgeois. Like most of her neighbors, she was a collector of dust-catching *Kitsch* — trinkets, statuettes, and similar frivolous objects that adorned both horizontal and vertical surfaces and turned apartments into obstacle courses for playful children.

Conrad and Johanna Berg had three sons and a daughter: Hermann, born in 1872; Carl, known as Charly, born in 1881; Alban; and Smaragda, born in 1886. Hermann followed his father into the import-export business and immigrated to New York City while Alban was still a child. There, he made his fortune as a junior partner of a large firm specializing in porcelain, toys, and linens.

The three younger Berg children grew up in relatively active and affluent surroundings. Their ebullient mother, who knew both English and French, took great interest in her husband's business, and determinedly maintained her good health and high spirits. Conrad Berg was her opposite, calm, quiet, and weakened by a failing heart. There were no great outpourings of emotion in the household, but neither was there any artificial formality. Johanna was a down-to-earth woman, with businesslike attitudes and a love of freedom for both her children and herself.

In his early years, Alban took after his mother. He was sturdy and plump, mentally quick, conscientious in school, and easily amused, even mischievous. As he turned thirteen, though, he suddenly came to resemble his father, both physically and emotionally. He grew tall and very thin, and began to exhibit the artistic, aristocratic good looks that were to stay with him until his death. He lost the robust good health he had enjoyed through his childhood and began to have difficulties with his schoolwork. His mind wandered, and he tended to get lost in romantic introspection. As he gave up interest in school, he discovered the arts. No amount of fascination or devotion could make him a genius, however. Alban was smart but by no means precocious.

The young Berg's emotional turns and mental waywardness must have frustrated his teachers. In 1895, the ten-year-old completed his five classes at the lower school and passed into the neighborhood *Oberrealschule,* a secondary school whose curriculum did not include instruction in the classics. He studied religion, German, French, history, mathematics, natural science, drawing, and gymnastics; later, he was taught physics, chemistry, and English. Through the first four years, Alban's grades were usually "satisfactory," sometimes "praiseworthy." But in the fifth level, German and geometry gave him problems; he preferred to write his own language without following rules of punctuation and syntax, and he had no patience for memorizing geometric proofs. He passed on to the next class only after repeating the geometry test.

His academic troubles continued, however, and he repeated both the sixth and seventh levels, stumbling over English, math, and, once again, German. Two years behind schedule, the nineteen-year-old at last passed his final examinations at the *Oberrealschule* in May 1904. He

took both oral and written tests; one of the assignments
was to write an essay entitled "Science Is Power."

Even in Vienna, the city in the world most vocifer-
ously proud of its cultural heritage, the fine arts were all
but ignored in the schools. Responsibility for investing
children with a love of music and painting rested with the
parents, and Conrad and Johanna Berg evidently met this
challenge with some enthusiasm, if not necessarily with
sophistication. When the old Burgtheater was demol-
ished, Conrad bought its pipe organ at auction and had it
installed in the spacious flat — not so much for its musical value as for its novelty as an object. But the instrument did get played, by the great composer and
organist Anton Bruckner, among others. Bruckner
would visit Tuchlauben 8 from time to time; Alban later
remembered the distinguished old Herr Professor kissing
his mother's hand. These visits were probably the child's
first close contact with a professional musician.

The children were taken to galleries, the theater, concerts, and the opera (where they sat up in the fourth
gallery). There was music at home, as well. Ernestine
Goetzlick, hired to be Smaragda's governess and valued
as the "family pearl," concentrated on teaching the children music and French. Smaragda was a gifted pianist;
she went on to study with Theodor Leschetizky, the
Czerny-trained autocrat who taught Ignacy Paderewski,
Artur Schnabel, and Ignaz Friedman. Simply by being accepted to study with Leschetizky, Smaragda practically
assured herself of a career in music. She went no further,
however, than to achieve a modest reputation as a
chamber-music player.

Brother Charly's gifts were vocal. Though there was
never much chance that he could or would earn his living
singing, his baritone voice was later to carry him into the

popular Udel Quartet, named for the director of the
chorus at the Vienna Opera. As a teen-ager, Charly sang
folk tunes as well as the great *Lieder* of Schubert, Schumann, Wolf, and Brahms for audiences of family and
friends, with his sister accompanying him at the piano.

Alban was the one of the three younger Bergs with the
least conspicuous musical talents. The boy was drawn to
the piano more by curiosity and by a desire to do what
his sister was doing than by any natural gift. Miss Goetzlick did teach him some rudimentary piano technique,
but Alban was no more thrilled by music than he was by
literature, poetry, drawing, or the theatrical presentations
the children devised under the governess's direction for
the amusement of their parents. As a child, he drew with
what he later called "a certain facility that I mistook for
talent." Then he decided he would become a great poet,
and turned his attention (often during class) to scribbling
verses and dramas of prodigious length and pomp.

If his industry occasionally failed him, his imagination
did not. Berg's favorite correspondent and confidant during his teen-age years was Hermann Watznauer, a Viennese civil servant who made the acquaintance of the Berg
family in 1899, when he was twenty-four and Alban was
fourteen. Some of the younger man's letters to his mature
and sympathetic friend went on for thirty handwritten
pages; they were full of the blood and tears of youth —
partly sincere, no doubt, but also stylish and self-consciously sensitive. In November 1903, Watznauer received
the following romanticized portrait of an evening at home
(the punctuation is Berg's):

> My dear Hermann, you left us on Thursday . . . melan-
> choly — as is unfortunately always the case with me —
> followed on the heels of gaiety!! I was attacked again by that
> old life-pain, which clings to me like some old inherited ill. I

had little to do — it was soon done — and then I felt the tug
of the piano. I wanted to hold on to the first impression
awakened in me by that poem of Hofmannsthal's: *"Hoertest
du denn nicht hinein, dass Musik das Haus durchdrang"* [Don't
you hear music ringing all through the house] . . . I got that
far, but could not get any farther — then I read a little in
Poesy and Truth — but it gave me hardly any pleasure! — At
last it was evening. Then, to the suffering of my soul was
added a physical pain; but it was still such as I consider a
beautiful pain. We dined. Then a little more music: Grieg's
magnificent *Autumn* Overture — just right for my mood —
then the many beautiful things from *Dalibor*. We went to
bed. I lay there with a heavy heart — I had that feeling,
when one clutches at one's oppressed heart and wants only to
plead: "Oh, please let it go slower — quite quiet and gentle — be still!" — and thus I went to sleep, in the happy conviction: for ever —

As was his habit in his high-drama years right after the
turn of the century, Berg signed his letter with a big
black cross.

The recipient of this Wertheresque *Sturm und Drang*,
Watznauer, was Alban's surrogate father, friend, mentor,
and catalyst. Few of Berg's schoolmates had time or patience for his poetic indulgences, which also went against
Johanna Berg's nature. To her, there was no such thing as
"beautiful pain," and, besides, there had been too many
domestic disruptions to allow her to keep her mind on
anything as impractical as *Poesy and Truth*. In 1899, the
family had moved out of the center of the city into a
larger dwelling in Vienna's VII District (then Breitegasse
8, now Karl-Schwerighoffergasse 8). There, on March
30, 1900, Conrad Berg died of heart disease; his youngest
son was just fifteen. He had sensed for some time that his
heart was going to fail, and had, with good reason,
worried about Alban's future. In the city and at the fam-

ily's summer retreat — the Berghof, near Villach in the
mountains of Carinthia — Conrad watched the relationship grow between his youngest son and Watznauer.
He called the frequent guest aside one day and charged
him with guiding Alban after his death. Watznauer's
friendship was to take the form not only of continuing to
listen to the youth's romantic monologues, but also of in-
troducing all the Berg children to the rich avant-garde
side of Vienna's culture, suggesting reading material,
and, it seems, inspiring Alban to put his first compositions on paper.

Conrad Berg's death left the family in a precarious financial position. Although Johanna Berg could manage
the shop herself, the main part of the business holdings
fell into the hands of strangers. Fortunately, both Hermann and Charly were self-supporting. Hermann proposed taking Alban with him when he returned to New
York, to introduce him to the world of commerce,
which, for want of stronger leanings, it was assumed he
would enter in search of a livelihood. Hermann's propo-
sition evidently came under serious consideration, but a
widowed aunt, Marie Bareis, offered to subsidize Alban's
continued schooling in Vienna. This aid, the income
from the store, and money gleaned from renting rooms
in both the Breitegasse flat and the Berghof made it possible for Johanna Berg to keep her youngest son and her
daughter with her.

The death of the father, whom he so resembled, seems
to have touched off Alban's interest in music. For a fifteenth birthday present (seven weeks before Conrad died),
Watznauer had given his friend the popular *Golden Book of
Music*. (Despite its elementary level and its superficiality,
the book meant so much to Berg that he mentioned it
with fondness a quarter-century later.) The bereavement

might well have brought on Alban's first attack of asthma, of which he would live in fear throughout his life. Like his dead father, and very much unlike his mother, Berg was constantly sensitive to any pains in his body and in those of his loved ones. His letters show that he was often ailing or treating some trivial disorder, and visits to various doctors were part of his routine. Those who knew him, however, say that he was thin and asthmatic, but was no more given to confinement than most Viennese.

Alban's first asthma attack is said to have occurred on July 23, 1900, at the Berghof; over the years, his bronchial ailments frequently came on while he was in the country. The siege on July 23 so concerned the fifteen-year-old that he took the number twenty-three as his number of fate (*Schicksalszahl*). But he recovered in time to return to Vienna and school that fall, and only English gave him pause during the first term. Nevertheless, for reasons of health or finances, Alban did not return for the second semester of the 1900–1901 school year, and he repeated the sixth level the following year.

The free time, and an encouraging push from Watznauer, led Berg deeper into music. He approached the craft of writing notes on paper with virtually no formal background in theory, counterpoint, and the other niceties of composition, but he did have a rich knowledge of musical repertory. Besides hearing live performances in concert halls and at home, he had polished his piano technique to the point where he could play four-hand music (two players at one piano) with his sister. Through his life, this remained one of his favorite forms of recreation. Later, he would read through original works and transcriptions at the keyboard with his wife, and he dubbed himself "the last of the great four-hand players."

By 1904, the year Alban finally left the *Oberrealschule,* the Bergs' library of piano music for two and four hands had reached impressive proportions. Many of the scores bore Alban's critical comments: Bach's suites were "singularly beautiful"; Beethoven's Opus 20 Septet rated as "beautiful, still youthful but already profound." Bizet's *L'Arlésienne* Suite was "the best orchestra work I know," a judgment that says more about Berg's lack of sophistication at this time than about Bizet's achievements in this particular score. In Alban's book, Tchaikovsky's Sixth Symphony was "not playable," perhaps because of the pianist's limitations more than the music's.

Berlioz's *Roméo et Juliette* and the *Symphonie Fantastique* were "mere fads" to the youth's ears, as were Brahms's Hungarian Dances, some of Richard Strauss, and even works by Mozart. But Strauss's *Macbeth* did have "lovely spots" in it; *Ein Heldenleben* was — for better or for worse — "ultramodern," and *Till Eulenspiegel* rated as "the most beautiful of all." In addition, *Till* had the definite advantage of being "not especially difficult" in its piano reduction.

Brahms was one of Berg's favorites. He found the Third Symphony *"wunderschoen,"* and considered the Fourth to be "a little more pleasing than the Second." Brahms's Trios, Opus 8 and Opus 101, were frequently on the Bergs' parlor programs, but the young critic's highest compliment was saved for *Ein deutsches Requiem:* "*This* is music." Brahms was to have a lasting effect on Berg. So, no less obviously, was Schumann, whose *Manfred* Overture was marked "very lovely, and not too difficult," and whose Opus 44 Quintet was "glorious . . . the scherzo a bit difficult."

Under these influences, Berg went to the piano with pencil in hand and wrote down his first compositions, virtually all songs that could be sung by Charly or Smaragda, accompanied at the piano by Smaragda or, when she sang, by Alban himself. The very first effort, as Berg later listed it for Watznauer, was "Heiliger Himmel," based on a poem by Franz Evers. The manuscript, copied out with the precision that would characterize all of the composer's handiwork, is marked Opus 1. Seven years later, the same number would appear for posterity on the Piano Sonata, the first work the professional composer judged worthy of publication.

The *first* Opus 1, however, shows how much Berg — who had not yet thought seriously of devoting his life to music — had learned from the masters, especially Brahms (who did not die until 1897, and was thus still "modern"), Schumann, and Richard Wagner. The very traditional harmonies are strong and secure. C Major reigns. And yet the song does not belong to proper, nineteenth-century drawing rooms; even here, Berg's feeling for drama expresses itself in unpredictable ways. The first phrase of "Heiliger Himmel" ("Summer dreams of purple evenings . . .") spreads a surprisingly wide-leaping vocal line over an accompaniment of chords that fade from *piano* back to *pianississimo*. Then, in a sudden shift ("The sword of Odin cuts through the clouds . . ."), the tempo picks up, and the piano introduces an assertive, martial theme, which the voice pulls forward, *fortissimo*. For many older, established composers, this kind of change would have seemed dangerous or frightening.

"Heiliger Himmel," "Herbstgefuehl" (text by Siegfried Fleischer), "Spielleute" (Ibsen), and "Unter den Linden" (Walther von der Vogelweide, the famous Minnesinger whose work figured in Berg's sixth-level curriculum), all date from the year 1901. They number among approximately 150 songs and ensembles for voices

and piano that Berg wrote between that year and 1908,
when the Piano Sonata became the "official" Opus 1.
From these, the composer later culled the Seven Early
Songs, but most of this music — including a few instrumental works — were unpublished and generally unknown through Berg's lifetime, and so remain today.
Some of the manuscripts were passed to friends, as gifts
or because Berg saw no future for them in the stacks on
his shelves. Over the years, collectors held a number of
these songs in safekeeping; others were split up and sold,
page by page, on auction blocks, and can probably be
counted as lost.

Berg had neither the hope nor the belief that these early
songs would ever find a place in history. He wrote them
for domestic performance, without any serious thought
of becoming a composer. He identified music with summer vacations, since he had already learned how much
easier it was for him to study and compose at the Berghof
than in Vienna. During the summers of 1903 and 1904,
Frida Semler shared in the spirited fun of the young
Bergs. Then an undergraduate at Wellesley College, near
Boston, Miss Semler — later Mrs. Mortimer Seabury —
was the daughter of an associate of Hermann and Conrad
Berg in the import-export business. Though she was a
paying guest at the Berghof, Frida and Alban became fast
friends, and their correspondence continued for several
years after they last saw one another.

A half-century later, Mrs. Seabury recorded her memories of that free and idyllic country life for the Newsletter of the International Alban Berg Society. Meal times
meant picnics on the porch, with fresh milk and eggs,
salads, and thick brown bread, whose doughy insides
were molded by the young people into statues or into ornate, personalized funeral monuments. The conversations

were filled with gossip about who was sharing which
villa with whom, and under what circumstances; singers,
writers, actors, and actresses who decided to summer at
the Ossiacher Lake might have thought that their private
lives went unnoticed, but nothing escaped the teen-agers
at the Berghof, especially the inquisitive Alban. Some
of the famous and near-famous befriended Alban,
Smaragda, Frida, and their companions. These Austrian
summers were an education for the innocent sixteen-
year-old American girl, whose ruse of trying to hide her
blushes by drinking from a glass of milk whenever the
table talk turned to sex was quickly detected and announced by Alban.

Mornings in the country were spent at the lake.
Dressed in black bathing trunks and a long-sleeved black
shirt, gingerly pushing his long hair out of his eyes,
Alban, conscious of his appearance, hardly looked ath-
letic. But he had the strength to swim several miles back
and forth across the lake without tiring. The only way
most of his friends could keep up with him was to row
the boat alongside him, as they kept a watch out for the
arrival of the postman, and fetched letters to be opened
and read on the water.

Afternoons were devoted to less strenuous pursuits —
music, reading, sewing, correspondence. Alban left lunch
to return to work on his songs; Frida remembered his
working on "Grabschrift" and the duet "Viel Traeume."
Smaragda and her brother tried out all his new compositions, then played four-hand piano music from their library — unless the piano happened to be usurped at tea
time by a paying customer who wanted to show off his
own keyboard agility with a popular waltz. To the
Bergs, this was both an amusement and an annoyance;
music was to them, wrote Frida, "a sacred thing."

On early evening hikes around the lake, Alban would
occasionally carry a book and a candle to read by, then
blow out the light and join the conversation when he had
finished his chapter. Modern German poetry was inspiration for new songs; recent or recently translated plays
provided evening entertainment, with the young people
dividing the parts and reading aloud in friendly competition to see who could be the most persuasively dramatic.
Highlights of the 1903 theatrical season at the Berghof
were Ibsen's *Hedda Gabler* and *Ghosts*. Schnitzler's *Reigen*
and Wedekind's *Erdgeist* — both too risqué to be acted
out — gave the friends plenty to talk about in 1904.
More than twenty years later, Berg was to go back to
Erdgeist and turn it and its companion piece, *Pandora's
Box,* into his second opera, *Lulu.*

Alban, Smaragda, and their friends often faced the
public with a humorous and artificial demeanor. During a
midsummer trip into Vienna, the Bergs and Frida Semler
were offered tickets to the State Opera — seats in the expensive orchestra section, not up in the top gallery,
where Alban and Smaragda usually sat poring over their
scores with the aid of a flashlight, and voicing running
critiques of the performance. That night in the coveted
orchestra seats, Alban and his sister tried to look appro-
priately bored and blasé, complaining loudly that all of
their friends were off in the country (though it is more
likely that they were up in the inexpensive seats).

And on visits to palaces or galleries, kingly staircases
would tempt the Bergs to put on their royal act, bowing
and addressing their unsuspecting "subjects," freely offering little children their unsolicited "royal blessings."
They could switch from the everyday Viennese dialect to
the courtliest German, adding all the appropriate titles
and inflections that can make the language so stilted and
formal.

These were not average Viennese teen-agers; they had little or nothing in common with the thousands of hefty, hearty Austrian students who plunged into the Danube each summer. They took the Viennese sense of propriety — a sense that may be genetic — and added to it their own artistic sensibility. They went further than most of their contemporaries would have dared to go in ridiculing the artificiality and class-consciousness that were part of their heritage and their language. But in no way had they turned their backs on their society. They may have thought themselves superior to the soldiers who gathered at the country dances and the sturdy women who dragged their offspring to the museums, but the Bergs were nevertheless present at those dances and museums, very much a part of their community.

At the same time, Alban was reaching beyond his small circle of family and friends, looking for private heroes. Three artists from the north — Ibsen, Grieg, and Strindberg — were among them, but Henrik Ibsen was, as Berg told Watznauer, "my living ideal." He paid honor to Shakespeare, Goethe, Dostoevski, and Balzac, but found a special combination of inspiration, entertainment, and perhaps even a degree of solace in the work of Ibsen.

At this point, Ibsen was at the end of his career. In 1900, the year Conrad Berg died, the playwright suffered the first in a series of incapacitating heart attacks. He died in 1906. There is no way to know whether Alban was aware of the remarkable parallels between his life and Ibsen's. There is no doubt, however, that the published poems and plays — including *A Doll's House* (1879), *Rosmersholm* (1886), and *Hedda Gabler* (1890) — were in the Berg library and were repeatedly read.

Ibsen was born on March 20, 1828, in Skien, a small coastal town near Oslo, the son of a prosperous and so-

cially ambitious shipper. Lavish town-and-country social
occasions filled the boy's early years. But when Henrik,
the eldest of five surviving children, was seven, his father's fortune was wiped out, and the family had to move
from a large villa to a remote farmhouse. There the boy
turned introspective, painting, drawing, reading, staging
puppet shows, and retreating from a society he found
hypocritical and petty. His hope for the future grew from
a profound self-reliance, an almost mystical belief in the
power of the individual, male or female. Before Freud
spelled out the functions and powers of sex in different
words and for different purposes, Ibsen dealt with the
same powerful father-husband-daughter relationships. If
women of the late twentieth century have tended to make
too much of Ibsen's primitive feminism, the treatment of
women in the plays was still fascinating to Berg, who
was growing up without a father in an age where the
"eternal feminine" of Goethe's *Faust* had disintegrated
into Otto Weininger's scandalous (and, thus, popular)
concept of the "feminine idea," whereby women exert
the wantonly sexual downward pull that leads thinking
men to nihilism.

Ibsen's conflicts stemmed from the pain of his family's
financial ruin, from personal disappointments (he failed
the entrance examinations to medical school), from public rejection, and from lifelong guilt. In 1846, he fathered
an illegitimate son by a maid in the apothecary shop
where he was an apprentice. Else Sophie Jensdatter, like
her young lover, had been born to a wealthy family and
knew the humiliation that could accompany the loss of
money. She was well educated and shared Ibsen's interest
in literature, but there was never thought of marriage.
For more than a decade, the father scraped to contribute
to his son's support. In 1858, the playwright married

Suzanne Thorenson. Neither their happiness nor the son they had together erased Ibsen's memories of his first child, memories that are reflected in the characters of his plays who harbor secrets of what society calls sins.

The parallels between Ibsen's life and Berg's are remarkable. Like Knut Ibsen, Conrad Berg was a merchant and trader; like the Ibsens, the Bergs moved up in the world, though the children of both families had to come to terms later with the loss of prosperity. Both Henrik and Alban escaped into private ideas and fantasies; both failed academically and moved into creative careers at least in part as a result of these failures.

And, like Ibsen, Berg knew the toll of private guilt. In September 1903, Alban, distraught over his academic failures, attempted suicide. He had written to Watznauer from the Berghof during the summer, "I'm too dull even for the joy of dying — joyless — I lack the great joy — I even lack the great suffering!!? — It could be so! — So I am a tentative seeker! Finding nothing!"

The suffering was not artificial, nor was it merely an impatient youth's displeasure at the thought of having to spend an extra year in school. The tragedy of that summer was most likely the birth of an illegitimate daughter, the result of Alban's liaison with a Carinthian girl. The mother may have been the daughter of a public official named Stiasny; the details of the birth and life of Berg's only child remain mysterious. Alban is said to have given the mother a sum of money or to have made payments toward the child's support. It would have been necessary, then, for Watznauer or members of the immediate family to know of the birth, since the eighteen-year-old father had no funds of his own. Berg never established contact with his daughter, though he could easily have kept track of her through Carinthian neighbors. All he kept was a

picture, taken in 1910 or 1911, a copy of which later came
into the possession of Erich Alban Berg, son of the composer's brother Charly. Erich Alban did not doubt that
the girl in the picture was his uncle's daughter. The
seven- or eight-year-old child, dressed in a middy blouse
and skirt, had inherited the dark, questioning eyes of her
father, her cousin observed.

The death of Conrad Berg, the decline in the family's
fortunes, his precarious health and failure in school, an
unhappy love affair, an unwanted child, an indeterminate
future — at eighteen, Alban reacted to these pressures by
trying to kill himself. He was probably at the Berghof,
and he probably used either pills or gas. (Smaragda
would attempt suicide with gas several years later.)
Berg's early biographers all mention the unfortunate
event in passing but offer no details; now, everyone who
could remember the circumstances is dead. There is no
question, however, that Alban was distraught and that
his situation seemed intolerable. But was he serious?
Frida Semler had spent most of the summer months of
1903 at the Berghof, and nothing in her brief memoir indicates that the active, amusing Alban was on the brink
of killing himself, or that he spent much time in lonely
brooding. Could this gesture have been simply another
dramatic act by the dramatic youth who called himself a
"tentative seeker" and enjoyed the role?

It is possible that Berg wanted only to act the role of a
suicide; that he was, in effect, asking for help and support
in life. The adolescent Berg was certainly given to theatricality. When he first sat for a professional photog-
rapher, at the age of nineteen (when he finally left
school), Alban studiously projected the image of beautiful, fragile sensitivity, drawing his big, dark cape around
him (a predecessor of the fur coat he would soon pos-

sess), to accentuate the soft, aristocratic, "artistic" features, full lips, and faraway eyes under floppy brown hair. (See picture following page 174.) His nails were bitten down to the quick. Still, the model who immediately comes to mind is Oscar Wilde; Berg's friends saw the resemblance and commented on it. There is just the slightest feeling of decadence in the photographs from 1904, but what Berg projects more than anything else is a confident aestheticism, a belief that life can follow art. He had not yet found manners or an art to follow or to adopt; he was still sifting through other people's styles and ideas. He sought guidance from Ibsen, Strindberg, Shakespeare, Brahms, Richard Wagner, and a more recent discovery, Gustav Mahler, as well as from personal friends, like Watznauer. Yet Alban was still without direction. He needed a sterner voice, a father figure who would make demands on him and tolerate no self-indulgence. By chance — or by an act of fate — he found just such a man.

Chapter 2

Student of Schoenberg

ARNOLD SCHOENBERG was a natural leader. There was something about the short, round, balding man that attracted disciples. Born in Vienna on September 13, 1874, he grew up struggling, and the family barely avoided poverty. The brash youth had had to leave school at the age of sixteen in order to work. He got a job as a low-level clerk in an unimportant bank and was fired when he signed a customer into the account books as L. van Beethoven. He was delighted to be free.

From that moment on, the twenty-one-year-old Schoenberg committed himself to music. He studied the violin, taught himself the cello, played chamber music with friends, and tried his hand at composing duos, trios, and quartets. He was not a virtuoso. When he found a job conducting a chorus of workers in a town near Vienna, he could not play the piano well enough to direct his singers to the correct pitches. When he stood in front of an orchestra, the players laughed at the way his zeal was confounded by an utter lack of technique. His musical taste extended to Brahms and Wagner — and stopped

there. In the late 1890s in Vienna, Richard Strauss and
Gustav Mahler were the avant-garde; but well into the
twentieth century, Schoenberg had trouble coming to
grips with Mahler's work.

The idea that this man, a one-time bank clerk who had
musical training from none of the right places, could
enter the rarefied world of the arts was far-fetched. To
make things worse, Schoenberg was a Jew. Even as formidable a figure as Mahler had had to convert from Judaism to Protestantism before the Viennese would officially offer him the position as director of their State
Opera. And, as far as anyone could tell, Schoenberg was
not even worthy to carry Mahler's batons or sharpen his
pencils.

But Schoenberg had a vision. In 1897, he realized that
Brahms was dead, not only physically but spiritually. He
recognized that the time had come for music to take a
new direction, and he found that direction in his own
imagination. The overripe sonorities of Mahler and
Strauss, issuing from oversized orchestras, seemed to
Schoenberg every bit as dangerous as did Viennese society's compulsive reliance on layers of dusty Kitsch.

If he was not precisely sure where he would lead
music, he was certain that he should be in command.
And his rise was startling, at least among those Viennese
artists and intellectuals who shared Schoenberg's sense of
dissatisfaction and knew that they had to make a decisive
move toward a new aesthetic if their cultural heritage was
not to die. As writer, teacher, musician, and painter, this
assertive newcomer boldly demanded and quickly earned
the respect and good will of many leaders in the humanis-
tic disciplines. In some respects, Schoenberg was the
most radical and adventuresome of them all, but he was
also a great compromiser. He decided that it was in the

best interests of himself and his art to convert to Protestantism, which he did. As the years passed, though, this
technical conversion would do him little good. He gained
recognition and some measure of acceptance from the
public by writing music that echoed Wagner and did not
even threaten to bring him nearer to his goal of "breaking
through the limits of a bygone aesthetic." As his mentor,
he chose the traditional composer Alexander von Zemlinsky, and married the older man's sister, Mathilde.
Needing money to live on, he moved his family to Berlin, where experimentation was more welcome than in
Vienna, and passed endless hours orchestrating some six
thousand pages of operetta, then moonlighting by scoring and leading light music in a cabaret. He did not hate
popular music; he professed admiration for Franz Lehár
and for the team of Gilbert and Sullivan, and he wrote his
own set of cabaret songs. But he hated the drudgery of
orchestration. He knew he had to do this work to earn a
living, at least for the time being, but he deeply resented
being diverted from his chosen course.

Schoenberg's fervor was messianic. He started out
alone, with fierce discipline and determination, constantly
battling poverty. He faced the past with love and the future with logic, always claiming that he intended to compose conventionally, but he could not. He made himself
into the thinker and the theoretician; Egon Wellesz, one
of his students, made the comparison between Schoenberg and Moses, referring to Schoenberg's unfinished
opera *Moses und Aron*. Like the prophet, the composer
searched for his truth, withstanding not only dissent, but
ridicule. "His was a difficult life," Wellesz wrote, "a life
full of tension, the anguish of which can be seen in his
paintings, an anguish so great that it burst open the
boundaries of tonality, and a superhuman energy was

needed for building up a new system of composition that, when completed, was his own creation."

There were very few people who could understand, share, and try to ease that anguish, at least to Schoenberg's satisfaction. These chosen few listened closely to the master's deep, dusky, compelling voice, which demands attention even on a scratchy tape made in the early 1930s. Among those people who were to listen, help, and ultimately serve Schoenberg was his junior by ten and a half years, Alban Berg.

In July 1903, Schoenberg, his wife, and baby left Berlin, where the cabaret had shut down, and moved back to Vienna, where they could save money by sharing a house with the elder Zemlinskys. In the same month, Berg was writing to Watznauer about the lack of hope for his future, admitting that "even music doesn't bring me the joy it used to." Back in Vienna in the fall, Berg began his second year in the seventh, and top, level of the secondary school. With the cooperation of his friend Paul Hohenberg, an aspiring poet, Berg finished the grade without much trouble. Hohenberg wrote assigned papers with such titles as "The Correct Path to Self-Knowledge"; Berg put his own name on them, handed them to the teacher, and came out with "praiseworthy" grades. So with several more songs written, much more Ibsen read, and very little schoolwork done, Alban was finally graduated. He admitted later that it was a mystery to him that he had ever managed to pass the tests.

Alban, without having to worry about going back to school in the fall, thrived during the summer of 1904 at the Berghof. He swam, took the sun, ate the country food, and drank the local beer. He read Goethe and searched for song texts among modern German poems. In his room, he told Watznauer, he was "a little child of

man set amongst gods and heroes," surrounded by busts
of Beethoven, Brahms, and his father, portraits of Mahler, Ibsen, and, again, Beethoven, and a reproduction of
Correggio's *Jupiter and Io*.

He could still be inspired to raptures that were denoted
in his letters by masses of dashes and exclamation points.
But as he matured, it was the beauties of the countryside
and woods more often than self-pity that led him to these
vivid excesses. His growing sense of irony was nurtured
by the work of Peter Altenberg, the eccentric Viennese
poet who was to become a close friend of Smaragda's and
whose texts were to inspire Alban's Opus 4, the Altenberg Songs for voice and orchestra. Berg was feeling
much more secure with himself than he had the summer
before, and he was definitely *not* fretting about what the
future might bring.

But the time had come for Alban to make his contribution, if not necessarily to posterity, at least to his family.
The fact that there was an urgent need of regular funds
for basic household expenses precluded his having serious
thoughts of a career in the arts. Although music, poetry,
and painting had all exercised their attractions on Berg at
one time or another, he had pursued none in a way that
would have indicated any professional or lasting ambi-
tions. He had never had an interest in following his father
and brothers into the import-export business. He had
thought of becoming an engineer, in part because he was
gifted in detailed drawing and sketching, but years of
training and apprenticeship would have been required before he could begin a scientific career.

So Berg did what so many insecure artists and poets
before him had done: he put himself into the service of
imperial Austria. Following the wishes of his mother, he
signed on as a probationary accountant for the government offices of Lower Austria. (The region, which in-

cludes Vienna, is low in the sense that it is down from the mountains.) After a year's apprenticeship, he was to receive an annual salary of six hundred kronen (about $400, or £100). In September and October of 1904, various documents were sealed, verifying that the aspirant was mentally, physically, and morally capable of undertaking his new assignments. On October 18, Berg enrolled in a course in public accounting at the University of Vienna, the successful completion of which was a prerequisite to his being named a full-fledged civil servant.

Berg entered his new life without complaint, but it was not the kind of activity for which anyone could have mustered much enthusiasm. Watznauer recorded the unpleasant working conditions in which the young man celebrated his twentieth birthday, writing down statistics on the buying and selling of pigs. Later, he was assigned to keep tabs on distilleries and their productivity.

His work was careful and diligent. The first year passed to the satisfaction of his superiors, and the apprenticeship gave way to a regular salary. To his superiors, he appeared motivated, although, in fact, Berg's new-found seriousness of purpose had nothing to do with the civil service. For at the same time as he had begun accounting for pigs and distilleries, the young man had been introduced to Schoenberg.

In October 1904, Smaragda spotted the following announcement in Vienna's *New Musical Press,* placed inconspicuously between a sarcastic comment on a *Parsifal* competition in America and the announcement that Professor Dr. Arthur Seidl would visit the Berlin University:

In the girl's *Gymnasium* [school] in Vienna (I District, Wallnerstrasse 2), from October 15 to May 15, between 5:00 and 9:00 in the evening, courses in music theory will be offered for professionals and serious amateurs by Arnold Schoenberg

(harmony and counterpoint), Alexander von Zemlinsky
(analysis and instrumentation), and Dr. Elsa Bienenfeld
(music history). The number of students will be limited.
Enroll by October 15.

Smaragda passed the announcement on to Charly, who
borrowed several of Alban's songs and went to see
Schoenberg. The teacher, who had just turned thirty,
looked over the work and sent back an invitation for the
young Berg to join his classes, free of charge. Though he
may have been no businessman, Schoenberg could spot a
gift. Like Berg, he was largely self-taught, and saw talent
in the Brahms- and Wolf-styled songs written out so
painstakingly by the young man who was, probably at
that very moment, sitting in an office counting pigs. Evidently without a second thought, Alban heard Charly's
news and arranged to attend his first professional-level
music class.

Berg later made a note for Watznauer of the first songs
that were laid out for Schoenberg's scrutiny: "Es wan-
delt, was wir schauen" (text by Eichendorff), "Liebe"
(Rilke), "Wandert ihr Wolken" (Avenarius), "Im Mor-
gengrauen" (Stieler), "Grabschrift" (Jakobowski), and
"Traum" (Semler). Berg never included any of these
songs among the works he counted worthy of publication.

Berg's musical limitations were obvious to both
Schoenberg and Berg himself. As Schoenberg later wrote
of Berg's early studies:

> In the condition in which he first came to me, it was impos-
> sible for him to imagine composing anything but songs . . .
> He was incapable of writing an instrumental movement, of
> finding an instrumental theme . . . Usually the teacher has
> no success in this area because he does not see the precise

problem — so we end up with composers who can't cope
with a single instrument . . . But I corrected the deficiency
and am delighted that Berg found his way to a very good
style of orchestration.

Characteristically, Schoenberg took full credit and almost made it seem as if *he* had done all the work. If,
however, the teacher had said that at that point in his life
Berg did not know what he wanted or needed, he would
have been right. Schoenberg decided that this quiet
young man should start at the very beginning in this
musical night school, with basic theory and counterpoint.
Schoenberg had already begun to break down the old
boundaries on his way to a new style with such works as
the string sextet *Verklaerte Nacht,* the early songs, *Pelleas
und Melisande,* the still-unfinished *Gurrelieder,* and the D
Minor String Quartet, Opus 7, which he was working on
through the end of 1904 and the first half of 1905. But his
teaching methods were strictly traditional, based on lessons to be learned from Bach, Beethoven, and Brahms.
"In art there is only one true teacher, aptitude," Schoenberg wrote. "And that has only one useful assistant,
namely, imitation." Examples from the masters illus-
trated lessons written out and eventually published in
Schoenberg's own textbook, *Harmonielehre;* the counterpoint classes followed Heinrich Bellermann's 1862 treatise
on the subject. Until his students had the firmest possible
hold on the concepts and solutions of the old guard,
Schoenberg steadfastly refused to introduce the new for
official scrutiny, though he expected that contemporary
music would be a constant part of his charges' lives.
Berg applied himself to Schoenberg's lessons and assignments with an enthusiasm previously foreign to him,
and external circumstances helped his cause. In the first

half of 1905, Alban, Smaragda, and their mother moved
from Breitegasse to the tree-lined suburb of Hietzing,
across the street from the parks of Schoenbrunn Palace,
to share the villa at Hietzinger Hauptstrasse 6 with Mrs.
Berg's older sister, Julie Weidman, whose husband had
died a few months before. The situation was perfect for
Alban; for the first time, he had his own place, a small
studio-house where he could pull the shades against all
distractions, brew pots of tea to keep himself from doz-
ing off, and devote nights and weekends to music. He did
not know it, of course, but during the two years he lived
on Hietzinger Hauptstrasse his future wife was living in a
large private villa right up the hill, and the flat in which
he would spend more than two decades of married life
was around the corner, only a few blocks away.

Aunt Julie Weidman, who had no children, died in
November 1905 without leaving a will, and her estate
went to her closest relative, Johanna Berg. It included
money, furnishings, and a great deal of property, including eight large apartment houses in Vienna. The real estate required a good deal of tending, which would later
become a tiresome burden, taking hours away from
Berg's composing. But the days of near-poverty had
ended, and, if it exercised careful management, the family
was sufficiently well provided for to be able to withstand
even the economic emergencies that were soon to be a
prelude to war.

The immediate effect of the inheritance was that Alban
was able to leave his government desk for good and devote his life to music. He submitted his resignation on
October 7, 1906, officially on grounds of illness and
physical strain, and by October 31 he was a free man
again. Schoenberg had ended his career at the bank by
registering an account to L. van Beethoven; Berg ended

his days as a public servant by declaring that the debts of all the farmers in his jurisdiction were irretrievable.

In Schoenberg's classes, Berg found inspiration and purpose, camaraderie and friends, the most important of whom was Anton von Webern. Born in Vienna on December 2, 1883, the son of a well-to-do mining engineer, Webern was extremely well trained, not just in relation to the other members of the Schoenberg class, but in comparison with composers throughout history. When he and Berg met in the Schoenberg school in the fall of 1904, Webern was studying musicology with Guido Adler at the University of Vienna; in 1906, a dissertation on the *Choralis Constantinus* of Heinrich Isaac made him Dr. Anton von Webern. Isaac (circa 1450–1517), a leader of the Netherlands school of polyphony, had served for a time in the court of Maximilian I, in Vienna. As editor of major parts of Isaac's music, Webern became intimately acquainted with the styles and inclinations of composers from the late fifteenth and early sixteenth centuries, a period about which his colleagues knew virtually nothing.

The friendship between Webern and Berg grew from their shared devotion to music and to Schoenberg, from their passion for poetry and literature, and from the fact, quickly evident, that they were the two most gifted of Schoenberg's pupils, despite their very different levels and backgrounds. The ties among the two students and their teacher deepened into lasting friendships; as Webern later wrote, "Friend and pupil; one was always the same as the other."

Although Webern left Schoenberg's class in 1908 and was in and out of Vienna on conducting assignments from that year on, the men remained joined as a spiritual triumvirate, to be broken only by war and death. Webern's life was full of struggles and idealistic quests. Characteristically, he pushed himself to write music that seems to exist somewhere above, in a rarefied atmosphere, while he was fighting a most earthbound battle to support his wife and children. He was killed in September 1945, in the small town of Mittersill, near Salzburg; he had stepped outside his son-in-law's small house to enjoy a cigar without disturbing his sleeping grandchildren, and was shot by an overeager American solider.

Webern and Berg were opposites. Both were born Catholic, but Berg was barely religious, and Webern was increasingly given to pantheism and mysticism. Webern was small — he came about up to Berg's shoulder. He had no interest in society, cafés, or the good life, and had no hope of ever experiencing it; Berg longed to be the *grand seigneur,* and lived the role as best he could. Webern existed just above the poverty level; Berg usually had enough cash, and when he did worry, it was usually about not being able to continue to live in the manner to which he had so happily become accustomed. Webern was a feeling *Mensch,* quiet but easy to talk with, approachable, warm; Berg was cool, aloof, reserved, and sometimes given to looking down his nose at the common herd.

The two were different musically, as well. They applied Schoenberg's theories in opposite ways. Berg, the romantic, looked to the past, and found a connection between new techniques and established traditions. Ironically, it was Webern, the trained musicologist and the expert in the fifteenth and sixteenth centuries, whose music moved most violently and irrevocably into the future. Though Webern took great care to connect his work, in conversation and lectures, with that of such past masters as Beethoven and Brahms, his music can bring to

mind the words of the artist Juan Gris: "No work des-
tined to become classic may resemble the classic works
which preceded it." René Leibowitz wrote that Webern's
work "represents the greatest advancement in the evolu-
tion of the art of music." No one would ever have said
that about Berg. Yet as different as their musical styles
and goals were, Webern and Berg were bound together
inextricably with Schoenberg, by private friendship and
purpose. They are the pillars of what has come to be
known as the New Viennese School of composition, as
opposed to the "old" Viennese school of Mozart, Haydn,
Beethoven, and Schubert. Unlike the earlier generations
of composers, the members of the New Viennese School
saw each other regularly, and actually had a school, for a
time. They passed ideas back and forth, musical ideas as
well as literary and practical ones. Yet, though Schoenberg, Berg, and Webern admired each other's works, it is
important to acknowledge that their differences are more
significant than their similarities.

Class hours were devoted to studying music of the old
masters, but Schoenberg's students were also expected to
keep abreast of what was new, and that meant going to
concerts, even if their empty pockets forced them to
sneak in through the back door. In May 1906, Berg and
Watznauer joined Zemlinsky, Schoenberg, and Gustav
Mahler himself in Graz for the Austrian première of
Richard Strauss's opera based on Oscar Wilde's *Salome;*
Berg went to hear and see it again and again, wherever
and whenever it played. Premières of Mahler's own
works were on the calendars, of course, and Berg attended Mahler's farewell performance, his conducting of
Beethoven's *Fidelio* at the Vienna State Opera in October
1907. And he was naturally at all concerts of music by
Schoenberg, including in these years the early songs;

Verklaerte Nacht; the Chamber Symphony, Opus 9; and
the public première of the Second Quartet, for voice and
strings, Opus 10, in F-sharp Minor.

It was probably at this performance of Schoenberg's
Opus 10 that Berg got his first impression of the opposi-
tion he might face if he, too, became "successful." Egon
Wellesz remembered the occasion:

> The atmosphere in the elegant and old-fashioned Boesen-
> dorfer Hall was tense from the beginning . . . The first
> movement had hardly begun when, enraged by the unex-
> pected C in the fifth bar, the music critic named Karpath
> jumped up from his seat and shouted, "Stop it!" Unper-
> turbed, the Rose Quartet went on; but it was in that scherzo
> that, after a *fortissimo,* the audience started laughing and its
> laughter drowned out the music. An elderly gentleman sit-
> ting in front of Mahler began whistling on a door key. I
> heard Mahler shouting, "I'll risk five florins (the fine for dis-
> turbing the peace) and box you on the ear!" "You are not
> here as director of the Opera, you can't order me to stop,"
> the man retorted. Mahler rose from his seat, but at that
> moment two young men, pupils of Schoenberg, rushed for-
> ward and carried the man out of the hall.

The next morning a Viennese paper reported, not in
the music pages but in a column devoted to urban crimes:

> The scene last night between eight and nine in the Boesen-
> dorfer Hall was unprecedented in Vienna's music history;
> there was a full-fledged scandal during the playing of a com-
> position whose creator has already caused public nuisance with
> his other works. But yesterday he went further than ever; it
> sounded like a cats' concert. All the same, the public sat
> quietly until the end of the first movement. Then, from the
> standing-room, shouts of approval brought on the ava-
> lanche, which ebbed and grew, finally, to a mammoth cli-
> max . . . Ludwig Boesendorfer was standing sadly in the
> lobby — it is so important to him that things go right in his

hall. A friend suggested to him, "Now they're supposed to play Beethoven, but air out the hall first!"

The outbursts infuriated Berg — and they were to become even louder and more violent. If the première of Igor Stravinsky's *Le Sacre du printemps,* on May 29, 1913, in Paris led to a riot that has become more famous than those that accompanied the works of Schoenberg and his colleagues, the Viennese audiences were no less rowdy than their French counterparts, nor were the Viennese police any less obliged to march in and calm enraged audiences.

At this time, Berg was a defender, not yet a defendant. In the 1906–1907 music season, he stood in front of the public, singing bass in a choir conducted by Schoenberg. A representative program of that ensemble included works by Haydn, Hassler, Senfl, Mendelssohn, Bach, and Brahms. In the winter of 1905, he had made his first out-of-the-parlor appearance, as composer and instrumentalist, accompanying his sister in his own song "Die Nachtigall" (to a text by Storm) at a home for widows and orphans. It would be a rash overstatement to call this a professional, public engagement, and, needless to say, there was no resulting outrage, only applause for the youthful Berg duo.

"Die Nachtigall" was among the first of his songs that would be presented publicly and preserved; Berg included it in his set, Seven Early Songs. The other pieces were written as a change and relief from the musical problems and puzzles he was assigned to solve for his lessons with Schoenberg. Considering that he had started those classes with virtually no preparation and no knowledge of what to expect, Berg had quickly become an eager disciple. Only the most single-minded and determined pupils kept coming back, as Schoenberg de-

manded more and more from them and tolerated less and
less disloyalty; so the small group that remained eventually moved to Schoenberg's living room.

Classes of only seven or eight meant that everyone in
the group received individual attention, and the meetings
became less structured, given over more to the students'
particular problems. As far as the teacher was concerned,
these problems were not limited to music. He felt perfectly free, even obliged, to regulate every facet of his followers' lives. If he did not approve of their friends, he
said so; if they were not dressing neatly and stylishly
enough to meet his standards, they also heard about that.
They were expected to conduct themselves in a manner
appropriate to students of Schoenberg, which meant
seriously and with dignity. Berg was even berated for his
handwriting. No matter that the young man always
turned out perfectly legible music manuscripts; his script
was not clear enough for Schoenberg.

Some young people rebelled against this kind of dictatorial rule from the man who was supposed to be only
their music teacher. But Berg, whether or not he was
consciously grateful, began his relationship with Schoenberg by accepting every suggestion or order unques-
tioningly, almost as if the master's word were gospel. He
wanted and needed this strong, sure, superior force. In
return for their complete obedience and trust, Berg, Webern, and a few others were allowed to think of themselves as Schoenberg's friends and, eventually, honored
by being asked to address the master with the familiar
German *du*.

Early in the summer of 1907, after two and a half years
of study, Berg completed Schoenberg's theory and counterpoint class and was judged ready to take on the
greater challenge of original composition. He wrote of
his promotion to Frida Semler:

Now, next autumn, comes composition. This summer I am
to work hard, partly composing out of the blue (I am making a piano sonata for my own benefit like that) and partly
repeating the counterpoint exercises (six- to eight-part
choruses and a fugue with two themes for string quartet with
piano accompaniment). Naturally, I enjoy it all very
much — and that's necessary; if I did not enjoy it I'd never
be able to do it. And of course Schoenberg's enormous ability gives one a grandiose panoramic view of the whole literature of music, and a healthy and accurate judgment besides.
And that's *good!*

Berg went on in that letter from the Berghof to spout
what were most likely Schoenberg's own thoughts on
musical fashion, as opposed to lasting quality, and the superficiality of the public's appreciation for even the works
of the masters, let alone new music. If the student was
paraphrasing his teacher, at least he did so with conviction and with supporting facts based on the history he had
learned in the Schoenberg school. And his new friends
and new sense of direction had led him to expand his literary tastes. He would never give up Ibsen, Strindberg,
Goethe, and Shakespeare, but at the age of twenty-two
he was also reading more Wedekind ("the really new
direction — the emphasis on the sensual in modern
works"); Homer; Cesare Lombroso, the Italian who made
the first attempts to explain criminal behavior in physical
and scientific terms instead of moral or social ones; and
Richard von Krafft-Ebing, the German neurologist and
psychiatrist who gave us the words "sadism" and "maso-
chism." The ideas of Sigmund Freud were also beginning
to permeate Viennese thought and gossip.

Berg had come so far so fast that he was deemed ready
to make his official debut as a composer. On November
7, 1907, with Alma Maria Schindler Mahler and Alexander von Zemlinsky among the honored guests, works

by Schoenberg's pupils were played in the Saal des Gre-
miums of the headquarters of the Vienna trade union on
Schwarzenbergplatz 16. Admission was by invitation.
Works by Berg, Erwin Stein, Rudolf Weyrich, O. de
Ivanow, Dr. Anton von Webern, Heinrich Jalowetz, Karl
Horwitz, and Wilma von Webenau were announced.
With the listing of his Double Fugue for String Quartet
with Piano Accompaniment (after the Manner of a Continuo) Berg was identified as a "student of counterpoint,"
indicating that the Double Fugue had been written as an
assignment for the class the young composer had completed several months before. No such qualification went
next to Berg's name for the program's listings of his three
songs, "Liebesode" (text by Otto Erich Hartleben), "Die
Nachtigall," and "Traumgekroent" (Rilke), though "Die
Nachtigall" was certainly written before the Fugue, since
Berg and his sister had presented it at the widows and
orphans' home in 1905. Berg himself played the piano
part in his Double Fugue for this Schoenberg-school reci-
tal, with a quartet including fellow student Jalowetz on
viola. The composer did not accompany his own songs,
however; that assignment went to his colleague Horwitz,
with a singer named Elsa Pazeller.

The review of the concert in the *New Vienna Journal*
was one of the most sympathetic ever received by the
Schoenberg circle, with words of praise not only for the
students' talents, but also for the teacher's thoroughness
and, by implication, his musical style.

Berg's own review of the concert was somewhat less
favorable than the critic's. He wrote to Frida Semler that
he was annoyed when the business of the outer world impinged on his creative work, especially when, as in the
case of the November 7 concert, the public expressed
what seemed to him to be misplaced enthusiasm. Berg's

Fugue was the most warmly received work of the evening, but in its composer's opinion it was by no means the strongest composition on the program. With the set of his songs, too, Berg learned that applause was not always a good reflection of musical value. "Traumgekroent," which he considered to be the best of the three, was coolly received, but "Die Nachtigall," according to Berg the weakest, was the most popular.

A year later, when Schoenberg's students again organized a concert of their own works with the master's approval, the critics lived up to the worst expectations and tossed sharp barbs. This time, on November 18, 1908, the event was held in the large hall of Vienna's famous Musikverein, the home of the Vienna Philharmonic Orchestra, which was not the ensemble hired by the students to perform the most important première of the night, that of Webern's Passacaglia, Opus 1.

Berg was represented by another work that qualified as a product of his apprenticeship, the Twelve Variations on an Original Theme for Piano, performed by Irene Bien. Several reviewers admitted to having difficulties in finding the theme and following the variations; only one reporter heard how much the young composer had inherited from the conservative Brahms.

Schoenberg himself remembered the early years of his association with Berg when, at the behest of Willi Reich, who was to become Berg's student and biographer, he traced Berg's progress. Schoenberg's reminiscences tell as much about the author as they do about the subject. These are the teacher's recollections from 1949, fourteen years after Berg's death, in Schoenberg's own English:

When Alban Berg came to me in 1904, he was a very tall youngster and extremely timid. But when I saw the com-

positions he showed me — songs in a style between Hugo
Wolf and Johannes Brahms — I recognized at once that he
had real talent. Consequently, I accepted him as pupil,
though at this time he was unable to pay my fee. Later his
mother inherited a great fortune [or what appeared to
Schoenberg to be a great fortune] and told Alban, as they
now have money, he could enter the conservatory. I was
told that Alban was so upset by this assumption that he
started weeping and could not stop weeping before his
mother had allowed him to continue with me.

He was always faithful to me and has remained so during
all his short life. Why did I tell this story? Because I was
greatly surprised when this soft-hearted, timid young man
had the courage to engage in a venture which seemed to invite misfortune: to compose *Wozzeck,* a drama of such extraordinary tragic [*sic*] that seemed forbidding to music. And
even more: it contained scenes of everyday life which were
contrary to the concept of the opera which still lived on
stylized costumes and conventional characters. He succeeded.
Wozzeck was one of the greatest successes of opera.

And why? Because Berg, this timid man, was a strong
character and faithful to his ideas, just as he was faithful to
me when he was almost forced to discontinue studying with
me.

He succeeded with the opera as he succeeded in his insistence to study with me.

Making the belief in ideas one's only destiny is the quality
which makes the great man.

And in the late 1930s, after Berg's death, Schoenberg
wrote as follows about his friend and former student:

Two things emerged clearly even from Berg's earliest compositions, however awkward they may have been: First,
that music was to him a language, and that he really expressed himself in that language; and secondly, the overflow-
ing warmth of feeling. He was eighteen at the time, actually

nineteen — it is a long time ago, and I cannot say if I recognized originality at that stage. It was a pleasure to teach him. He was industrious, eager, and did everything in the best possible way. And — like all those young people of that time — he steeped himself in music, lived in music. He went to all operas and concerts and learned the repertory; he played four-hand piano at home and learned to read scores. He was enthusiastic and unbiased, receptive to everything beautiful, old or new, in music, literature, painting, sculpture, theater and opera.

I could do counterpoint with him in a manner rare among my students. And I mention especially the five-voice Double Fugue for String Quintet [*sic*], which was full of ingenious spots. I guessed what levels to which he could be pushed: when the Fugue was finished, I told him to add a piano accompaniment in the style of a continuo. Not only did he execute this assignment excellently, but he found ways of adding a further host of minor devilries.

The instruction in composition that followed proceeded effortlessly and smoothly up to and including the Sonata, Opus 1. Then problems began to appear, the nature of which neither of us understood then. I understand today: obviously Alban, who had occupied himself with contemporary music, with Mahler, Strauss, perhaps even Debussy (whose work I did not know), and certainly with my music — certainly Alban had a burning desire to express himself in a way different from the classical forms, harmonies and melodies with their proper schemes of accompaniment. He wanted a style more in accordance with the times, which would reflect his own developing personality. There was a lapse in his creativity . . .

Unshakable conscientiousness and reliability were very characteristic of Berg. Whatever he undertook he executed with painful exactitude — thought it through from the ground up and then corrected and proofread it carefully . . .

And then he was the truest and most affectionate of friends. His power of invention was inexhaustible when it

was a matter of preparing a pleasant surprise for someone; it
was on the same plane as the intensity of his composing.

When did Alban Berg stop studying with Arnold
Schoenberg? In one sense, in 1908, when he handed in his
"journeyman's work," the Piano Sonata, called it Opus
1, and declared an end to his apprenticeship. On a more
casual basis, however, their work together continued
until 1911, when Schoenberg left Vienna for Berlin and,
in fact, referred some of his less experienced students to
Berg, so that the younger composer could begin his own
teaching career. But in a very important way Berg never
stopped calling Schoenberg his teacher. Even after he no
longer submitted manuscripts for Schoenberg's approval,
Berg continued to want and actively seek his master's en-
dorsements, and he suffered when the criticism was
harsh. Both Webern and Berg admitted that they saw
Schoenberg as a father figure, and both were pained even
as adults when relations with their mentor occasionally
became strained. The two students, neither of whom was
very much younger than his teacher, assumed the roles of
protectors, shielding Schoenberg from financial hardship,
defending him against the press, acting as intermediaries
and, sometimes, apologists on his behalf.
　　Berg in particular spent a good deal of time that might
otherwise have been devoted to composition working as
Schoenberg's personal assistant and secretary, preparing
performances, writing essays on the older man's music,
and lobbying for both monetary support and acceptance
of Schoenberg's work. For at the same time as he was authoritarian, Schoenberg was also magnetic. He demanded
complete devotion, and often received it. Gradually, Berg
learned to remain "in service" to Schoenberg as friend
and advocate without giving up his own musical in-

dependence; Webern, ironically, was never able to free himself from Schoenberg's musical grip to the extent that Berg managed to. Yet Schoenberg was the most important figure in Berg's life during his early years of maturity; without this teacher and disciplinarian, Berg might never have become a composer. The younger man recognized this debt and, difficult as the task was, spent his life trying to repay it.

Chapter 3

Friendship and Love

B<small>UT</small> S<small>CHOENBERG</small> could not be everyone and everything to Berg. The young man still depended on his family, with whom he moved from the suburban peace of Hietzing back into the city, to a flat at 11 Vordere Zollamtsstrasse, near the customs building, in 1907. He had his old confessor, Hermann Watznauer, who was rising in a civil service career. He had his school friend Paul Hohenberg, by now a published poet. And then there was the exciting café crowd of poets, artists, and writers, many of them close friends of Smaragda. They went to Vienna's legendary coffee houses for wine, beer, and "large browns" — coffee with milk — and for intellectual stimulation. Fortunately, they were not in the position of the many Viennese who were driven into the cafés by the city's severe shortage of warm, comfortable housing.

The "in" spots changed. For a while, Berg preferred the Casa Piccola, on the Mariahilferstrasse, Vienna's longest shopping street, with everything from block-long department stores to yard-wide book and antique shops.

Later, after the architect Adolf Loos designed the interior
of the Café Museum, across the Karlsplatz from the new
home of the antiacademic Secession art movement, the
friends started to congregate there. The furnishings have
since been changed, but the Café Museum still has the
look and the ambience it had in the second decade of the
century.

The most memorable nights were those when Berg
went with his sister and sometimes Charly, too, to the
Loewenbraeu, a place for food and beer behind the
Burgtheater. There, the young musician met the enor-
mously influential Viennese social critic Karl Kraus, the
poet Peter Altenberg, the writer Stefan Zweig, the architect Loos, and the artist Gustav Klimt, who had just been
named president of the Secession. Alban and Charly were
welcome because they came with Smaragda, the family
intellectual. In addition to being a skilled pianist,
Smaragda was unusually well read, witty, and persuasive;
she was also more of a social rebel than either of her
brothers. Though she was barely twenty, her opinions
were valued by the older artists and writers of the Loewenbraeu circle. Alban had less to say, but with his
newly won self-confidence as a musician, he could meet
these famous people knowing that he was, or soon would
be, more than simply Smaragda's brother.

One of the men who frequently came under discussion
at these cultural round tables was Mahler. Berg had been
part of the mob of young enthusiasts who had laid siege
to the conductor's dressing room after Mahler had led the
Vienna première of his Fourth Symphony, in 1902; the
baton Mahler had used that night was to remain one of
Berg's most prized possessions. At the time of the Fourth
Symphony, Mahler's reputation rested primarily on his
being the lionized director of the Vienna State Opera and

the husband of one of the city's femmes fatales, Alma
Maria Schindler. Several more years were to pass before
even the Schoenberg circle would think of Mahler principally as a composer; the première of the Sixth Symphony, in 1906, marked an important turning point in
drawing attention to Mahler's creative powers.

To Berg, every contact with the man who personified
the Vienna State Opera and its grandeur was unforget-
table. When Mahler left the Opera for New York, in
December 1907, Berg was among about two hundred
people who congregated at the West Station at 8:30 A.M.
to shake his hand, wave farewell, and watch the hero's
train pull out of sight. There would be other meetings,
one in the fall of 1910, only a few months before Mahler's death. Mahler learned that Berg was an aspiring
composer and asked if he also took the podium. When
the answer was a definite no, Mahler replied, "Only
composing! That's the way to do it!"

There were new friends, a new direction, and new
vitality in Berg's life — places to go, things to do, much
to learn and see. But Berg wanted more. "I hope that
when I go out into the big wide world, I'll find an honorable, wonderful young woman who will be devoted to
me and who will show me the way to glory," the
twenty-one-year-old composition student wrote to Watznauer in the fall of 1906. A few months later, he spotted
someone who seemed to meet those requirements, in the
standing-room at the concert hall in the Musikverein and
later in the highest, least expensive seats and standing-
room at the Opera. She was Helene Karoline Nahowski,
daughter of Franz Nahowski, a civil servant, and his
wife, Anna Nowak. In the words of Altenberg, "She
looked like a tall, thin, ash-blond Russian student, only
very tired from unfought battles." She was strikingly
beautiful. At that time, her blond hair hung almost to her

waist; later she would pile it up, leaving tendrils to curl
gently around her face. Her features were even and
strong. She was not merely presentable; she was stylish.
She kept her figure by eating very little, and that reluctantly.

Altenberg noticed her before Berg did, and wrote two
sketches of her, one of which sounds remarkably like the
composer Alwa's Hymn to Lulu in Berg's second opera:

H.N.

In your eyes I read your life —
I don't need to know anything more, this is all.
And your voice is my music in the world!
Seeing your hands makes me thank fate —
and to comfort you makes me tremble deep inside!
You are displayed in the world like a cut flower,
which stares defiantly at hardy plants!
You alone fill me with longing, God's honorable torment!
The others can be enjoyed when they're there,
and left for dead when they're far away!
But the poet's desire and need radiates from you,
and his flames feed on this fuel!
When you speak of love songs, I hear them sung;
When you speak of love poems, I have read them!
When you speak of beautiful women, I see them,
When you speak of men, I die of despair!
          And the world is dark for me —
The power, the power, power of consecration without oath!
          That is the spell you have over me!
You are troubled by a thousand secret battles fought here
                    and there,
but they are dew and sun to me,
in which I patiently observe and understand you,
like a mother taking in the riddles of her beloved child —
Do not go away! Because if you leave me,
your own magic is dimmed —
and there remains a world which will treat you brutally!

If Altenberg, the irreverent bohemian poet, loved Helene Nahowski — and there is no evidence except these
poems that their relationship went beyond friendship —
Alban Berg did also, at once. Initially, they merely
glanced at each other across crowded concert halls; she
could hardly have missed the tall, thin young man who
went to so many of the same places she did. Then, on
Good Friday of 1907, Berg finally managed to meet Helene by convincing her brother, Frank, to lure her into
the garden at a certain hour in the afternoon, and their intense and curious relationship began.

Helene was only a few months younger than Alban;
she was born on July 29, 1885, on Hetzendorferstrasse,
in the Meidling section of Vienna. She grew up with her
two sisters and her brother at one of the best addresses in
the suburb of Hietzing, in a villa at Maxinggasse 46, with
a large lawn and parks on two sides, a five- or ten-minute
walk from the lesser villa where the Bergs had lived from
1905 to 1907. She was widely rumored to be the illegitimate daughter of Emperor Franz Josef (her brother, Franz
Josef, called Frank, was named for the emperor), and the
resemblance she bore to the Hapsburgs was evident to
knowing observers. She was a member of that artistic
circle which included Altenberg, though probably more
because of her beauty and grace than for her own ideas or
accomplishments. She studied singing with dreams of
someday performing at the Opera, and she could manage
passably at the piano. Over the years, Berg praised her
voice and her musicianship. That she made no career for
herself does not seem to have been a loss to art.

As a child, Helene found a Prince Alban in a book of
fairy tales, and dreamed about being carried off by him.
As a twenty-one-year-old, she found another, living
Alban. The two joked about the make-believe prince in
several of the hundreds of letters, walks in the park, visits

to concerts and museums, and excursions with friends
that marked their romantic courtship. Both believed in
love at first sight; she gave it an almost mystical tinge.
On the frontispiece to her collection of nearly five
hundred of the letters that Alban wrote to her over the
years, Helene wrote, "For twenty-eight years I lived in
the Paradise of his love. His death was a catastrophe I
only had the strength to survive because our souls were
long ago joined together in a union beyond space and
time, a union through all eternity."

And in the first letter Helene Berg chose to include in
this volume (she controlled both the selection and the
editing of its contents), her new friend and husband-to-be
quoted Theodor Storm's poem "Schliesse mir die Augen
beide," which he was setting to music for her:

With your dear hands
O close my eyes.
Beneath its touch
All suffering dies.
Wave after wave
Now sings the smart.
No ripple more,
You fill my heart.

"One good thing about the image in this song," Alban
wrote; "it gives me an excuse to send you the letter you
scorned last night. Again and again, I kiss that hand of
yours, my most glorious Symphony in D Minor!"

The letter is undated, but it was probably written in
April or May of 1907, soon after Helene and Alban met.
It was followed by another, more soulful letter, in which
Alban asked:

Isn't it enough for you, Helene, if one man throws himself at
your feet? A man with a soul — real deep feelings, I mean —
and a body and mind, too, as good as anyone else's. To

make your happiness complete, do you really need a man
friend to flatter you and several boring girl friends? Can't I
become everything to you? . . . Oh, how I long to be alone
with you for once, for hours and hours, with nobody else
around, so that our hearts could open and melt into each
other, so that peace and serenity could pervade my being at
last, so that I need not feel forever only the "suffering of
love."

Berg was smitten, though the remarks in his letters and
the few of Helene's replies that are extant and available
are relatively cool, sometimes even distant. His ardor
grew, however, and by June 1907, writing to her had
become a regular and important part of his life. "Well, I
really *am* in love," he wrote at that time. "I can't go to
sleep any more unless I first have a little chat with you,
even if only by letter."

Much of their communication had to take place by
post. For one thing, Helene had another suitor, Raoul,
who had been out of Vienna during the first weeks of Alban's energetic courtship. Also, Franz Nahowski decided
that the musician was not an appropriate companion for
his daughter. At first, the young couple's meetings had
been easy and casual; Helene went freely around Vienna
and had a large circle of friends. But as she began to
single out Alban and to meet him privately, her father in-
tervened, and the lovers had to arrange to rendezvous at
railway stations in town or near their respective summer
homes (hers at Trahuetten, between Vienna and the
Berghof), at museums, or in parks. They passed mes-
sages back and forth with the cooperation of Helene's sister Anna, who, along with her mother, was sympathetic
to Alban's cause. When they had to rely on the mails,
Berg became an expert on the Austrian postal system,
timing deliveries to the minute and growing anxious

when the postman was delayed or when a letter was a day or two later than he anticipated.

Alban never seriously doubted that Helene was the young woman for whom he had been searching; Helene, who was more experienced in the games of suitors, was not so easily convinced — or, if she was, she coyly kept it to herself. Her father, who had begun with reservations, grew increasingly less fond of the persistent musician. Johanna Berg, however, was eager to give the young people her blessing. In 1907, Smaragda married well; her husband was Adolf von Eger, son of the president of an Austrian railroad company. From the beginning, that pairing proved more successful financially than emotionally, but it seemed to Johanna that it was high time her impressionable youngest son started a family of his own, too. Alban, however, knew from Shakespeare that the course of true love never did run smooth. Johanna should have known that it never runs according to a would-be grandmother's wishes.

Just meeting Helene, however, affected Berg tremendously, and his emotions began to follow the sine-wave pattern they had traced before he came under the stabilizing influence of Schoenberg. But he made significant creative advances, especially in the private, recreational songs he wrote outside Schoenberg's classes. He still had no real reason to believe that he would ever be able to survive as a composer or be self-supporting. Nevertheless, each work represented a new musical conquest; each piece invariably moved away from its predecessor, if not always to a higher level, at least to a different one. From the time he was twenty until the end of his life, Berg's work never stood still or recapitulated.

The Seven Early Songs are especially revealing of this rapid-fire progress, even though they were compiled and released much later, for reasons more practical than artistic. In 1928, when he was beginning serious work on *Lulu,* Berg realized that it would be a while before his next première and that it would be to his advantage to keep his name before the public. He dipped back into his files and combined seven songs from his student days, songs that would in no way offend listeners' ears and would recall the tradition from which he had grown. In order to make the first performances of these songs as big an event as it could reasonably be, Berg decided to orchestrate them, rather than leave them with the original piano accompaniments. It was in this larger version that they received their first performance, on November 6, 1928, in Vienna. Universal Edition published both the voice-piano and the voice-orchestra scores in the same year.

Berg's impressionable youth did not shame him, and he never denied the musical past that nurtured him. If anything, the orchestrations of these songs tie them even more closely to that past, accentuating their debts to Strauss and to Mahler, and separating them from the relative sparseness that would become a trademark of the "new school." It would be hard to imagine Schoenberg or even Webern having agreed to resurrect works such as these Seven Early Songs to represent them during their maturity. Berg not only brought the music out and set it before the public; he gave reason to believe that he reveled in the process.

Schoenberg went to the first Berlin performance of the Seven Early Songs, in the spring of 1929, and cabled his congratulations to the composer. Berg replied with pleasure, admitting that the songs of his youth still had special meaning for him, that he associated them with Schoenberg's classes, and that the success of the orchestrated version of the songs made memories of his student days even more vivid. By 1928, of course, there was no question that Berg could set the songs with orchestra. But between 1905 and 1908, even if he had wanted to follow the leads of Mahler and Strauss and set songs with the support of a large instrumental ensemble, he would have had technical problems; he was not ready for such a challenge.

Three of the seven had already been performed; "Die Nachtigall," "Traumgekroent," and "Liebesode" had been Berg's entries in the concert of music by Schoenberg students in November 1907, the event marking his formal debut as a composer. Four were "new." From his private collection of well over one hundred songs that had not been performed outside his living room, Berg chose "Im Zimmer" (text by Johannes Schlaf), "Sommertage" (Paul Hohenberg), "Nacht" (Carl Hauptmann), and "Schilflied" (Nikolaus Lenau). Though it is hard to date them precisely, the songs were written between the middle of 1905 and the summer of 1908, in the second, third, and fourth (and final) years of Berg's most intensive and basic study with Schoenberg. Alban and Smaragda had performed "Die Nachtigall" in 1905. "Nacht," the first number in the published order, is generally thought to have been written last, in the spring of 1908; its style tends to confirm this dating.

It is impossible to know with any certainty whether Berg submitted these particular songs to Schoenberg's classes, but the odds are that he did not. They were probably written during summers at the Berghof, when the young composer was free from exercises in theory and counterpoint and from the instrumental assignments Schoenberg was giving in order to teach his student the rules of orchestration. These songs were written for sheer

pleasure. And just as they show where Berg started and
where he came from, they point surely in the direction he
was to follow.

Much as it would have pained him to admit it later,
Berg started from the most romantic side of Richard
Strauss. Having taken more than half a dozen trips to
hear *Salome* in 1906, Berg could never have denied this
early affinity to that leader of the early-twentieth-century
vanguard, even though he changed his mind and told
Webern in 1911 that he was "disenchanted" with
Strauss's songs and even with the opera *Der Rosenkavalier*. Here, again, Berg shared Schoenberg's tastes; by
1911, Mahler had replaced Strauss on Schoenberg's list of
admired composers.

But as much as the Seven Early Songs owe a debt to
the great German art-song tradition, from Schubert and
Schumann through Brahms, Hugo Wolf, and, of course,
Mahler, the music was clearly born of Strauss. They are
full of Strauss's (and Wagner's) willingness — even
eagerness — to ride great climaxes. They are packed with
Straussian expansiveness; in only two or three measures,
the introductions of several of the songs seem to open
doors on vast, mile-high vistas. Naturally, the added orchestrations underline these qualities; the Seven Early
Songs are better known in their fully orchestrated versions than in their original chamber forms, and for good
reason. The symphonic accompaniments, making use of
different combinations of instruments in every song, give
the music new color and motion, so that it seems to spill
out of its confines, like a stream impatiently rushing into
an ocean.

"Nacht," the opening song, acts as a door-opening
metaphor: both the beginning of Carl Hauptmann's text
("Clouds are fading over the darkening valley,/mists are

floating, waters murmur softly,/Now, all at once, the veil
is lifted;/Oh watch, watch!") and Berg's setting of it
suggest the opening moments of Béla Bartók's *Bluebeard's
Castle,* with its anxious promise of opening doors.

The vista revealed here in the poem's last twelve lines
had been seen by Strauss and Wagner. In the second
song, "Schilflied," Mahler's influence is more evident,
especially in the transparent orchestration and the
sweetness of the treatment of Lenau's nostalgic text. Divided strings accompany the third song, "Die Nachtigall," giving a great feeling of depth and proportion
that looks back to Brahms, an impression strengthened
by the traditional cadence and the song's straight A-B-A
form, with the first verse of the poem repeated verbatim
at the end.

"Traumgekroent," the fourth song, is a setting of
Rilke's famous "That was the day of the white
chrysanthemums,/I was almost afraid of their magnificence . . ." Berg's music plays on the words' nervousness. And the orchestra moves according to Strauss; a rising line in the lower strings under the words "you came
sweetly and softly" predicts a parallel but even more
magical moment in Berg's last work, the Violin Concerto. "Im Zimmer," the fifth of the Seven Early Songs,
accompanies Schlaf's poem with special attention to
woodwinds, horns, harp, and percussion. The Marschal-
lin could sing this song to her young lover, Octavian;
there is a remarkable parallel here to *Der Rosenkavalier* in
particular and to Strauss's music in general, especially to
the composer's more domestic aspect.

"Liebesode" (to Hartleben's text), though not the last
of the seven songs in their probable order of composition, is the one that bows most deeply in the direction of
Schoenberg, both in the music and in the choice of text.

("In the arms of love we slept blissfully./At the open
window the summer wind listened,/and carried peaceful
breathing out into the bright moonlight . . .") Schoenberg, too, was drawn to images of night winds and
moonbeams, especially as described by the poet Richard
Dehmel. And the last of the orchestral series of Seven
Early Songs, "Sommertage," bows again in the comfortable direction of romanticism and heads for a rich, grand
cadence, in which Berg was not even afraid to let the
cymbals ring out on the singer's last note.

The assignments Schoenberg gave the twenty-two-
year-old Berg were not merely exercises, though the
same purposes probably could have been met through
simple, repetitive *études* in counterpoint and orchestration. Schoenberg's top priority was to move Berg away
from his vocal island and get him to adapt his obvious
talents to instruments. The teacher could not make his
student stop writing songs completely, but he could re-
fuse to pay attention to them during class hours. So all of
Berg's works for Schoenberg were instrumental, beginning with the Double Fugue for String Quartet with
Piano Accompaniment (after the Manner of a Continuo).
The manuscript of this, Berg's vehicle for his debut as a
composer-pianist, has been listed as lost, but all or parts
of it may eventually turn up, either in the piles of papers
in the Berg estate or at auction.

The Twelve Variations on an Original Theme for
Piano represented Berg at the second concert of music by
Schoenberg's students, in 1908, and, though never published, were printed in a facsimile version in H. F. Redlich's 1957 biography of the composer. The Variations
were dated 1908, which would make them contemporaries of the Piano Sonata, Opus 1. But the relative insecurity of the Variations would indicate either that they

were written (or started) quite a bit earlier or that, for
some reason, they never received the same amount of
care and time Berg devoted to the Piano Sonata. In the
Variations it is possible to recognize what Schoenberg
meant when he said that Berg urgently needed to work
on mastering his instrumental style. It is one thing for a
piece to be difficult to perform; it is something else when
the music feels and sounds awkward even after the difficulties have been mastered.

Here, too, we can feel how much happier Berg was in
those years when he was dealing with words and voices
than when he threw himself into the more abstract instrumental realm. The ancestors of the Variations are
Brahms's sets of piano variations and his "Haydn" Variations for orchestra, most notably in the use of thirds and
sixths, the parallel motion, and the very grand piano
style. Schumann also figures in Berg's Variations, especially in the technical writing for the piano (though here
Berg had not yet learned his lessons well) and in the
rhythmic displacements and some harmonic progressions. Berg knew the principles of variation tradition,
which would have figured prominently during his first
weeks of work with Schoenberg. He had the courage to
veil his theme and to vary the mood of the music from
section to section. And he was bold enough to challenge
himself and the pianist with new problems in each variation, for example, the scale passages in Variation I and the
canon of Variation III.

But the solutions to these problems are not always satisfying to either performer or listener. The harmonies
tend to be awkward; cadences are often precipitous; the
dramatic gesture is chopped off; and the warmth and expansiveness that characterize the songs seem to have been
repressed by technical and expressive insecurities. Berg

was aiming for a style that would hold on to drama and
romanticism without going along with the layers of indulgences they had come to imply. Naturally, it took
him a while to find the path to his new manner of communication.

What is surprising, though, is that he was so far along
by the time he finished the Piano Sonata, in 1908. He
started the Sonata during the joyous summer of 1907 at
the Berghof, "out of the blue . . . for my own benefit,"
while repeating some exercises from his counterpoint
class and channeling a good deal of his mental ingenuity
into finding ways to arrange meetings with Helene Nahowski and to inspire her to write more frequent letters.
Yet the difference between the Piano Sonata and anything
that might be called an exercise (including the Double
Fugue with Piano) is amazing. The Sonata showed that,
at twenty-three, Berg had come into his own as a composer, which also meant that he had reached emotional
maturity. Schoenberg must have realized this, and surely
the teacher influenced Berg's decision to make the Sonata
his official Opus 1. As such, it served as the last work of
his apprenticeship. Berg's work with Schoenberg would
continue, but he was no longer identified as a student. Increasingly, he was on his own.

Webern reached a similar point during the same year of
his studies with Schoenberg. His Passacaglia for Orchestra, Opus 1, actually marked the end of his formal instruction. Despite the fact that Webern's Passacaglia has
come to be performed more often that Berg's Sonata, the
Passacaglia has less of a feeling of adventure. (This could
be precisely the reason why it so frequently represents
Webern on symphony orchestra programs.) Webern's
journeymanlike work is polished, lyrical, wholly professional, and self-contained. Berg's wants to move on,

gives a feeling of dramatic unrest, tackles problems and fights battles too large to be won or lost in the course of a sonata movement.

Berg sat down to write a sonata at the Berghof, feeling confident enough to try something on his own initiative other than a song, and knowing that such a project brought back to Vienna after the vacation months would please Schoenberg. The young composer achieved his goal. The piano sonatas of Mozart, Haydn, and Beethoven each takes its name from the structures of the first movement. The sonata form is the exposition of ideas, their development, and a recapitulation as a neat return, usually following a harmonic scheme sanctioned by time and custom. When modern listeners speak of a sonata, they have come to mean a piece in several movements, usually three, with the first in a moderate or moderately fast tempo, the second slow, and the third fastest of all. In the second half of the nineteenth century, composers began to take great liberties with the sonata form, but Berg's original thoughts for his first sonata had been traditional; he planned a three-movement work, but could not get the second and third movements to present themselves. When he mentioned this problem to Schoenberg, the teacher said to go no further; Berg had evidently said all he had to say on his musical subject. Opus 1 stayed a single movement, fulfilling all the requirements of sonata form (including the vestigial repeat of the exposition), and stopping when its point was made.

Actually, Berg had said quite a lot. To begin with, as opposed to the Twelve Variations on an Original Theme, the Sonata is written expertly for its instrument; though not simple, it is idiomatic and rewarding to the performer. It has a taut, self-controlled feeling, yet, in a manner not unlike Stravinsky's (but in a very different idiom), it is full of small but telling dramatic gestures. These gestures, which have an energy and direction that can be quite independent of their formal purpose or placement, show the beginnings of one of Berg's musical hallmarks. Gone are the long phrases that swept around the Twelve Variations and the Seven Early Songs. In their place stand multipurpose fragments that can be built together into longer phrases or used separately, both horizontally and vertically, melodically and harmonically. To be sure, Mozart often used parts of his principal themes as points of departure for development sections, but Berg took this idea one or two steps further when he used the sections of the original statement as germs for an entire work. The opening phrase, three measures in three-quarter time, gives the analyst everything he needs to work with: an opening pair of fourths outlining the interval of the seventh; a retreat downward, again using the fourth; and a concluding (cadential) minor second. At no point in the Piano Sonata are the cadences anything but straightforward; the work is in B Minor, and Berg made sure that no listener would ever have cause to doubt it.

The cadences and the strict sonata form are proof that it is not the treatment of the material that sets the Piano Sonata apart from its predecessors but, rather, the material itself. No student will miss the arrival of the second theme; history says it should arrive in the key of the dominant (the fifth tone of the scale), and it does, only reluctantly, by way of a ninth chord built on the pitch A. Just as clear as the form are the composer's instructions to performers. Characteristically, Berg filled his score with painstaking indications for accents, changes in dynamics and tempos (making it very clear how each new pace should relate to those that went before). He even tried to head off potential misreadings; at the approach to the recapitulation, he suspected that even the best-intentioned and most sympathetic pianist might want to hold back a bit, so he wrote in a warning against slowing down (*"Nicht schleppen!"*).

Etta Werndorf played the world première of the Opus 1 Piano Sonata on April 24, 1911, in the Ehrbar Hall; the program also listed string quartets by Webern, Horwitz, and Berg (the Opus 3), and Webern's aphoristic Pieces for Violin and Piano, which were particularly challenging to listeners' ears and minds. This time, not even Berg was lucky with the press. Paul Stauber reported in the *Illustrierte Wiener Extrablatt:*

> After a long hiatus, the Society against Art and Culture [a jibe at the Society *for* Art and Culture, which was generally identified with Schoenberg and his circle] took up its routine exercises Monday evening in Ehrbar Hall. The group's leaders, lacking talent, imagination, and taste . . . have named the director of Viennese cacophony, Mr. Schoenberg, as their patron and have adopted the cause of his youthful followers . . . Mr. Berg had written a piece for piano (immodestly entitled Piano Sonata) that has traces of talent and musicianship. But the joke is no longer funny. It is now clear that not only the untalented but also the gifted students with vague futures are being dragged down a primrose path that can never lead to art or culture. And therefore only the strongest protests possible are suited to describe the travesty of Monday evening.

The critics raged. The public was enraged. Much as the Viennese loved their scandals, those that took place at Schoenberg's concerts were too much even for them, since they violated the sacred ground of music. Today, Berg's Piano Sonata seems to pay homage to the past, remarkable as it was in the young composer's development. But the critics and audiences of 1911 noticed that it also owed a debt to Schoenberg's Chamber Symphony, Opus 9; that, for them, was enough to cause a riot. The musicologists had solved the problems they might have faced earlier by deciding simply that the music was impossible: Schoenberg's early (1899) Opus 4, the string sextet *Verklaerte Nacht,* befuddled the analysts by using the "nonexistent" inversion of the ninth chord where the ninth sounded in the bottom voice. There might have been a crisis had the scribes not concurred that, since the rules said that the ninth could not be used in the bass, they would forget the sextet altogether. They decided that nothing out of the ordinary was happening. Clearly, however, something was.

Chapter 4

A Musical Revolution

IT IS HARD to argue for inevitability in art. It was no more inevitable that the one-line melodies of plainsong would be harmonized according to strictly developed rules than it was that Beethoven would write his Ninth Symphony. It was similarly no more inevitable that cavemen would try to conquer the animals they hunted by painting their images on walls of stone than it was that Duchamp would paint his *Nude Descending a Staircase.* If Bach had not written his cantatas, if Beethoven hadn't written the *Eroica,* if Stravinsky hadn't written *Le Sacre du printemps,* would someone else have done so?

Yet there are times, moments in the life of society and thus of the arts, too, when traditional structures and ideas have been so completely explored, and when the pressure around them has built to such a point, that radical changes have to be made. Specific creations are not inevitable; change is. Schoenberg liked to tell about the day a World War I army colonel came up to him and asked whether he was really *the* Arnold Schoenberg, the controversial musician. "Somebody had to be. Nobody

wanted to. So in the end I agreed to take on the job," was
the composer's reply. It was obvious to Schoenberg and
his followers that certain aspects of musical expression
(such as the solid tonal cadence and key signatures of
sharps and flats) had lost their usefulness. The immediate
task that Schoenberg, Berg, and Webern faced was not so
much to define the new style in full — that process
would be able to take care of itself — as to put themselves in a position where they would be free to accept
new ideas; where they would not be, in a sense, trying to
fit new sounds into old molds.

Western music had been moving in one general direction for a thousand years. Chants were made from scales
of seven physically related tones; the seven that ran C, D,
E, F, G, A, B, and back again to C came to be called C
Major. When two notes could be sounded together to
pleasing effect, a chord was formed, and harmony as we
know it had begun. Within the realm of that simple C
Major, a B-flat could add interest and variety to both
melody and harmony, so it gained official recognition.
The church slowly gave its blessings to the use of other
"accidentals" (F-sharp, E-flat, and so on), and the kings
and nobles who paid for the music finally learned to love
what had initially assaulted their ears. "Chromaticism,"
the free use of these "foreign" pitches, peaked in the
Renaissance, then was brought back to life by Johann
Sebastian Bach. In C Major, the use of an F-sharp or a
B-flat gave easy access to a different key, and the process
of modulation was born. One piece could have sections
in both C Major and G Major, for instance, but always
according to one shared set of rules. Modulation, in particular, had to be strictly regulated lest the music go out
of control and lose its way back to the home key.

The story of Western music since 1685, the year Bach

was born, is basically the story of harmonic expansion. Once Claudio Monteverdi and his colleagues of the pre-Bach Baroque settled into key structures and relationships of the kind that we still identify (with our tradition-oriented ears) as basic, the pattern for future development was set. Bach took more harmonic liberties than his mainstream precursors; Beethoven went further than Bach; Schubert and Schumann risked even more. As the number of admissible pitches increased, as the harmonies became richer and thicker, so did the performing forces. Change was born of pragmatism and necessity. Mozart was able to command more performers than Bach had. Beethoven needed more musicians than Mozart (and was so widely respected that there was usually a patron to pay for the added players). A Schumann symphony performed by the same number of players used for a Bach suite sounds anemic.

As Schoenberg said, somebody had to do it. An individual had to take the first step. On the charts of the broad course, it matters less exactly who was responsible for adding the flute or the second trumpet to the previously "standard"-sized orchestra than that it did happen, and that the symphony orchestra slowly filled out to its still-current nineteenth-century dimensions. Yet there have been certain seminal moments, certain events that seemed to ignite fireworks which could not be missed by either musicologists or the general public. One such moment was the sounding of the famous "Tristan" chord — the first multinote grouping in Richard Wagner's opera *Tristan und Isolde* — with all its ambiguities. It was not at all obvious where the "Tristan" chord (basically, F, B, D-sharp, G-sharp, or two seemingly unrelated fourths) came from, where it was inclined to go, and whether it would ever get there. In an operatic epic built on sex and passion, it was terrifying to traditionalists to think that they might be denied the fulfillment of a complete cadence on a comfortable triad. *Tristan* opened on to new realms in which no one was extremely secure. But once these realms had been opened, their existence could not be ignored.

The "Tristan" chord was only nine years older than Schoenberg, twenty years older than Berg. But by the time these composers were old enough to come to terms with their inheritance, they had to face a large body of post-*Tristan* expression, from Anton Bruckner's translation of all-stops-out Wagneriana into the symphonic medium, to Richard Strauss's virtuoso tone poems and Mahler's highly dramatic and even neurotic distillations. Even in conservative Italy, in the old-fashioned and ever-conservative world of opera, Verdi and Puccini managed to make their devotees' blood run hot while underlining their theatrics with harmonies that would not have been accepted before *Tristan*.

Schoenberg, Berg, and Webern grew up on what then seemed the rabble-rousing creations of Mahler and Strauss, with their huge orchestras, their oceanic sonorities, their unprecedented lengths. Naturally, the first inclination of the new generation had been to carry the thoughts of their ancestors several steps further; for his *Gurrelieder,* which was not completed until 1911, Schoenberg had to have special music paper made to accommodate all the different instrumental and vocal lines.

But an end had been reached; there was a level of expansion beyond which it was impractical, useless, and ultimately thankless to reach. No composer wants to write music that will never be performed, and the *Gurrelieder,* for example, is rarely programmed because of the difficulties and expense involved in engaging the choruses·

and oversized orchestra, rehearsing them all separately and together, and, indeed, fitting them all onto a stage. Since every element in the *Gurrelieder,* Beethoven's Ninth Symphony, or *Tristan* hinges on every other, nothing could be changed without affecting everything. The sacred old rules were worthless; once one element went, the others crumbled, too. If the ear said that there was neither room nor use for further growth, the mind said that the forces that had led music to expand had to be rearranged, if not forgotten, before new styles could emerge.

By virtue of his personality, his vision, and, in fact, his lack of training, Schoenberg was the person willing and capable of implementing some of the most important changes in the new music. But the process was tortuous and frightening; recalling what he and Berg went through with Schoenberg during the decade beginning in 1906, Webern spoke of "feverish struggles and decisive necessity." Impatient as the musical explorers were, however, they had to proceed deliberately, freeing themselves, in effect, from one antiquated rule or element at a time. The first to go was the traditional triad, the three-note chord built from thirds; in its place came chords constructed of fourths, which had their own tendencies and implications. Next was the key signature; with so many accidental sharps and flats spread throughout the music, it had become meaningless, even bothersome, to have the symbols at the beginning to indicate that they would be in force throughout the work.

Then tonality began to fall. This was the epochal event, the catastrophe. Tonality's demise was inevitable, yet it has left such a gap that the whole of twentieth-century music has been a quest for something satisfying to take its place. Schoenberg, Berg, and Webern realized

they had no choice but to let the bulwark fall; Webern
said, "It is really dead . . . [and] there is no point in continuing to deal with something dead." His matter-of-factness, however, should not minimize the gravity of the
situation faced by the New Viennese School. Schoenberg
was finding it tremendously difficult to follow new directions in his own music, let alone verbalize them for his
students. He was waging a battle and calling on young
people to support his cause, without knowing what his
specific goals and targets were or would be. He compen-
sated for the amorphous state of his art with his authoritarian manner. And the proclamations were not coming
only from Schoenberg's side; Webern, commenting on a
radio broadcast by a composer named Rinaldini, argued
that "at present people are squabbling over whether tonality should be given up. *He* may be squabbling," Webern said, "but we see it quite plainly and don't need to
squabble . . . Nobody has gone beyond our style, and
there is no need to discuss the others, who are merely rewriting old music." Webern was the most loyal of disciples.

There was, of course, more than one way to avoid the
forgeries of rewriting old music. The methods tried and
adopted by Schoenberg, Webern, Berg, and their followers were among many that were attempted in those
difficult decades. If it was generally conceded that Beetho-
ven-style tonality had lost its effectiveness and its time-
lessness, there was no unanimous choice of what would
replace it. And yet more than one person hit on the same
idea. Schoenberg, Berg, and Webern were gradually
coming to realize that, without cadences, key signatures,
or tonal bounds, each note in the chromatic scale (that is,
C, C-sharp, D, D-sharp, E, F, F-sharp, G, G-sharp, A,
A-sharp, B, and back to C) was beginning to demand

equal treatment; the hierarchy that had been implied by the old key structures was no longer meaningful. A young musician named Josef Hauer came to similar conclusions; but in 1915, when Private J. Hauer tried to explain his ideas to his superiors in the Austrian army, he was ridiculed and thought to be in need of psychiatric help. The officers sent him to Egon Wellesz for a second musical opinion; Wellesz listened with interest to Hauer's talk about twelve-tone rows that would function as compositional blocks in the same manner as the ancient Greek *nomoi,* or melodic patterns. In the consultant's judgment, Hauer was sane, if not sophisticated. Hauer obtained his release from the army office, and Wellesz spread the word through the Schoenberg circle of this fascinating concept of composing with twelve notes, every one equal to the others. Later, when both men had formulated their ideas more clearly, Schoenberg and Hauer were in contact directly. But with this early, somewhat vague concept of twelve-tone composition, Hauer had made his one contribution to music history.

Certain ideas were in the air, beginning to be talked about and studied by a number of people. One of the amazing things is that these ideas were current in and circling around Vienna, bastion of conservatism and the hearth and home of operetta. One might have expected the new ground to be broken in Berlin or Prague, where society concerned itself more eagerly with the avant-garde, or in London or even America, where the roots of the old Germanic tradition were not so deep and where change might therefore have been more easily facilitated.

But it was in Vienna that people recognized that change was inevitable, and that as blessed as the old monarchy, economy, religion, home life, language, literature, painting, and music had been, the entire culture was on

the verge of upheaval. Not even the subconscious was
safe; the much-discussed theories of Dr. Freud made even
dreams and fantasies the objects of scrutiny. If the majority of the Viennese tried to retreat into their overstuffed
eastern European–Victorian parlors to listen to the songs
of Schubert in nervous self-satisfaction, an eloquent
group of rabble-rousers was ready to make it difficult for
all but the most cloistered conservatives to shut out
change. As is usually the case, the sharpest and most per-
ceptive critics of the culture were members of the inner
circle. Wagner, Hugo von Hofmannsthal, Max Rein-
hardt, and Strauss could be described as "freaks of realism" because of their beliefs in the power of theatricality
and their demands for real animals onstage, trees that
looked like trees, and blood that looked like blood. But
their roots in reality were as shallow as Heinrich Heine's
and as fictional as Werther's when compared with those
of Karl Kraus.

A well-to-do Jew of Bohemian ancestry, Kraus saw his
city as "a proving ground for world destruction," much
as Adolf Hitler was to say that Vienna had been his "hardest, but . . . most thorough school." Kraus established
himself as the prophet who would hold up a mirror to
show the Viennese their own faults; his weapon was language, not glass. In 1899, having turned down the much
sought-after position as chief satirist for Vienna's *Neue
Freie Presse,* Kraus started his own radical periodical, *Die
Fackel (The Torch),* and printed 922 issues of the small red
booklet over the next thirty-seven years. In the beginning, such important members of the loyal opposition
(loyal to Kraus and his view of history) as Altenberg,
Houston Stewart Chamberlain (the husband of Eva Wagner, daughter of the composer), Richard Dehmel, Egon
Friedell, Else Lasker-Schueler, Wilhelm Liebknecht,
Adolf Loos, Heinrich Mann, Schoenberg himself, Frank

Wedekind, Franz Werfel (who would be Alma Mahler's third husband, after her divorce from Walter Gropius), and Hugo Wolf were allowed to contribute to Kraus's extremely popular journal. But after 1911, Kraus wrote all the copy himself — usually while everyone else slept, since he lived an inverted life, working all night and sleeping all day.

In his single-minded search for integrity, Kraus attacked virtually everyone: the police, the aesthetes, Zionists, all vestiges of imperial *alt Wien,* and anything with the slightest tinge of superciliousness. His writings defy proper translation and have never become widely known outside Austria, not least because he pointed his finger locally, at his own countrymen. Kraus was most vitriolic in his criticism of journalism, which he despised in its traditional form. "There is no baseness which the press would not be ready to falsify and pass off as a magnanimous deed; there is no crook on whose head it would not place the laurels of glory or the oak-wreath of citizenly virtue, whenever that served its purpose," he wrote. He was particularly disgusted by journalists who jumped on Mahler's bandwagon only as the composer-conductor was dying, and by reporters who were writing Mahler's obituary at the same time as they were telling concerned callers that his condition was improved. Schoenberg and his students shared Kraus's views on this and the great majority of cultural issues, even though they did not always agree with his aesthetic choices. Kraus derided the operettas of Lehár as crowd-pleasers, signals of further degeneration of society, but adored Jacques Offenbach (and translated *La Périchole* into German). Like Schoenberg, Kraus had two categories for music and all the arts: good and bad, or, as he preferred to say, true or false. Truth was artistic, but falsehood was not only inartistic; it was evil.

It was, naturally, Kraus who decided whether a truth was artistic, and one of the few whose truths he found consistently artistic was the architect Loos. "Adolf Loos and I — he literally and I grammatically — have done nothing more than show that there is a distinction between an urn and a chamber pot, and that it is this distinction above all that provides culture with elbow room. The others, those who fail to make this distinction, are divided into those who use the urn as a chamber pot and those who use the chamber pot as an urn."

Schoenberg expected his students to share his reverence for Kraus. The composer felt that he was the writer's brother-in-music, that Kraus wrote of a mission which he, Schoenberg, shared. "I command the language of others; mine does what it wants with me," Kraus said. "I have learned more from you, perhaps, than a man should learn, if he wants to remain independent," Schoenberg wrote to Kraus in a presentation copy of *Harmonielehre*.

Berg eagerly awaited the arrival in the post of each new copy of *Die Fackel;* he read it thoroughly, discussed it with his friends, and kept old editions in specially marked boxes. Still, he was not so unquestioning of Kraus as his teacher was. Berg respected and enjoyed the writer's work, and he looked forward to meeting him in coffee houses for evenings of literate and irreverent talk. But Berg was young enough to want to take in a variety of opinions.

He was not nearly so shaken by the inevitability of change in his art as Schoenberg and Webern were, nor could he quite share the feelings of fear and urgency that followed their realization that the old musical laws were obsolete. Through the hours he spent in the Schoenberg classes and in conversations with his fellow students on subjects both practical and theoretical, Berg thought and talked about the issues that occupied his friends' minds. But he was not alarmed. Perhaps he did not yet know enough to be afraid. He was not resisting change, but neither was he desperate for it. What the poet Stefan George called the "air of a different world" aroused Berg's curiosity, but he was not yet stifled by the old atmosphere.

His mind was filled with counterpoint, composition, Schoenberg, and Helene Nahowski. Early in 1908, the important Vienna Exhibition of the avant-garde attracted all of the city's young intellectuals, though, to Berg's great disappointment, he and Helene did not see the show together; her escort was Paul Hohenberg. Afterward, however, the young lovers did talk about the radical new art, especially the contributions of their strange friend Gustav Klimt. Here was a man whom Helene's father would never have considered acceptable company for his daughter. The stern protector of the young lady's reputation might have heard about one of Berg's nights out with Klimt in the fall of 1907, when, along with Smaragda, Loos, and a flashy woman called "La Bruckner," they started at the Fledermaus cabaret and moved on to the Z-Keller am Hof, where, as Berg confessed in a letter to Helene, "things became fairly confused for the next few hours." Attracted by La Bruckner's "wonderful hands," and transported by the glow of wine, Berg was, at least in his own opinion, indiscreet.

Klimt must have smiled knowingly at the young man's confusion, however innocent, passing, or, for that matter, sensuous the goings-on had been. And the artist would have laughed uproariously had he known about the gratuitous confession Berg sent to Helene and the remorse that obviously accompanied it. Klimt loved love. Alma Mahler, who went through a stormy romance with

him (and also with his colleague Oskar Kokoschka),
wrote of Klimt:

> He was . . . already famous at thirty-five [in 1897, when she
> was eighteen], and strikingly good looking. He was tied
> down a hundredfold, to women, children, sisters, who
> turned into enemies for love of him. And yet he pursued me
> to Italy . . . In Venice, in the bustle of the Piazza San
> Marco, we finally saw each other again. The crowd con-
> cealed us and his hasty whispers of love, his vows to rid
> himself of everything and come for me, his commanding
> request to wait for him . . . I was deaf to all his pleas to visit
> his studio.

Alma Mahler was vain, opportunistic, and not always
accurate in her reminiscences, but she was not overstating
Klimt's energies for passion. The man who is generally
remembered as the first "modern" Viennese painter was
born in 1862; his father, like Johanna Berg's, worked in
gold and silver. Klimt learned the craft but preferred to
use his precious metals in pigment form, painting them
on canvases in lushly erotic, Byzantine images of female
bodies. Klimt scandalized the Viennese, and they adored
him for it. They even granted him the honor of a commission from the Viennese Ministry of Education to paint
three pictures for the ceiling of the main hall of the University of Vienna. But when the first of these, *Philosophy,*
was unveiled in 1900, a tremor rocked the city government, and eighty-seven professors petitioned successfully
to prevent the iconographic clusters of naked shapes from
ever floating above their scholarly heads. Naturally, this
scandal did nothing but help the artist's business, and,
though the main hall of the university went without
Klimt, his works became coveted, and there was no
shortage of rich ladies presenting themselves to the
painter as high-paying models.

The Viennese, particularly the women, found Klimt's work as irresistible as they found Freud's ideas. Klimt projected his women into a strong yet romantic dream world, heavily overlaid with jewels and ornament. The painter's rich visions wore the layers of imagination and subconscious into which Freud's theories delved so mercilessly. There was not a hint of denial or abstention, no inhibition or repression, no social rules. The portraits speak the names of the two great preoccupations of a complacent society: money and sex.

Klimt had no desire to live among the people whom he painted. He secluded himself in a studio in Hietzing, not far from the Nahowskis' villa, but far enough from the main streets so that the painter could let his garden grow wild, could wear long, flowing robes, and share his life with Emilie Floege for twenty-seven years without bothering to marry her. Emilie prospered as a dressmaker to Vienna's fashion-conscious society ladies; to be dressed on canvas by Klimt or for a gala occasion by Emilie Floege was the dream of many a wealthy matron.

Klimt was the first president of Vienna's Secession, the movement that began in the house where Berg was born. In 1897, the Secession made a formal break with the tradition-bound Imperial Academy. The dissenters took as their motto "To the Age Its Art, to Art Its Freedom." Two years later, with funds from the industrialist Karl Wittgenstein, father of the philosopher Ludwig, Josef Olbrich designed the Secession's palace-museum on high-priced land at the central Karlsplatz; a gold cupola of intertwined foliage (immediately dubbed "the gilded cabbage") topped the building's bulky mass. By 1900, though, Klimt and his fellow would-be drop-outs were so accepted by the establishment that their work was included in the Paris International Exhibition.

The City of Vienna still does not support the Secession
Museum or list its events on cultural calendars, but the
movement's acceptance never depended on official sanc-
tions. Even at the Wiener Werkstaette, the arts-and-crafts
center that projected Secessionist principles into the design of furnishings, utensils, and fabrics, the artists had
failed as rebels. In the eyes of some, their work was fully
as vapid as the society people who were rushing to pur-
chase it. Loos was the spokesman for the radical purists,
and he went so far as to write an essay, "Ornament and
Crime," in 1908, proclaiming, "But the man of our own
times who from an inner compulsion smears walls with
erotic symbols is a criminal or a degenerate . . . Just as
ornament is no longer organically linked with our culture, so it is also no longer an expression of our culture . . ."

Early in 1918, Klimt died from the paralyzing effects of
a stroke. Left in his Hietzing studio was an unfinished
canvas, *The Bride,* whose details caught the artist in an act
of voyeurism. The left side of the picture is filled with
knotted, floating bodies. On the right side waits the
virgin, her scarf, a feature characteristic of Klimt, seeming to separate her head from her pale body, her legs
spread, knees bent, and her genitals painted in graphic detail. When he suffered his fatal stroke, Klimt was carefully covering up his young bride with one of his richly
ornamented skirts, hiding the erotic layers from public
scrutiny.

Soon, Berg would be doing something comparable in
his music, obscuring the personal, programmatic elements so that it would take many years and some luck for
anyone to prove that they were really there. He may have
remembered Klimt's cover-ups when he planned his
own, for Klimt was to Berg what Kraus was to Schoen-

berg. The younger composer never made the same kind of declaration of dependence to Klimt as Schoenberg made to Kraus; Berg's primary allegiance was to Schoenberg, and such pronouncements were not part of the Berg-Klimt friendship. But the brand of aesthetic and artistic purity espoused by Schoenberg and Loos did not suit Berg, and he knew this relatively early in his career.

Berg and Klimt were very much part of the new Viennese society. It was not all that far away, in the end, from the old society, which they both held in mild contempt. The painter and the composer were unusual enough, each in his own way, to be considered harbingers of aesthetic breakthroughs, but they were conservative enough to be successful and accepted in their own time. They projected radically different personal images as adults, but their art was as similar as their lives were different. Each time Berg saw a new work by Klimt, he sensed a deep, spiritual attachment, a likeness that had not yet manifested itself in his music but was soon to do so.

Chapter 5

Marriage

SEX, LOVE, AND FAMILY LIFE were very much on Berg's mind, and, in fact, were creating some problems in the household. Smaragda's marriage to Adolf von Eger lasted less than a year. Johanna Berg and her youngest son were disturbed not just by the brevity of that liaison, but also by Smaragda's increasingly public lesbianism, which, though accepted in the Kraus-Loos circle, was far from being considered normal by most of the family's friends and neighbors.

Berg's sense of propriety was offended, and he had as little to do with his sister as possible, even though they were again sharing their mother's flat. Smaragda was in need of professional advice; in October 1908, she tried to kill herself by sticking her head in a gas oven. While Johanna nursed her back to health, Alban tried to be supportive. But from this time on, he did little more than tolerate Smaragda and her female friends, and privately he looked on them with more scorn than pity, no matter how broad-minded he felt when such matters did not concern him so closely.

And Smaragda's affairs reminded Berg of his own, which seemed to be going nowhere. Helene was still seeing Raoul and was not allowed to see Alban, who was frequently left waiting for her on a street corner or in a park long past the designated hour for their secret rendezvous. He continued to write to her, sometimes two or three times a day, and the pair arranged to run into each other in the company of friends or at concerts. But Berg longed to spend time alone with her, and even as she began to warm to his advances and seemed to grow less fond of Raoul, their chances for building a lasting relationship became dim indeed.

But there was some good personal news. At the beginning of July 1908, Berg was declared exempt from the draft. Standing over six feet tall and weighing only 140 pounds, he was in no way a hearty physical specimen, and he made sure he would be dismissed by following the age-old practice of exhausting himself right before his medical examination. On June 30, he spent the night partying; at ten in the morning on July 1, he appeared before the medics and was declared unfit.

He was free, then, to leave Vienna for the country. But his health declined, and on July 23, eight years to the day since his first asthma attack, he suffered another particularly severe one. He was tended immediately by a doctor who had just arrived at the Berghof's tea garden by boat from the other side of the lake — a doctor who had earned from the young people the name "Professor Slivowitz," by virtue of his regular drink. He was the already well-known Sigmund Freud. The diagnosis was an allergic reaction to blossoms and pollen, but it was not the diagnosis as much as the doctor himself who impressed the patient. Berg had found some justification for his own superstitions and soul-searchings in Freud's theories

on psychology and the unconscious, and took the opportunity not just to answer all the doctor's bedside
queries, but to pose some questions of his own. Through
his life, Berg shared with Schoenberg the Freudian belief
that physical ailments were psychologically induced.

The rest of the summer he spent regaining his strength,
tending an injured wrist, and putting on "the happy family act," as he described it to Helene. Hermann Berg was
visiting from America, as he did almost every summer
during these years, energetically undertaking projects to
put the grounds of the Berghof in order. Charly was
there with his wife, Steffi, and their son, Erich Alban. So,
of course, were Smaragda and Johanna. "We make an interesting contrast," Alban wrote to Helene. "Mama over
two hundred pounds, Hermann two hundred twenty-
four pounds, and huge Erich; then Charly, Smaragda and
me, pale as lilies, emaciated, looking as if we had come
straight from the famine in Java. All this intensive family
life makes me pretty irritable . . . so it's back to my
beloved cigarettes and my brandy."

Near the end of August, Berg was well enough to
travel. Though he never relished the prospect of being
away from home, he accepted an invitation to visit
friends in Venice, a short and popular trip for touring
Viennese. He found the "hidden, romantic, quiet cor-
ners" of the city, slid down the canals by night in gondo-
las, and swam to the Palazzo Vendramin-Calergi, where
Wagner had died twenty-five years earlier and where
Berg experienced "moments of melancholy sweetness."
He also found romance, though he did not want it; a
Viennese girl named Ridi gave him chase, but, though he
was flattered and tempted, he remained faithful to
Helene.

Back in Vienna in September, Berg continued in pursuit of Wagner and Helene, arranging to have her accompany him to a performance of *Siegfried* at the Opera, with Felix Weingartner conducting. The two young people looked forward to the prospect of annoying the maestro who had succeeded Mahler as director of the Opera and was thus regarded with suspicion or worse by the former director's supporters.

In July 1909, Berg and Helene traded Wagnerian references by post between their summer houses, with Alban claiming to be afflicted by *Schwarzalben,* the black dwarf-slaves of Alberich in *The Ring* operas. "I can see a sweet teasing smile on your face that I should compare myself with the hero Siegfried," he wrote, "but I think you know what I mean! . . . Here are the *Schwarzalben,* striving for riches, fame and power, while I stand against them with my striving for the highest, for Bruennhilde-Helene, symbol of spiritual and moral perfection."

At the end of July, Berg packed his bags for his first pilgrimage to the Wagnerian shrine of Bayreuth, a trip paid for by his brother Hermann. The prospect of making the journey alone and the problems he was having in arranging a rendezvous with Helene along the train route took the edge off his excitement, but he was nevertheless overwhelmed by a performance of *Parsifal* on August 8, 1909. In retrospect, however, he found Bayreuth itself an "empty delusion," and never went back. He was offended by the intermission frivolities, by the social atmosphere that was, in his mind, inappropriate for *Parsifal,* and by the audience ("mostly Bavarians and Americans"), who looked to him like caricatures out of the satirical Bavarian magazine *Simplicissimus.*

Despite the rigidities of some of his personal attitudes, Berg was in the process of making a significant musical breakthrough. The Four Songs, Opus 2, were sketched

during the summer of 1908, although they were not finished until the spring of 1910. Like the earlier songs, they
were begun as a private project, but they grew in stature
to the point where the young composer decided to make
them his official Opus 2 and, notably, his last works for
voice and piano after a decade of exploring the style.

They are at once a beginning and an end — the end of
Berg's dependence on Mahler and Strauss (and Brahms
and Schumann) for inspiration, and the beginning of a
new, dramatic language. Though all four songs take only
a total of about eight minutes to perform, they travel
a great distance. The first, based on an excerpt from
Friedrich Hebbel's poem "Dem Schmerz sein Recht"
(beginning with the line "Sleep, sleep, nothing but
sleep"), is full of quiet despair and longing for death; one
has the feeling that the speaker is too tired for emotion,
has passed that point. Once — only once — the dynamic
level of the song hits a *forte;* otherwise, it hovers around
piano, pianissimo, and even below. Opus 2, Number 1,
begins and ends lyrically, with a slow, rocking motion in
the left hand of the piano that is reflected in the vocal line.
The key signature indicates that the song is in D Minor;
the music itself never departs from the home key.

But after only three minutes of Hebbel's *"Schlafen,
schlafen,"* Berg's Opus 2 moves away from the romantic
tradition of the German *Lied.* The last three songs in this
set are based on poems from Alfred Mombert's cycle *Der
Gluehende.* The Hebbel verse shares the theme of sleep
with the Mombert trio, but the second, third, and fourth
songs of Opus 2 have a new feeling of mystery in both
texts and settings; they are Expressionistic and more dramatic.

Opus 2, Number 2, to Mombert's "Schlafend trage
man mich," lasts only eighteen bars, and Opus 2, Num-

ber 3, "Nun ich der Riesen Staerksten ueberwand" (I overcame the strongest of giants), takes only twelve bars. Number 2 is in G-flat (six flats in the key signature); Number 3 is in C-flat (seven flats); but in neither case does the key signature have much hold on the music, and anyone who sees the score may think Berg put in so many flats because he found it more efficient to cancel them out when necessary than to write them in all the time. "Nun ich der Riesen" lets no phrases for piano alone interrupt the straightforward delivery of the text. Furthermore, Berg made sure that the singer would announce his bold conquest at the right tempo by suggesting that the song begin "not hastily, but rather in the tempo of spoken words" in the printed score.

After the giants have been overcome and the hero can "totter through the streets in the throes of sleep" at the conclusion of the third song, Number 4, "Warm die Luefte," comes as a three-minute, twenty-five-measure dramatic cantata, divided into three distinct sections. First, very lyrically but in such a chromatic idiom that the voice is constantly dealing with major- and minor-second competition from the piano, the singer hears a nightingale; the piano responds with a flutter of arpeggios. Freely announcing himself in imitation of the bird ("I want to sing"), the singer recounts a tale of lost love:

"Up high in the mountain forest
Cold snow melts and oozes,
A girl in a gray dress
Leans against the damp trunk of an oak,
Her tender cheeks are sick,
Her gray eyes feverishly stare

Through the giant, menacing tree trunks [piano *glissando,* with the right hand going up the black notes of the instrument while the left hand goes down the white keys].

"He still isn't here. He's leaving me to wait . . ."
[*fortissimo*].

Finally, with low, loud thuds on the piano, the song switches mood again; "Die!" the singer orders. Berg wanted the word sung "without any tone." And at once the feeling is sweet and calm again: "The one dies while the other lives:/That makes the world so profoundly beautiful."

"Warm die Luefte" may be the most striking and important song Berg ever wrote. With Opus 2, Number 4, he dispensed with the vestigial key signature, which no longer signified anything of import and was making the writing more difficult rather than easier. He used a kind of dramatic gesture that might have been called "word painting," had Schubert not given that phrase a prettier, more minuscule connotation; Berg's paintings have a stronger, more violent impact than the babbling of a friendly brook of the nineteenth century.

And, consciously or not, Berg played a kind of game with the fourth song of Opus 2. It not only sums up what was happening in the last years of the first decade of the twentieth century; it predicts an important facet of the techniques of twelve-tone composition. All four of the Hebbel and Mombert songs are derived from the same chord, but that chord is not clearly revealed or given its place of honor until the very end of the final song. It is a tower of fourths, arranged at that cadence as B, F-sharp, E-flat, A, D, and it is a chord that so captured Schoenberg's imagination that he used it as an example in his *Harmonielehre*. Ironically, Schoenberg had used the same chord in works dating from 1908 and 1909, and even as early as 1900 in "Erwartung." Evidently it was Berg's treatment of the chord and his thorough examination of all its possibilities that intrigued Schoenberg. Furthermore, it was becoming more and more obvious that harmony, to whatever extent it had a future, rested on chords built from fourths instead of from the traditional thirds.

Berg had his Opus 2 Four Songs and his Opus 1 Piano Sonata published in 1910 by Robert Lenau, in Berlin. The composer was embarrassed because he had to spend his own money to bring his music before the public, and asked Webern not to spread the word that he had resorted to a vanity press. But he was proud that he had designed the covers for both works himself, in *Jugendstil* script, and this led him to tell his friends about the project and take credit for it, despite his initial reluctance.

Once again, musical progress gave Berg added confidence in other areas of his life; he reached the point where he was determined to marry Helene Nahowski. Helene, too, was convinced that this was the right thing for both of them, though she did not fully share her lover's sense of urgency. This served only to increase Alban's ardor. They were both twenty-five, old enough to decide for themselves, even if they both still lived at home. But as Helene withdrew from her other beaux, her father's reservations about the young Berg turned into active dislike. The musician was, according to Nahowski, intellectually inferior, impoverished, sickly, and part of a family given to immorality.

Helene told Alban what her father had said about him, and Berg exploded. In July 1910, the Nahowskis vacationed at a spa in Styria. After the father returned to work in Vienna, Alban joined the women. From Tobelbad, near Graz, with Helene sitting next to him to give him courage and cool his ire, Berg wrote a lengthy letter to Franz Nahowski, refuting, in numerical order, each of the reasons the older man had given for keeping him from becoming a member of the family — indeed, from seeing Helene at all.

In refuting the charges against him, Berg was unable to avoid certain exaggerations. He compared his relationship with Helene with that of her sister Anna and Arthur Lebert, a manufacturer of emery paper, whose forthcoming marriage had received full parental approval. Trying to sound mature and reasonable, he ended up sounding petulant and resentful. He lied about his accomplishments in school and his affiliation with the University of Vienna, and defended the "profession" of music.

> It is true that during the last three years I have taken afternoons off to be with Helene, squandering precious hours waiting in the street, but that does not justify your assumption that I am idle . . . You say you don't give a whit for "vocations" and consider music at best a frivolous entertainment . . . There are a hundred times more musicians . . . than there are emery-paper manufacturers . . . A glance at any newspaper will show you that there are musicians who command just as high an income as court councillors, generals, manufacturers and land-owners. . . .

Nahowski had found out that the Bergs' houses were mortgaged.

> Were they completely ours, we should be multimillionaires — which, of course, I never said we were . . . The fact that I myself have no income at the moment does not mean that I am incapable of earning . . . There are musicians who provide for themselves and their families by orchestrating operas and operettas, or earn money by making piano reductions, giving lessons, accompanying singers, etc. I could do any or all of this, but Helene agrees that I should wait.

In truth, Berg could have done some of these, but he would have been taxed to convince anyone that he was sufficiently competent at the keyboard to coach singers or to do anything that involved performance.

He offered to provide Nahowski with a certificate from the health authorities attesting to his good health.

> Do you really think that a man who is neurasthenic or in any way infirm could have been pulled through the exertions of body, mind and spirit that I have and still put on weight? That I could stand in snow up to my ankles, as I have often done — waiting for Helene?

And on the charge of family immorality — specifically his sister's lesbianism — Berg defended his heritage.

> So we come to the root of your attacks against my family. Had I the time, I would make this long letter two or three times as long and deal in detail with homosexuality: those afflicted by it and those who, because they are not so afflicted, treat these sick people as criminals. Perhaps your slurs, if I hear any more of them, will one day force me to take the matter up. For the moment, I only say that there can be few families without at least one problem child. It is not my business to ask which of your children comes into this category, except that you seem to regard Helene as one — because for the last three years she has been "going out" with a man she is not officially engaged to . . .
> I felt obliged to shake off the dirt which has been flung at me for the past three years. And now, as I hope this letter will have proved to you, the unbreakable bond between Helene and myself gives me the right and the power to consider myself engaged to her.

Franz Nahowski did not even bother to read the letter. While Alban stayed in the country, nervously tracing the epistle's progress and doubtless assuming that the postmen realized the value of those particular pieces of paper, the addressee tossed the letter, unopened and unread, onto his daughter's bed, which may have been just as well, considering the borderline truths to which her suitor had resorted, not to mention his frequent if inadvertent sarcasm.

Berg anxiously awaited a response, but none came. At the end of July or the beginning of August, he returned to his family's summer house, where, without Helene's reassuring presence, he suffered and waited. Finally, the couple's persistence won out, and late in August 1910, Helene cabled Alban that they had her father's permission to announce their engagement. The reluctant paternal blessing came on the condition that the pair be wed in a Protestant ceremony instead of a Catholic one, so that the divorce, which Nahowski thought inevitable, would be easier to arrange. Alban and Helene agreed to the stipulation and happily returned to Vienna in the fall, free to spend time together and plan a spring wedding.

Berg was now ready to make a change in his musical style, as well. By the time the printing of his Opus 1 Piano Sonata and his Opus 2 Songs was completed to his satisfaction (that is, perfectly), he was tired of the music. He wrote to Webern that he was "almost ashamed of my old pieces." A string quartet was on his mind, and though Berg was working on both it and the songs concurrently for a time, the quartet that was to become Opus 3 was, in the composer's opinion, both different and important.

Berg's first String Quartet (which was probably only his second attempt in the genre, following the Double Fugue, to which he added a piano continuo) received its first performance on April 24, 1911, just before Berg's wedding and Mahler's death. It was on a program that also included quartets by Webern and Horwitz, as well as Webern's Pieces for Violin and Piano. "The idiom was mishandled by Mr. Alban Berg," reported the critic Stauber, despairing that such a piece could ever be called a string quartet. After this single performance the String Quartet faded into oblivion until 1919, when Webern wanted to present it and persuaded Berg to revise it slightly. The composer made a few further changes in 1924, just before the Opus 3 was published by Universal Edition. A decade after he wrote it, Berg confessed to Webern that he was still strangely partial to his String Quartet, and so, ultimately, were a number of other people. The Havemann Quartet performed the work on August 2, 1923, at the first International Festival for Chamber Music in Salzburg, and it brought Berg his first measure of international acclaim.

In Salzburg for that performance, Berg was delighted by the Havemann Quartet, "four fair-haired, cheerful, enthusiastic and hard-working musicians." On the morning after the concert, he called it "artistically, the most wonderful evening of my life . . . They played with indescribable beauty . . . and I revelled in the lovely sounds, the solemn sweetness and ecstasy of the music . . . The 'wildest' and 'most daring passages' were sheer harmony in the classical sense . . . At the end, there was almost frantic general applause . . . not one sound of booing . . . General opinion was that I carried off the prize."

Even then, Berg was unaccustomed to being the center of attention or to hearing the sound of applause unpunctuated by booing and hissing. And his Salzburg success was witnessed by two or three dozen members of the foreign press, as well as by a number of personal friends, including Emil Hertzka, the director of Universal Edition. Schoenberg had repeatedly begged his publisher to take on the works of his students Berg and Webern, but his pleas came to naught on Berg's account until that night in Salzburg, when Hertzka requested the Quartet, and, of course, received it at once. Other ensembles, including the Pro Arte Quartet and the Hindemith Quartet, asked the composer for permission to perform his Opus 3, and concert series in Copenhagen and Stockholm requested that the Havemann group include Berg's work on programs in those cities. With this exposure and with the Havemann Quartet touring Germany with the piece, the Opus 3 became Berg's calling card in most European centers.

The String Quartet was the last piece Berg wrote under the day-to-day influence of Schoenberg as teacher, and no matter how much guidance the teacher may have offered, solicited or not, the work is still purely Berg's own. This is the first piece written in what is immediately identifiable as the composer's mature style. It is almost defiantly original; it comes out of the great German string-quartet tradition of Haydn, Mozart, and Beethoven, but it does not need to thank any predecessor for either inspiration or information.

The work is in two movements (thus upsetting the early critics, who thought it had to be in the four movements of Mozart and Haydn in order to be a real string quartet); the second part can be thought of as a development of the first. This idea was not new; its closest relative is Mahler's Eighth Symphony. Theodor Adorno, a friend and pupil, called Berg's process "liquidating the sonata," meaning that the technique of sonata construction runs all through the Quartet and that there is no longer any clear line between the presentation or exposition of ideas and their development.

More interesting, though, than a step-by-step recount-
ing of the relationships of the motives and their harmonic
implications is the overall effect of Berg's Opus 3. Any
feelings of stress and nervousness that come through in
the Piano Sonata have been alleviated here, replaced by a
kind of naturalness and ease that indicate both maturity
and complete control of the material.

And the Quartet takes certain qualities of the Four
Songs, Opus 2, and advances them, suggesting that, as
comfortable as he had been and still was with the human
voice, Berg had reached the point where he could think
instrumentally, and had spotted some elements he could
not yet assimilate into his vocal style, or that seemed better suited to treatment by instruments. The rhythms in
the Quartet are both more varied and more inevitable
than those of the Four Songs. Although in his first work
without key signature, the Opus 2, Number 4, song
("Warm die Luefte"), Berg painstakingly avoided connections with strong tonics or key centers, they abound
in the Quartet. Opus 3 still lacks sharps or flats in the
key signature's ruling position, but there is rarely a moment within the work when Berg completely avoids the
suggestion of a home key — even though that tonic
might be remote and is subsequently both denied and
dislocated. He no longer needed the old tonic-dominant
systems to give the work structure; this he found through
motivic relationships and repetitions both literal and
varied. But neither did he feel the need to avoid the
home-key feeling entirely. He would not bow to the old
rules of harmonic motion and progressions, but when
they wanted to present themselves, he welcomed them
without anxiety.

Ironically, at this time both Schoenberg and Webern
were professing to have problems with the new, keyless

style known as "atonality." (Clearly, there is no such
thing as "atonal" music — music without tones — but
this is the word that has come to be associated with
works that do not lie within the boundaries of traditional,
key-oriented harmonies, and it is far too late to eradicate
this misleading expression from the working musical vo-
cabulary.) On a theoretical level, and also on a practical
one, it seemed impossible for a composer to write extended pieces of music without a tonal center to grasp
and return to, especially when there was no text to give
the music a structure and minimal duration. A song, after
all, has to go on at least as long as it takes to sing all of the
words.

Schoenberg was attempting to deal with these issues in
his classes, often without success. Webern had come up
against them in his own writing, and had turned to producing such tiny pieces that the only logical extension of
the style would have been total disappearance. The Five
Movements for String Quartet, Webern's Opus 9, were
written at about the same time as Berg's Opus 3. But
though Berg evidently had no trouble extending his
Quartet's two movements to more than eighteen minutes, Webern retreated and said all he had to say in his
Five Movements in a total of less than eleven minutes,
with the middle section lasting not even sixty seconds.

Though his approach was less theoretical, Berg was
dealing with the problems in a different way from that of
his colleagues. If Webern and Schoenberg were intent on
rejecting any suggestion of tonics and their magnetism,
Berg found that he rather enjoyed these nostalgic occur-
rences, and as long as he could keep them from overtak-
ing the idiom and turning it Wagnerian, he was glad to
allow in his music references to the past. He felt no ob-
ligation to write music that was determinedly new, and

had no desire to ignore his heritage as an Austrian composer. Schoenberg and Webern wanted to pull up roots
and relocate themselves in brand-new musical territory;
Berg's sense of continuity kept his stylistic progression
smoother and more gently flowing.

Emotionally, his mind was lyrical at the time, too,
because he was to marry Helene Nahowski on May 3,
1911. The day before the ceremony, Helene wrote to her
fiancé:

> My dearest and nearest!
> Tomorrow is our wedding day. I am setting out with you
> into "the land of marriage" full of confidence and high pur-
> pose. I will always be a prop and support to you, a faithful
> and loving companion, both here and over there "in the
> other world." Gladly and of my own free will I give up ev-
> erything that made my girlhood so full of beauty, hope and
> happiness — my modest "art." I quench my own flame, and
> shall exist only for and through you. Now we shall be
> together for ever.
>
> Amen.

They were married in the Swiss Reform Church on
Vienna's Dorotheergasse. Photos show that the two families were on sufficiently good terms to sit for the camera
in the garden after the short ceremony. The happiness of
the bride and groom was marred two weeks after the
wedding by the death of Mahler, whom they both idol-
ized as composer and conductor, and by the knowledge
that, following a short honeymoon at the Nahowskis'
home in Trahuetten, they would have to separate again
and return to their respective family dwellings (the Bergs
were by now at Nussdorferstrasse 19 in the VII District
of Vienna) because they could not find a suitable place to
set up their own household.

Finally, during the summer, Helene's mother found a

roomy corner flat on the first floor (a few steps above
street level) of a sizable, eight-family building at Trauttmansdorffgasse 27. The newlyweds would be very near
Helene's family and could still have a good Hietzing address, but in the low-rent part of the suburb. The flat had
an entry hall, a drawing room, a good-sized kitchen, one
bedroom, a bath, and a large porch for a sun room. A
bay window in back looked out on a well-tended garden,
and the street was quiet enough for Alban to be able to
work.

The papers were signed, and the young couple's
mothers prepared the flat with curtains, wallpaper, and
various household items. It was the Bergs' first and only
home; Trauttmansdorffgasse 27, Apartment 1, was their
city address until Berg's death, in 1935, and the widow
kept the apartment nearly unchanged until she died,
forty-one years later. In 1978, BERG still marked the buz-
zer by the outer door.

Strange as it seems, Helene kept — or thought she
kept — the promises she made in the letter she wrote the
day before her wedding, to be "a faithful and loving
companion, both here and over there 'in the other
world.' " For better or for worse, Helene Berg, wife and
widow, was to have significant influence on music history. Willi Reich observed the couple and wrote, "No
one could completely grasp what she meant to the *artist*
Alban Berg no less than to the *man*. Beyond her delightful relationship to the man, Helene not only accompanied
her husband on most of his journeys, but — with her
finely cultivated heart and spirit — became the critical adviser of the composer in his work. Her presence gave the
artist the peace and comfort of a relaxed home life, and
the quiet necessary for undisturbed creative work."

But these lines were written by Berg's student and biographer well before Helene died, on August 30, 1976, at the age of ninety-one. Only then did the truth become known: what had been believed to be a perfect marriage had been far from ideal. Alban and Helene had not been characters in a drama of domestic perfection, even though it might have appeared to the world that they were.

Chapter 6

Work for Schoenberg:
The Altenberg *Lieder*

THE RUSH OF artistic advances at the beginning of the second decade of the twentieth century was exciting and inspiring, but Berg needed money to support himself and his new wife. Until he could find a publisher, he had no hope that his income from composing would even approach his expenses. Nor could he continue to pay out of his own pocket to have his works printed. Fortunately, many of Schoenberg's students were trained for tasks that could bring in at least food money. As part of their class-work, and also out of sheer good will, they had proof-read their teacher's scores, making sure they were flaw-lessly prepared for the printer, and had made piano reductions of important works. Berg, for example, worked on reducing Schoenberg's *Verklaerte Nacht* into a one-piano version, although that hundred-page effort was never published and may have been intended as nothing more than an exercise.

The first assignment along these lines that was handed

to Berg was a reduction of the last movement of Mahler's Eighth Symphony for four-hand piano. Though it is known that he worked on this project under Schoenberg's watchful eye, there is neither a contract with Universal Edition nor a credit on the published version to verify Berg's involvement. From the beginning, however, he was very good at this kind of work — too good, perhaps, for it tended to get in the way of his own artistic progress. In January 1912, Schoenberg advised Berg to stop wasting his time with piano reductions that involved a movement here or a hundred pages there, and in the future undertake only assignments in which he would get sole credit for reducing complete works. The first full work to which Berg was assigned by contract through Universal after this was nothing less than Schoenberg's own huge *Gurrelieder,* which was not even completely composed when the agreement for a piano reduction was signed in September 1911. Berg worked for more than a year, trying to compress all the parts of the outsized orchestra into something that could be played by two hands on one piano. When he finally sent a first draft to Schoenberg, who had moved to Berlin by this time, Schoenberg sent back orders to cut it even more, leaving only the absolutely crucial elements.

This project, which continued through Berg's wedding, his honeymoon, his move into an apartment of his own, Mahler's death, and Schoenberg's relocation in Germany, was both taxing and time-consuming. It demanded Berg's time and energy to a degree where neither the fee nor the small recognition for those who do this sort of musical dirty work could compensate. And to make matters worse, there were several weeks during the period Berg was working on the *Gurrelieder.* when he thought that both Webern and Schoenberg had dismissed

him from their lives. Though Schoenberg had reason to
be particularly well disposed toward the student who was
working so tirelessly on his behalf, he was annoyed with
Berg, for reasons that are not clear now and may not
have been clear even at the time. Berg and Webern were
again communicating cordially by the middle of August
1911, when Schoenberg was preparing to leave for Berlin. In a letter, Berg admitted to his old classmate that,
having been busy with the wedding, Mahler's death and
funeral, the trials of outfitting a new apartment, and so
on, he had indeed been casual about keeping in touch
with Schoenberg. But that should not have been enough
to explain the teacher's short temper, especially after Berg
finally found the time and the courage to try to make
amends, going repeatedly to Schoenberg's rooms in Hietzinger Haupstrasse 113 (very near the Bergs' new flat),
where he was put off, left waiting on the doorstep, or ignored.

Schoenberg's moodiness came as no surprise to Berg,
but he was nonetheless unhappy when he was the cause
and when his apologies and explanations were not welcome. He was particularly hurt when he found out that
Schoenberg was planning to leave Vienna. The teacher
may have been planning to go without even saying farewell, but then, on practically no notice, he ordered Berg
to take care of all the physical details and arrangements
for his move and to keep track of a lawsuit in Vienna in
which he was still involved.

Concerned about both his own finances and Schoenberg's reputation, Berg continued to undertake menial
chores for Universal Edition, and also began to teach a
few students whom Schoenberg, feeling more friendly,
had referred to him just before his move. The assignments coming from the publishing house dealt primarily

with Schoenberg's music — a piano version of the last two movements of the String Quartet, Opus 10, which Schoenberg ordered be "absolutely easy to play," and a four-hand reduction of the early *Pelleas und Melisande* orchestral work. Berg also undertook the piano reduction of Franz Schreker's *Die ferne Klang,* an opera that, though now long forgotten, impressed the young composer and influenced his own thinking about operatic subjects.

A year after he moved to Berlin, Schoenberg still had not found people whom he could trust as copyists and proofreaders, so those tasks continued to fall back to Berg and his fellow ex-students in Vienna. In a letter to Emil Hertzka at Universal, Schoenberg declared that the première of the *Gurrelieder* would not take place early in 1913, as planned, unless Berg and several others were summoned instantly and put to copying the parts. In November 1912, Berg was overseeing the preparation of "sixty-six voices (without the strings)" of the *Gurrelieder,* and was none too happy about it. He told Webern that he never would have agreed to undertake the task had he not seen that it was necessary to the première, and that he was having to do all the correcting himself because he was the only one intimately acquainted with the music.

Anticipating the first performance of the *Gurrelieder,* which, thanks to Berg, would take place as scheduled, Hertzka asked Schoenberg for a written guide to the piece, a kind of semitechnical introduction aimed at prospective concertgoers. Universal Edition often published such guides to herald important premières of works by their composers. Schoenberg would not write this guide himself but recommended Berg for the job. Berg accepted the assignment, of course, partly for money, partly for Schoenberg, incidentally because a well-produced guide might turn some attention his way, and largely because he was beginning to feel quite possessive toward the *Gurrelieder* and was proud that he knew the work better than anyone except the composer himself. There followed an exchange of letters in which Berg and Schoenberg debated the possible directions such a project might take, as well as the purposes of any such guide, who might be expected to read it, and so on. Schoenberg finally suggested "a loose, aphoristic form," and by December 1912, Berg was working on his first musicological assignment for publication.

Hertzka had expected the *Gurrelieder* guide to run to about forty pages; Berg's went to eighty and kept growing. Schoenberg tried to assuage his panicked publisher, advising him to take Berg's work seriously. At the same time, he tactfully suggested to Berg that he cut out a few of the musical examples. Only Webern, who loved musical detail as much as Berg did, was rooting for a longer guide. Finally, Universal agreed to a compromise, and at the end of 1913 two guides were published, one an extensive study of 100 pages and 129 musical examples; the other, a much smaller version dealing only with the music's main themes.

Meanwhile, Berg became involved in other facets of the first performance of the *Gurrelieder,* soliciting help from subscribers to help underwrite the costs of assembling singers and instrumentalists for the giant work, and taking over some rehearsals of both the men's and the mixed choruses. Berg had reservations about his ability to conduct rehearsals; he told Webern that he had agreed only when he realized that his alternate was a Dr. Weigl from the Opera, for whom Berg obviously had no use.

The novice conductor got some advice on rehearsal techniques from Webern, which may have been unfortunate; it was precisely Webern's slow and pedantic style of preparation that made him unpopular with performers. True to form, Webern suggested that Berg proceed very slowly, perfecting only a few measures at a time. Schoenberg added some guidelines too; he thought it would be very good for Berg to get the practical experience of directing the choruses, and his warnings still apply to any conductor in any situation: "Speak as little as possible. Don't be witty . . . The real art rests in getting the *piano* and the *forte* exactly correct; everything else follows from that."

So Berg's responsibilities extended into the actual realization of the *Gurrelieder,* finally even into persuading the conductor, Schreker (who was also an ardent admirer of Alma Mahler's), to adopt the correct tempos, and running into the orchestra to correct mistakes in the impatient musicians' parts. When the performance finally took place, in Vienna's large Musikverein hall, on February 23, 1913, Berg could take personal pride in its extraordinary success both in comparison with other premières of Schoenberg's music and in objective terms as well. Numerologists could say that Schoenberg's number of fate (thirteen) and Berg's (twenty-three) were vibrating together to good effect. Webern wrote to Schoenberg that he had been overwhelmed by the work. And after all that effort and worry, Berg expressed gratitude to his teacher "for having been able to help arrange a concert that had such a wonderfully great success."

In addition to worrying about Schoenberg's musical survival, Berg concerned himself with his teacher's material well-being. Just before Schoenberg's departure for Berlin, in spite of the strains in their relationship, Berg sent out an appeal for friends and concerned members of the musical community to help keep Schoenberg from "coming to grief for lack of the necessities of life." About forty people responded to Berg with pledges of assistance, but the call turned out to be a false alarm; by the time it had circulated, Schoenberg had departed for Berlin and was, for the time being, in better circumstances. Later pleas on Schoenberg's behalf, however, were to be truly urgent, and consumed a good deal of Berg's emotional and physical energy.

With their teacher settled, Schoenberg's students redirected their efforts toward a book to honor the master. It was published in 1912 by Piper Verlag in Munich, with articles on all aspects of Schoenberg's art, including his painting. In the valedictory, "To the Teacher," Berg extolled Schoenberg's influence on his pupils' lives, referring to "genius," a "miracle," the "secrets of Divinity," and condemning skeptics to being "smashed on the rocks of their spiritual sterility." Berg mentioned to Willi Reich in later years that he suspected this essay might have been a bit fulsome. But Berg responded lyrically to any opportunity to tell the world about Schoenberg, no matter how much drudgery was imposed on him or how much personal indignity he suffered because of the moods of his teacher. Especially when he was away from Schoenberg, Berg could forget the older man's peculiarities. Even while he was heavily involved in the work on the *Gurrelieder,* Berg wrote to Webern:

> How despondent you must be again, far away from all those divine experiences, having to forgo the walks with Schoenberg and miss the purport, gestures and cadences of his talk . . . Twice a week I wait for him . . . before his classes at the Conservatory begin, and for fifteen to thirty minutes we walk in the midst of the noise of the city, which is made inaudible by the road of his words . . . Then twice a week at his house in Ober St. Veit, when to each lesson I bring the continuation of the *Gurrelieder* work, see his new paintings, and look at songs by Mahler.

With Berg paying so much attention to Schoenberg and his work, it would seem reasonable to expect that Berg's own music would have shown signs of the influence of his teacher. But something closer to the opposite was the case. Berg did have trouble stealing time from his secretarial work for Schoenberg (with and without commissions from Universal Edition) to produce a new work of his own. Yet 1912 saw the birth of one of his most original and dramatic creations, the Five Orchestral Songs after Postcard Texts by Peter Altenberg, Opus 4.

As a matter of fact, Berg had been considering the possibility of a large symphonic work with voices, on the scale of Mahler's symphonies and, of course, of the *Gurrelieder*. Though sketches do exist for the first movement of a symphony that looks like an homage to Grieg, as well as to Mahler, Berg was never to write a work that would fall into this particular category. Instead, his efforts in the summer of 1912 resulted in these Altenberg *Lieder*, his first mature work involving orchestra, his first product as a graduate of the Schoenberg school, and the most unfairly criticized of all his major creations.

The cue for the Altenberg Songs was the last song in Berg's Opus 2, "Warm die Luefte." Further inspiration came, then, from Webern's move toward orchestral miniatures in his Opus 6 and Opus 10, and from Schoenberg's Five Orchestral Pieces, Opus 16, as well as his early operas, *Erwartung* and *Die glueckliche Hand*. Berg had watched all of his friends' pieces take shape. Furthermore, by this time he was already beginning to think of an opera of his own. His marriage to Helene had put to an end any jealousy he might have felt toward the nonconforming Altenberg (whose real name was Richard Englaender), after those writings dedicated to the new Mrs. Berg appeared in the poet's 1911 volume called *Neues Altes (Something New, Something Old)*. Altenberg remained a friend of the Bergs until his death, in 1919.

By setting to music Altenberg's aphoristic *Postcard Texts,* Berg could again conveniently honor his predecessors, from Mahler and Strauss back to Beethoven. Neither Schoenberg nor Webern was comfortable expressing himself in songs with orchestral accompaniments, especially in light of the problem they called "singer versus orchestra," but Berg was eager to make an attempt. The use of the voice gave him confidence to deal with the instruments. And Berg's first orchestra was large enough to please even Mahler; it included piccolo, two flutes, three oboes (one alternating with English horn), three clarinets (one with E-flat clarinet), bass clarinet, three bassoons (one with the contrabassoon), four horns, three trumpets, four trombones, tuba, timpani, percussion (including triangle and tam-tam), glockenspiel, xylophone, harp, celeste, piano, harmonium, and a full body of strings. Yet the complete collection of instruments rarely sounds together, and even when a large number of people are playing, their tones are quieted through the use of mutes, certain kinds of bowing and articulation, and a wide range of other devices intended to add color and subtract decibels. In a sense, Berg was writing chamber music for orchestra; he was not interested in the *fortissimo* surge of the symphony, but in the variety of subtle sounds he could produce by calling on many small groups from within the large ensemble.

There is every reason to suspect that Schoenberg carefully monitored the progress of these pieces; even that he had something to do with their conception. "Go ahead and write at least a few songs," he advised Berg in a letter of February 13, 1912. "It's good to let poetry lead you back into music. But then, turn to the orchestra." Schoenberg had not forgotten that one of his favorite students had yet to test himself with a full orchestra.

There is also some indication that Schoenberg helped Berg with some technical problems. In the autograph version of an early draft of the fourth and fifth Altenberg Songs, specifically Number 5, measure five, a short vocal phrase is written in a hand that is not Berg's, and could well be Schoenberg's.

Still, Berg was moving in directions untried by Schoenberg or Webern, let alone by Mahler or Strauss. Although he subsequently allowed the songs in his Opus 4 to be performed individually, he thought of them very much as a cycle, and they are best tied together into an uninterrupted whole of about ten minutes' duration. In the context of the complete cycle, the introduction does not seem long, even though the voice does not enter until the twentieth measure and takes only eighteen bars to present the text. Yet when the large orchestra creeps in *pianississimo* to begin the Opus 4, it chimes quietly and rhythmically, like the Indonesian ensemble called a "gamelan," setting the exotic, mysterious, and suggestive mood of the whole work. The voice, too, comes out of nowhere, first wordlessly, with instructions in the score to indicate that the note be "sung with lips lightly closed (*ppp!*)," then with another "note sung with open mouth (*pp!*)," both "to start and finish with just a breath!" Only then does the singer actually start to present the text, with a wide-leaping melody that demands both agility and a sure, broad range.

There are many things in the score of Opus 4 to suggest the works of Webern, particularly the brevity of the individual songs (the second lasts only eleven measures), the low-level dynamics, and the lack of help the singer receives from the instruments in the quest for pitches. But there is a very significant difference, too, between these songs and Webern's works of the same period. Webern had a way of making even the shortest piece sound complete in itself. Berg's orchestral songs, on the other hand, seem to be mere suggestions of larger musical ideas; although they do not need to be extended, even the shortest seems ready to burst with implications, and even the quietest, most thinly scored moments are full of hints and suggestions that could be developed and discussed for hours. The unusual texts are as full of dramatic suggestions as the music is:

> Soul, you are more beautiful, profounder, after snowstorms.
> And you have them too, child of nature.
> Over both, there still lies a breath of melancholy gloom
> until the clouds blow away!
>
> After the summer rain did you see the forest?!
> All is glitter, quiet, and more beautiful than before.
> See, woman, you too sometimes need summer storms!
>
> Over the brink of beyond your gaze wandered musingly;
> Never a care for house and hold!
> Living a dream of life — suddenly, all is over.
> Over the brink of beyond your gaze wandered musingly.
>
> Nothing has come, nothing will, to still my soul's longing.
> So long have I waited, waited so long, ah, so long!
> The days will slip stealthily, and in vain my
> ash-blond silken hair flutters round my pallid face!
>
> Here is peace, here my tears flow, my heart weeps out its
> sadness!
> Here I give cry to my unfathomable, measureless sorrow,
> that would consume my soul . . .
> Behold, not a sign of mankind, not a soul around me;
> Here is peace! Here the snow drops softly into pools of water
> . . .

In addition to being Berg's friend, Altenberg was a writer of texts that were marvelously well suited to the composer's mood and needs. Conductor-composer Pierre Boulez has called the Opus 4 Songs a "unique, flighty union of irony and sentimentality," a union clearly dependent on the texts, and a special combination that was to be a distinguishing factor in Berg's music from the Opus 4 forward. Irony had been made an equal partner with romantic feeling.

This irony, not common in music but certainly no enemy of the art, comes closest to the surface in the second of the five Altenberg Songs, where the middle section of the cycle begins with three short pieces enclosed between the two longer ones. (Numbers 1 and 5 in the cycle are also notably more dependent on orchestral interpolations than their shorter companions.) The text of Number 2 is obviously ironic, and it could even sound caustic. On the word *"schoener"* (more beautiful), Berg wrote a vocal run and a trill, suggesting not so much beauty as cosmetic artifice.

In only twenty-six measures, the third song deals with lost time; too much gazing into infinity, the poet warns, and life can fly by. Some energetic analysts have speculated that Berg was consciously working in a twelve-tone system of composition in this song, but this is an exaggeration. He had no developed system except the idea that his universe, his musical "great beyond," consisted of the twelve notes of the chromatic scale; so all of these notes appear in both the first chord and the last, which builds up, pitch by pitch, over the course of the final seven measures.

Again, the fourth song talks of the singer's being passed by, in a miniature drama to which Berg gave a lonely sounding, dry accompaniment. The twelve-tone chord that ends the third piece gives way to a lone high note on the flute, and the singer's "ash-blond silken hair" blows against the breeze of instruments, recalling the exotic, Asian mood of the cycle's introduction.

Finally, the fifth song in Opus 4 reminisces on elements of the first, with its instrumental introduction and epilogue, and its return to expansiveness. The singer is still alone, where "the snow drops softly into pools of water," and where all freedoms are possible. The composer, however, significantly limited his own freedom by setting the text in the form of a passacaglia, a Baroque device used, for instance, in Bach's famous Chaconne for solo violin, where lines vary continuously above or around a theme that runs over and over again. This was the same form Webern used for his Opus 1 for orchestra, and it would reappear at crucial moments in Berg's later works. The idea of continuous variation was crucial to Schoenberg and his followers; obviously, it is a basic tenet of all music, extremely closely tied to the techniques of twelve-tone composition, in which a predetermined line of twelve pitches is varied and turned in every possible direction. The finale of Opus 4 is still far away from the actual twelve-tone techniques, but something does appear here that forecasts Berg's last completed work, the Violin Concerto. Dealing with peace and loneliness at the end of a cycle full of irony and searching, Berg turned back to longer, broader phrases full of tonal suggestions. In 1935, he was to do the same thing near the end of the Concerto, to depict a beautiful soul in eternal rest.

When Berg sent the manuscript of the Altenberg *Lieder* to Schoenberg at the beginning of 1913, the teacher responded with irritation. He was impressed with the orchestration, but was put off by what he considered "obvious attempts to find something new and different." Schoenberg admitted that he might eventually come to understand the Songs better, but at the time he found them "awkward."

There is some irony in Schoenberg's remarks about the quest for the new, since he was in fact more energetically engaged in such a search than Berg was. The younger man saw no irony, however, and even managed to read his mentor's words as praise. Schoenberg did include some of the Altenberg Songs on a concert planned for the spring, though not without reservations. A singer had to be found, and since Marya Freund was to sing Mahler's *Kindertotenlieder* on the same program, Schoenberg approached her first. He said matter-of-factly that he was not fond of Berg's Songs, but that since he had decided to put them on the program, either Miss Freund would have to sing them or he would find someone else. Freund begged off, followed by other singers, both male and female. This caused further difficulties because Berg insisted that the fourth song be sung by a woman (which the text clearly calls for). Then there were delays in preparing the instrumental parts, scheduling rehearsals, and even agreeing on a final date for the event. All involved faced the evening of March 31, 1913, with trepidation.

Schoenberg's presence in Vienna for the première of the *Gurrelieder,* and, therefore, his availability as conductor, had been the main impetus for planning this concert, which would take place under the auspices of the Academic Association for Literature and Music, one of several organizations sympathetic to the work of Schoenberg and his circle. Schoenberg's final design for the concert was submitted to the sponsor on March 10; he took great care to pace the evening so that the "dangerous" works would be first, "while the public is still fresh," with Mahler's *Kindertotenlieder* last, where they would not overpower the songs by Berg and Zemlinsky, and would provide an incentive for the audience to stay until the end.

After much preparation, at 7:30 P.M. on March 31, in

the large hall of the Musikverein, the concert started —
and never finished. It turned into one of the great scandals of twentieth-century music. According to one report
in the press, whistles, hissing, and clapping set off the
first brawl in the second balcony after Schoenberg's Opus
9, just before the intermission. During the break, supporters and detractors took their sides, and when they returned for the Altenberg Songs, they were ready to fight.
There was laughter and yelling, and Schoenberg finally
stopped the orchestra and called for the police to remove
the noise-makers. Webern shouted his support for
Schoenberg from his box seat, otherwise reserved citizens
climbed around and over their companions in order to
get a better aim at their cultural enemies, and even the
police commissioner could do nothing but order the concert stopped, to the great relief of the frightened musicians, who expected to be the objects of a frontal attack.

The report in the sophisticated *Die Zeit,* on April 2,
dealt with more theoretical issues:

Anton von Webern and Alban Berg, whose works created a
scandal . . . are friends and hangers-on of Schoenberg and
have been in contact with him for about ten years. From the
beginning, both have had boundless admiration for their
master, of the kind not even Richard Wagner could expect
from his devout supporters . . . Their devotion has also
taken the form of helping Schoenberg in material ways, since
he has seen bad days . . . It would not be necessary to speak
of this publicly if Schoenberg had not felt himself obliged to
pay back his young students and use his influence for performances of their works, despite the music's triviality. He has
repeatedly expressed this opinion of the works . . . Still
another example of how little stock Schoenberg puts in his
students' work: at the rehearsal for the concert the musicians
agreed that they would not perform Berg's piece. They be-

lieved that the public should not be faced with such music. Schoenberg, who had involved himself in other substantive issues, simply said, "Gentlemen, the programs have been printed, and it is too late to leave the work out." Yet at the performance he called for official action at the first sound of hissing.

Fueled by innuendoes from the press, a controversy blazed. Members left the Association for Literature and Music, not wanting to be associated with an organization that allegedly supported the avant-garde without discretion. Cartoons and editorials appeared in the papers. The incident ended in police court, where the hearing resulted in more laughs than sentences. Wellesz remembered that an operetta composer told the judge, "I laughed too. Is one not supposed to laugh if something is genuinely funny?" Another "expert" witness, a doctor, was called in to testify that the music's effects on the audience had been damaging to listeners' nervous sytems, and had even led to "severe depression."

On the way back to Berlin from Vienna, the conductor Hermann Scherchen ran into Schoenberg in the train's dining car. "The master, whose face was usually so peaceful, wore a downright war-like expression," Scherchen told Willi Reich. "He looked at me, his eyes blazing with anger, and asked, 'What do you think of the scandal?' Then, without waiting for my reply, he added, 'I should have had a revolver with me!' "

Chapter 7

Four Pieces for Clarinet
and Three for Orchestra

BERG WAS BOTH ANGRY and hurt at the reception handed him and his Altenberg *Lieder*. He responded to the article that had appeared in *Die Zeit,* but his rebuttal was never printed, and he may never have found the courage actually to mail it. To Webern he wrote, "The whole thing is so loathsome that I would like to fly far away." It was still on his mind in July 1914, when he wrote to his wife, "I haven't lost faith in the things I wrote before, even though you didn't care for all of them. I know you would like the Quartet (Opus 3) if it were performed today. And the Altenberg *Lieder* . . . if you heard them sung properly and all together — in less disturbing circumstances!"

But the Altenberg Songs were not soon to be heard under any circumstances. The fifth song, "Hier ist Friede," did appear in a piano reduction (not made by Berg) in a special issue of *Junge Tonkunst* (roughly, *Music of the New Generation*) published in 1921 by the Dresden

magazine of the avant-garde called *Menschen*. It was reprinted in *Musical Quarterly* in 1949. But the songs were
not performed as a complete cycle until 1953, when Jascha Horenstein resurrected them for broadcast on the
BBC. That presentation led, belatedly, to their publication by Universal Edition.

Even a quarter of a century after their publication,
however, the Altenberg *Lieder* are still not among Berg's
best-known works, though in terms of both style and
dramatic appeal they should have come into favor. *Wozzeck* and the Violin Concerto became the works most
frequently performed and most immediately identified
with their composer, followed by the Lyric Suite for
string quartet. The neglect of the Opus 4 Songs is inexplicable; the work that became Berg's Opus 5, however,
remained obscure for good reason.

The Four Pieces for Clarinet and Piano, Opus 5, are
oddities in Berg's output. To be sure, this composer was
never given to repeating himself. After his student days,
he did not seriously return to writing songs for voice and
piano (the exceptions were "occasional pieces," meant to
serve specific purposes and events). After the Opus 1 Sonata, he never went back to the solo piano. Even within a
genre, the works differ radically; the Lyric Suite is a distant cousin of the early String Quartet, Opus 3, and *Der
Wein,* for voice and orchestra, is in no way a sequel to the
Altenberg Songs. With all this, though, it is still hard to
understand how and why Berg decided to write for the
combination of clarinet and piano in the spring and early
summer of 1913.

There are two possible explanations. At the age of
twenty-eight, Berg was still a young man, with every
reason to envision a long life before him, and with no
reason to think that everything he wrote had to be of

equal import or that he could not spend his time experimenting. Furthermore, his money-earning chores of
copying, writing, and editing would naturally have made
it difficult for him to set aside the time to plan and execute a large-scale work, even if he had had such a project
in mind, which, at this point, he probably did not.

And then there was still the problem of size, which was
very much on Schoenberg's and Webern's minds, and
therefore also, at least tangentially, on Berg's. Both of the
older composers had been dealing in ever-shorter musical
time spans; by denying tonality, they had come to believe, they were also denying themselves the luxury of
musical expansiveness. Berg was not particularly concerned with this question, but he was aware of the problem. Musical cohesion and unity had to be found on two
levels: the smaller one, governing one or two phrases;
and a larger one, stretching over long movements and
complete works. For centuries, tonality had solved these
problems, but the old systems were no longer helpful.

When he wrote the Four Pieces for Clarinet and Piano,
either Berg had found no reasonable alternatives to the
guidelines of tonality, or he was genuinely drawn to the
idea of aphoristic music. The second possibility does not
suit his musical personality; if miniatures appealed to him
for a moment, subsequent works were to show that their
lure did not last. The Clarinet Pieces are, to use the common term, among the most "atonal" music Berg ever
wrote, including the twelve-tone compositions. Whereas
in earlier works, including the Opus 3 Quartet, and in future ones he had and would let tonality and its suggestiveness claim its due, in the Clarinet Pieces he fought the
strong pull of tradition. Berg could never separate himself from the magnetism of thirds and sixths as Webern
could, so there are moments even in the Clarinet Pieces

when the ear tunes to a home key, major or minor. But for Berg, the Clarinet Pieces are unusually free-floating.

They are still rooted in history, however. The idea of miniatures for a solo instrument with piano goes back through Debussy to Schumann and Beethoven. More immediate models were works of his friends: Webern's Four Pieces for Violin and Piano, Opus 7; Schoenberg's Six Little Piano Pieces, Opus 19; Webern's Six Bagatelles for String Quartet, Opus 9, which had been dedicated to Berg and which, though commonly dated 1913, had probably been written earlier. The closest links are between Berg's Opus 5 and Schoenberg's Opus 19. Berg originally intended to write six pieces, to match in quantity both Schoenberg's piano work and Webern's Bagatelles, but he stopped at four. The Opus 5 was dedicated to Schoenberg — the first in a series of works with which the student would publicly honor his master. Interestingly, the Opus 5 is very probably the first work of Berg's maturity written without any comments or suggestions from Schoenberg.

The question remains: Why the clarinet? Webern's pairings of violin or cello with piano were certainly more traditional; because there are always more string players than wind players on the solo-recital circuit, Webern's sets of tiny pieces had more chances for exposure than Berg's would ever have. And there is no indication that Berg knew a clarinetist who might want to perform his Pieces, or that he had any special familiarity with the instrument. Clarinets had naturally figured in the orchestra of the Altenberg Songs, but no more prominently than flutes or horns.

But Berg proved that he could write for the instrument as if he had mastered it through years of practice. The little Pieces burst with orders for a wide variety of articu-

lations, wide leaps from one end of the range to the
other, and sudden, surprising shifts in dynamics, exploit-
ing the possibilities of the clarinet as only a virtuoso
knows them. Like Webern's music of the time, Berg's
Clarinet Pieces are cushioned in softness, skirting utter
inaudibility (as when the pianist is asked to push down
the keys without actually sounding the notes, at the end
of the fourth piece). Again characteristically, however,
Berg's music would not be so comfortably contained,
and almost violent explosions mark both the first and the
last parts of the Opus 5.

These Pieces are close relatives of the Altenberg Songs,
and both Opus 4 and Opus 5 trace directly back to the
last song of Opus 2, "Warm die Luefte." Where the impact of the Altenberg Songs is more intense, in both text
and accompaniment, than the earlier Mombert song, the
Four Pieces for Clarinet and Piano enhance the more abstract, Expressionistic elements, as they manifest themselves in a purely instrumental idiom. Webern's tendencies at the time were self-effacingly antidramatic. Even if
Berg had been attracted by this vision of detachment, he
would have had to deny his personality in order to imple-
ment it. The Clarinet Pieces do occasionally seem to try
to exist out of time, as many of Webern's shortest pieces
seem to do, sounding both endless and nonexistent. But
though Webern had mastered this art of musical haiku,
Berg could not keep his music from wanting to go on
and say more. The Clarinet Pieces tease more than they
satisfy.

Even in this realm of the atonal miniature, Berg used
the outlines of traditional forms. By stopping with four
pieces instead of the planned six, he arrived at a little sonata, with an allegro beginning, an adagio slow movement, a scherzo with a bona fide trio, and a rondo finale.

The required exposition-development-recapitulation can be charted in the first movement; at the same time, the whole allegro can be thought of as a development of small melodic entities. Having returned to the concepts of continuous variation and unending development, Berg avoided themes in the sense of expanding melodies, and chose to build his structures out of small elements that would vary constantly within the larger phrases.

Here, as in the Altenberg Songs and the Opus 2 set, the first and last of the Clarinet Pieces stand out. This may seem inevitable to listeners accustomed to the traditional progressions of the four-movement sonata, but it is anything but a natural occurrence. The fourth piece of this set again marks the turning point, much as the Opus 2, Number 4, veered away from what had gone before. It seems as if Berg had decided to take a stylistic leap forward without waiting to tie up and fill out the work in progress. The last of the Four Pieces for Clarinet and Piano points toward the Lyric Suite and even toward the rondo structures so favored in the opera *Lulu*.

Berg had doubts about his new work. He wrote to Helene from Vienna on July 11, 1914, while she was taking the waters at Carlsbad, "As for the Clarinet Pieces, they aren't very striking in form, but are equally important (compared with the Altenberg Songs) in intention . . . If I didn't know that a proper judgment can be delivered only after a work is finished, I should despair every other day."

Schoenberg also had questions and reservations, which had much to do with cooling the relationship between Berg and his mentor for several difficult years. In June 1913, the Bergs went to Berlin to spend a week with the Schoenbergs; it was a pleasure for the friends to visit, and the two composers had business to discuss, as well. Berg was trying to find sponsors and supporters for a series of three concerts to be conducted by Schoenberg in Vienna during the next winter season; the series never materialized. Schoenberg had arranged for Berg to hear a rehearsal and performance of his epochal work *Pierrot Lunaire* while the younger man was in Berlin; though the song cycle had had its first performances in 1912, it was new to Berg.

Pierrot, one of the most important works of the century, caught Berg off guard. A year later he was still baffled and moved, telling Schoenberg, on July 20, 1914, "I only know that on the two occasions when I heard *Pierrot* I was conscious of the most profound impression ever made on me by a work of art . . . and I cannot imagine that with my small technical ability . . . I shall ever be able to comprehend this work which seems to me like a miracle of nature."

The "small technical ability" had evidently been pointed out to Berg by Schoenberg, with no mercy, on the younger man's last day in Berlin. Whatever Schoenberg said prompted a groveling response, mailed only a day or two after the Bergs returned home to Austria: "But I must thank you for your censure just as much as for everything you ever gave me . . . I need not tell you . . . that the great pain it caused me is a guarantee that I have taken your criticism to heart. And if I succeed in my resolution, this pain too will have lost its bitterness and will become one of those memories which . . . despite their depressing sides are full of profound, though serious beauty."

Whatever provoked Schoenberg may well have been quite incidental. Wrath came easily to the master; he was capable of labeling as traitors those former friends or students who, he felt, had ignored him or proven unfaithful.

And his disapproving outbursts did not always stem from artistic considerations, though in this case the implication is that the dissent began on musical grounds and continued from there. Schoenberg had been less than fully won over by the Altenberg Songs. Then, after he put them on the program in Vienna, rehearsed them, and defended them (however halfheartedly), it was they that had stopped the March 31 concert and led to ridicule of Schoenberg and his own art in the hostile press. Berg had been able to read Schoenberg's criticism of the Altenberg Songs as a compliment. He then went ahead to work on the Four Pieces for Clarinet and Piano, which, in size and aphoristic nature, would probably not have been what the teacher would have assigned to this student at that time. Then, too, only two years had passed since Berg's marriage, after which Schoenberg had treated the groom coldly. Schoenberg was neither the first nor the last creative leader who expected his followers to be married to their art, not to other human beings.

There are plenty of reasons why Schoenberg could have scolded Berg. Among the younger man's penchants and habits that Schoenberg found particularly unappealing were his fondness for the French Impressionists (including Debussy and Ravel, whose work Berg knew better than Schoenberg did), his tendency to write bleak music (for instance, the new Pieces for Clarinet and Piano), his lack of what Schoenberg considered to be reasonable productivity, and what were referred to as his "lack of self-discipline" and his "unreliability" — though it does seem strange that Schoenberg would have entrusted so much of the work on his own scores to someone whom he found unreliable and undisciplined.

Remorseful, and determined to win back his master's approval, Berg returned to work that summer at Helene's

family home in Trahuetten, aiming to satisfy one of
Schoenberg's long-standing edicts: "Every student of
mine should have written a symphony." Berg was thinking of a gay suite, but what he wrote was the Prelude (or
Preludium) to the Three Orchestral Pieces. After trying
to work on a fuller, one-movement symphonic work at
the same time as the Prelude, which was demanding to be
written, he shelved the idea of the symphony in favor of
the project that was moving with more vitality. The new
work would be the large-scale piece both he and Schoenberg had in mind, but it would also be a personal statement, not something someone else had assigned. He explained to Schoenberg in March 1914, referring to what
would become the March in his Three Orchestral Pieces,
Opus 6, "If what I write isn't what I have experienced,
perhaps my life would be turning toward compositions
that would be purest prophecy. But I don't have this in
me . . . and if I'm absolutely forced to do otherwise, the
result would probably be not a march of upstanding people parading happily, but, at best, a . . . 'march of the
asthmatics,' of whom I am one and, it seems, will always
remain so."

By June 8, 1914, Berg could let Schoenberg know that
he had "made a plan for my life," which included using
his time more efficiently and trying to be better organized. Since Helene took the cure in Carlsbad during the
summer of 1914, while Berg stayed in Vienna, the progress of the Three Orchestral Pieces can be traced in their
letters. On July 8, Berg was proud of "lots of important
and beautiful ideas coming to mind"; on July 10, he was
concentrating on the March, "thinking of it all day, and
even if I am not actually working on it, it is still seething
inside me." Enjoying his privacy and his ability to concentrate on creative work, Berg resented the hours (about

twelve each week) designated for his students. He was never as committed to teaching as Schoenberg was and never tried to influence his students to the degree he himself had been influenced during his days in class. Berg had none of the capacity for authoritative self-display that makes a good teacher, and, as he wrote to Helene, "giving lessons is a terrible strain . . . I have to think myself completely into my pupils' ideas, to hire myself out, as it were, and it is extremely hard for me to find my way back from there into my own thinking."

On July 11, Berg told his wife that his new work would be dedicated to Schoenberg, who had in effect ordered it as a birthday present. Since he was doing little other than composing and teaching, his letters during Helene's weeks at the spa were filled with musical details. Helene appreciated this, and wrote that she wished her husband would communicate his thoughts about his work more freely. Berg was delighted by her urgings.

> Now my work will really thrive . . . Why haven't I talked to you about this before? The urge to do so has often been strong, but one feels terribly shy about baring one's innermost feelings, even if one has already done so in music . . . Still, I would have overcome that shyness long ago, if you had given me a nudge in that direction. But you didn't say you wanted to hear about the work. In fact, I felt very flattered and honored and in a way deeply pleased by your saying (my proud little girl!) that you didn't want to "intrude on me." So I kept quiet about it.

Berg promised that the March would soon be ready to serve as the third of the Orchestral Pieces; the second, Riegen (Round), was barely begun, but was planned as a "very tender but cheerful dancing piece." The March had grown to greater proportions than Berg had envisioned: "Once again a long movement after so much short stuff.

It's longer than the five Altenberg Songs put together."
By using the Prelude, which he had drafted the previous
summer, as an opening for the Orchestral Pieces, however, he calculated that he could save some weeks of extra
work, and the prospect for an early completion of what
would become his Opus 6 was encouraging.

Musical issues gave way to practical ones in the correspondence, then, as Helene prepared to leave Carlsbad
and meet her husband in the country. A letter of July 15,
1914, however, brought an unpleasant foreshadowing of
Berg's future: "You know my two warts; the one on the
sole of my foot is completely healed. The other one on
the big toe has begun to hurt again, so I started squeezing
it. Soon it lost quite a lot of its core, and last night I
scooped out the crater very professionally . . . At night I
woke up with great pains . . . (which finally subsided)
. . . Now I think the wart has completely healed."

It was his asthma that frightened Berg throughout his
life. But it was an abscess that led to his death.

No amount of determination or organization could
help Berg meet his self-imposed deadline of finishing the
Orchestral Pieces in time to present them to Schoenberg
for his fortieth birthday, however. Apologetically, he addressed a letter of dedication to his teacher on September
8, 1914, trusting that Schoenberg's "paternal benevo-
lence" would allow him to "accept my good intentions"
in lieu of a completed work. "The close study of your
Orchestral Pieces, Opus 6, was an immense help and has
sharpened my self-criticism more and more," Berg
wrote. "This is the reason why I have not been able to
complete the second of the three pieces, Riegen, in time,
and why I have had to leave it until later, when I shall
probably succeed in changing what is wrong with it."

Even contemporary commentators noted with some

dismay that there was no response from Schoenberg to this dedication, nor, for that matter, any comment at all on Berg's Opus 6. Schoenberg had heard the young man's promises, but he did not see that Berg was becoming any more industrious or self-sufficient. As late as November 1915, Berg still felt obliged to explain to his teacher that he was not, and had not been for some time, financially dependent on his relatives. This was not true; he was receiving an allotment from his mother in return for managing some of the family's property in the city. He augmented that sum by giving lessons three afternoons each week and through sundry "projects: planning and preparing concerts; the final corrections in *Harmonielehre*; production of the brochure *Arnold Schoenberg* . . . work on the *Gurrelieder*; and in addition the versions of the two songs out of the F-sharp Minor Quartet [by Schoenberg]; part of the four-hand version of Mahler's Eighth Symphony; transpositions of the Strauss songs — and only my own short Orchestral Songs, Opus 4, and the even shorter Clarinet Pieces, Opus 5, in the space of two and a half years!"

Much as he felt that he had to defend himself against Schoenberg's charges of sloth and dependency, as he approached his thirtieth birthday, Berg had turned the projected symphony into one of his most challenging and important works. A note at the end of the printed score of the Three Orchestral Pieces, Opus 6, indicates that all three sections were finished at Trahuetten on August 23, 1914. Berg wanted to use his number, twenty-three, but the middle piece was in fact not finished and sent to Schoenberg until a year later. Whatever Schoenberg thought of the work, he must have seen at once that his admonitions and encouragement had brought results. The teacher wanted the pupil to write something that would be significant in the international stream of musical progress, and that is exactly what Schoenberg received when he unwrapped the packages that arrived in the mail carrying Berg's Opus 6.

The contrast between this work and everything Berg had written to date is stunning. As impatient and unsettled as the Clarinet Pieces are in sound and feeling, there had been little in them to indicate that Berg's next opus would shift direction so vehemently and masterfully. The Altenberg Songs, Berg's first adult attempts at dealing with the orchestra, suggest the dramatic potential that manifests itself in the Orchestral Pieces. But after the scandal that surrounded those Opus 4 songs, who would have thought that Berg would move not just in the direction of an even larger orchestra, but also toward complexities not hinted at in the earlier score?

The only one of Berg's earlier works that can be counted as a direct predecessor to the Opus 6 is the String Quartet, Opus 3, and parallels here can be found more in the realms of imagination and emotion than on the strictly technical level. Somehow, with all the difficulties he faced in writing the Orchestral Pieces — and he admitted to Schoenberg, on July 20, 1914, "I have to ask myself, again and again, if what I express in them, and what compels me to brood over certain bars for days on end, is any better than my last compositions" — Berg managed to produce the work that was so necessary, but that neither Schoenberg nor Webern had been able to find; the work that drew the line between the mainstream of the late nineteenth and early twentieth centuries and the avant-garde faction called the New Viennese School.

The link was Mahler. In the end, Schoenberg, Webern, and Berg all held this man in the highest esteem, but in different ways. Schoenberg had come to him relatively late, but Berg had always been drawn to him. At first, he was lured by the glamour and excitement that surrounded premières of Mahler's works; they were Events, the right places to be and to be seen, and the right things to talk about. In his early music, Berg kept Mahler at arm's length. The fact that the Altenberg Songs pair voice with orchestra harks back to Mahler's similar settings, though the style of Berg's Opus 4 had very little to do with Mahler's sound and technique.

But there was a strong current running between the two men. Berg was socially sensitive; he wanted to be accepted, and, more than the iconoclastic Schoenberg or the introspective, intellectual Webern, he was vulnerable to society's ever-shifting sense of style. The young Berg liked the fact that Mahler was married to the beautiful and intelligent Alma Schindler; later, the composer was proud that his own wife, Helene, and the widowed Alma had become friends. And Alma Schindler Mahler Gropius Werfel, to list the names of the woman who seems to have been an inspiration to many who were important in the arts of the early twentieth century, must have recognized in the young Berg some of the same qualities she had loved in her first famous husband: compassion mixed with irony, especially self-irony; an undercurrent of sentimentality; a hint of emotional instability; a powerful and sharp mind, combining analytical capabilities with flights of unrestricted fancy; a combination of playfulness and overriding pessimism. In addition Berg, unlike Mahler, was not merely handsome but almost beautiful. Alma picked Berg out of the Schoenberg circle and welcomed him to her table and her salons, where he watched her manipulate the men who loved her for her cleverness as much as for her dark beauty.

In the Three Orchestral Pieces, the Berg–Mahler connection reached the musical surface. Theodor Adorno, who (with Reich, Gottfried Kassowitz, Hans Erich Apos-

tel, and Fritz Heinrich Klein) was among Berg's favored
students, suggested that the Opus 6 should sound like a
simultaneous combination of Mahler's Ninth Symphony
and Schoenberg's Orchestral Pieces. But the relationships
with Mahler's Sixth Symphony are the stronger ones.
Berg had a special love for this work; he wrote to Webern, "I don't need to tell you . . . there is but one
Sixth, in spite of the *Pastoral*." The most obvious reference to Mahler's Sixth comes with Berg's use of the hammer blows, the notorious whacks that, no matter how
long and hard musicologists fight about how many
Mahler really meant to use, are the hallmark of the Sixth,
which Berg found so inspiring. In the Orchestral Pieces,
as in Mahler's symphony, the hammer hits in the finale,
first three times (starting *fortississimo*) at the movement's
huge climax, and again *fff* right at the end. Berg marked
his climactic measures in the finale *Hohepunkt* (high
point), as if anyone could miss it. The sounds of Berg's
hammer blows, like Mahler's, hit the listener in the pit of
the stomach. In the Orchestral Pieces, they also have the
effect of smashing the thick, dense mass of sound into a
thousand fragments.

In further tribute to Mahler, the last of Berg's Three
Orchestral Pieces is a March; it has the fanfares and drum
rolls that the earlier composer stylized similarly in his
symphonic marches. The central Round, which Berg
wrote last, also pays homage to Mahler's stylized waltzes
and *Laendler* (waltz steps slowed for heavy-footed German peasants). And even the Prelude, with its proces-
sional for percussion, both tuned (timpani) and untuned
(drums), spans the distance between Mahler's Third
Symphony and the percussive extravaganzas of the 1920s
and 1930s, which culminated in the work of Edgar
Varèse.

There are more French links in the Three Orchestral Pieces than might meet the eye. The score looks like Mahler, but the ears pick up suggestively Impressionistic sounds and devices, Debussy-like in their melodic outlines, but Ravel-like in their bravura use of the large orchestra (four flutes, four oboes, four clarinets, bass clarinet, three bassoons, contrabassoon, six horns, four trumpets, three trombones, tuba, the huge percussion section with two pairs of timpani and a hammer with nonmetallic sound, glockenspiel and xylophone, celeste, two harps, and strings *stark besetzt,* that is, as many as possible).

With all these players, with the relative expansiveness of the Orchestral Pieces (they last more than twenty minutes in most performances, and the March takes as much time as the two other movements combined, as Berg predicted it would), and with all the ties to Mahler and the French, what remains of Schoenberg? Everything, and surprisingly little. With the Three Orchestral Pieces, Berg declared independence from his former teacher (and even more strongly from Webern) to a much greater degree than is suggested in most discussions of the New Viennese School.

But, of course, Schoenberg's lessons had been responsible for setting Berg off to explore his own private creativity, so even if the Three Orchestral Pieces could never have been written by Schoenberg or under his direct influence, they could not have been written without him, either. In this music, Berg took what he learned about motivic development and repetition and extended it with great sophistication into the realm of rhythm, so that rhythmic motives act as signals even more engagingly than their melodic counterparts. On a practical level, Berg decided to adopt Schoenberg's practice of marking the principal and subsidiary voices with $H^{\overline{}}$ for *Haupt-stimme* (principal voice) and $N^{\overline{}}$ for *Nebenstimme* (secondary voice), to indicate what should stand out in performance and which lines could be left to fend for themselves in the dense fabric. These markings are more important than they might seem at first glance, since without them it is extremely unlikely that any performance of the Three Orchestral Pieces could come near what Berg had in mind. The music is extremely difficult for individual players and especially for the conductor, who has to deal with a remarkable number of simultaneous rhythmic, harmonic, and melodic events, and who must create order — or as much order as possible —from a score that could easily translate into chaos. Berg himself admitted to Adorno that the Three Orchestral Pieces contained music "more complicated than anything ever written before." They may not be as large as Schoenberg's *Gurrelieder* or as finger-twisting for particular instrumentalists as certain passages in Strauss's symphonic extravaganzas, but considering his Opus 6 as a whole, Berg was not exaggerating in his claim. Even the conductor who religiously serves the dynamic markings and the signs indicating which lines take precedence runs the risk of presenting his audience with not much more than prepared aural nonsense if both he and the orchestra are not on constant guard.

After Webern conducted the first performance of two of the Three Orchestral Pieces (Prelude and Round, which Berg sanctioned for presentation as a pair, separate from the concluding March) on June 5, 1923, as part of the Austrian Music Week in Berlin, Berg revised the scoring in places, simplifying and thinning it out. The first complete performance of the Opus 6 took place only after *Wozzeck* had propelled Berg to fame. Johannes Schuler, the conductor who so pleased Berg with an inventive and careful presentation of that opera in Oldenburg in 1929, wanted to go on to present the Three Orchestral Pieces. Berg was gratified by the request, but he cautioned Schuler that "a performance of these Orchestral Pieces, which, though short, are very difficult, is an impossible matter in the usual concert procedure, where a work like this has to be rehearsed along with a symphony, a concerto and an overture or orchestral songs — all in two rehearsals." Nevertheless, Schuler was bold and reassuring to the composer, and the performance went on.

Schuler asked Berg to write some program notes, but all the composer had time to produce were some "quickly marshaled analytical remarks," which were turned into prose by Dr. Fritz Uhlenbruch. They indicate that Berg was particularly aware of the symphonic structure nested in his Three Orchestral Pieces: "The Præludium would represent the first movement; 'Reigen' contains the scherzo and the slow movement (in that order!), and the March could be considered the finale." Furthermore, the composer noted, each piece fell into two symmetrical parts. "In the first piece several groups of bars in the first and second parts correspond to one another as mirror images . . . In 'Reigen' the binarity is given by the sequence of scherzo and slow movement . . . In the third piece the binarity results from the juxtaposition of the 'march-like' group and the 'march' itself."

As he sketched his thoughts about the Three Orchestral Pieces for that 1929 performance, Berg must have looked back on his Opus 6 as a relic from a forgotten time. So much had happened in the intervening fifteen years that the composer's life had changed drastically. The Three Orchestral Pieces were finished just in time to seem to set off a fury of upsetting events.

Chapter 8

War

On June 28, 1914, the Serbian terrorist Gavrilo Princip assassinated the Archduke Francis Ferdinand, heir to the Austrian throne, and his wife. Austria-Hungary set forth ten demands through which anti-Austrian agitation was to be suppressed. Serbia conceded on all but two points, and requested reference to the peace tribunal in The Hague. Austria adopted an all-or-nothing stance.

Germany stood behind Austria; Russia supported Serbia. Britain, France, and Italy proposed mediation, but Germany refused, and on July 28, Austria declared war on Serbia. That day, Webern wrote to Berg, "So, war! Are you amazed?"

On August 1, Germany declared war on Russia, and on August 3, on France. The Germans invaded Belgium, violating a treaty of which Britain had been a signatory, and England declared war on Germany on August 4. The Bergs were in Trahuetten. "Even here one feels the effects of the outbreak of war," Berg wrote to Polnauer.

"Everyone, man and horse, must prepare. Perhaps even we good-for-nothings will have to report."

"I must go to war, I must. I can't stay out any longer," Webern wrote on September 3. Schoenberg felt similar obligations; Berg was not as ardent. His patriotism was aroused, and he told Schoenberg on August 24 that he felt it "shameful to be only an onlooker at these great events," but he had little desire to fight. Still, political matters occupied his mind, affecting progress on his work, and when he sent the first and third of the Three Orchestral Pieces to Schoenberg on September 8, Berg said he sometimes felt it was "even downright wicked to be thinking of things other than the war."

During the first months of the conflict, the twenty-nine-year-old Berg was called up for another physical examination, but was still considered unfit for service, mostly because he was too tall and too thin. In one way, he was disappointed; he did not like to be told that he was a weakling. But his freedom allowed him to continue his work and tend to pressing tasks relating to the administration of his family's property. The last two months of 1914 were consumed by trips to and from the Berghof, where personnel who had been called to military duty had to be replaced. Berg looked forward to the end of the war and the Austrian victory, which he was sure would come. Safely disqualified, at least for the time being, he thought about military service. "Can I be of use? I had to run for a tram today, and had asthma all the time I was on it . . . I shall join the army as a volunteer on the condition that they fight only in the afternoon and let me sit down all morning," he wrote to his wife on November 1, at the beginning of one of his trips to Carinthia.

The war made traveling more difficult and crowded

than usual. "I breathed more freely in the surroundings of the dining car," Berg wrote to Helene. "It's not out of snobbishness that I don't like the common people. Perhaps it's only the appearance and smell of the third class . . . You feel as if the wheels were jumping across the sleepers, not gliding along the rails. And then the dirt and the constant smell from the W.C. I don't feel well at all!"

Though he was not a pacifist, Berg had no use for the trappings of war. But he spent some of his lonely hours at the Berghof in the following weeks devising a weapon that, he wrote to Schoenberg, "will give us such an ascendency over our enemies that we should be able to beat even a superior power." He intended to send his plans off to the War Ministry, but eventually turned his inventive imagination to a more peaceful device, a telegraph-style machine that would allow a composer to record the most subtle fluctuations of tempo as an incontestable guide for future performers. This machine might have been sold in tandem with the music typewriter Schoenberg had devised, but neither of these inventions was ever seriously developed.

Berg continued to view the war with patriotic disgust. Prices in Vienna had soared, and he considered stocking up on food at the lower country prices while he was around the Berghof. He followed the army's advances and retreats on a map, and instructed Helene to do the same. But he was depressed by the military hospitals and by the lines of wounded, and struggled to grasp the implications for the future of the growing conflict.

I sometimes feel here as if I were living outside this world, my petty interests against the maelstrom of the war [he wrote to Helene on November 8]. My head is just not big enough to take it all in. You read "Tsingtow fallen," and five minutes later you have forgotten about it, instead of rushing off into the mountains or swimming far into the lake to weep one's heart out, which would be more appropriate.

All these minor events in the war seem more overwhelming than any we've ever experienced before, or perhaps shall ever experience again. Yet they are only tiny fractions in this piece of world history, and in the end you take no more notice of them than of some war you learned about at school. How impotent the human spirit is!

Gradually, he came to believe that the war would last longer than a few weeks or months, and on December 31, 1914, the first New Year's Eve he had spent away from home and family, he wrote to his wife that he was frightened.

I couldn't imagine that the task of war would be fulfilled all that quickly: the task of making the world clean! . . . Our corrupt condition — by which I mean the aggregation of stupidity, avarice, journalism, business spirit, laziness, selfishness, capriciousness, deceit, hypocrisy and all the rest — hasn't changed at all. Sometimes there are things which look or sound like an improvement, but they turn out to be merely a set of clichés that would go well into cheap lyrics for singing, howling or spitting by our society of operetta enthusiasts . . . This muck-heap has been growing for decades, and in its midst there is still no trace of cleanliness. Believe me, if the war ended today, we should be back in the same old sordid squalor within two weeks.

On New Year's Day, 1915, Berg wrote to Schoenberg in the same gray mood: "Life *outside* goes on just as usual . . . As if nothing had happened, people in Vienna live completely without restraint, operettas and farces 'adapted to the times' are produced, and every theater and cinema is filled to the bursting point . . . If the war is to do what it is supposed to, and act as a cathartic, it is

very far from its end. The dirt remains, only in different
form."

The problems of everyday life went on. Schoenberg
was again in financial straits, and, with the aid of Alma
Mahler and her wealthy friends, a concert was arranged
for April 26, 1915, in Vienna's Musikverein, where
Schoenberg would conduct Beethoven's *Egmont* Overture
and the Ninth Symphony in Mahler's rescoring (with
some alterations by Schoenberg for the occasion). Berg
had second thoughts about the advisability of improving
on Beethoven, but afterward he reported that the concert
had been an artistic success, even though Schoenberg
realized little or no financial gain. Many Viennese disap-
proved of the combination of the controversial Schoenberg and the great Beethoven, however, and a disturbing
report of the concert appeared on May 1 in the *Ostdeutsche
Rundschau,* a Vienna-based daily:

> The way this promotional event turned out finally lifted the
> veil of alleged distinction that a group of musical politicians
> . . . had cleverly spread over [Schoenberg] . . . Surely even
> the most convinced opponents of this fellow, who for some
> time has been the constant cause of the most repellent phe-
> nomena in Viennese musical life, cannot have expected so
> complete a fiasco . . . as this crazy attempt at conducting
> . . . But now we see clearly how the string-pullers in this
> comedy are biased — people of whom we shall take due no-
> tice in the future . . . At the end, a hare-brained godless
> group planted themselves in front of the podium and, with
> the help of certain familiar louts of the concert halls, carried
> on wild applause; Talmudic casuistry deduced from this that
> the episode had met the public favor.

Berg clipped and saved this outburst, one of the first of
many blatantly anti-Semitic diatribes that would finally
result in Schoenberg's self-exile to America.

Webern enlisted in the army early in 1915. Schoenberg was called for a physical examination on May 20 of the same year, and, unfortunately, was found fit to serve. He enrolled as a one-year volunteer in the middle of December. The day before Schoenberg's medical appointment, Berg communicated to Webern his anxiety about their teacher's future. But a German submarine sank the *Lusitania* off Ireland on May 7, Italy declared war on Austria-Hungary on May 23, the war continued to spread, and soldiers were desperately needed. With the help of a letter from the Hungarian composer Béla Bartók, Schoenberg's students and friends managed to obtain the master's release from the army, at least until further notice, on October 20, 1916. They based their pleas on matters of health (Schoenberg had a mild asthmatic condition), and on precedent. Many prominent musicians, including Max Reger and Hans Pfitzner, had, by virtue of their importance to the community and through the intercession of influential friends, been exempted from military service. After his release, Schoenberg was called up again, in September 1917, for light duty; he went without complaint, and was re-released a month later on medical grounds.

Berg faced the increasingly serious situation with growing passion and with traces of panic. Italy's entry into the war had meant that older men were being called up, even those who, like Berg, had previously been declared unfit. In a letter to Schoenberg, Berg blamed his bad luck on Italy's having become involved on the twenty-third of the month, and cited a theory by the German biologist and Freudian disciple Wilhelm Fliess that the life cycle of males runs in periods of multiples of the same number, twenty-three. Webern suggested in his rational way that since Berg had to go to war he should try to join a regiment in Peggau, but Berg decided that it

would be better for him to find a way to remain in or
near Vienna, ostensibly so that he could continue to tend
his mother's property, but actually because he wanted to
be nearer home. For a while, he considered joining the
artillery. And by June 20, 1915, he wrote to Schoenberg
that he felt he was entering "a not unlucky phase" in life.

The Bergs went to Trahuetten, where the composer
worked on his Opus 6 before returning to Vienna to
report for duty. His first call was to a medical inspection
at eight-thirty in the morning of Friday, August 14. He
was declared fit to serve, as he reported to his wife, "like
everybody else, without even being examined. When
asked if I had any ailments, I said 'no' — again, like all
the rest." He entered the army the next Monday morning
in Huetteldorf, from where he would be assigned to a
battalion. Instead of falling into a depression, he spent his
last weekend as a civilian having breakfast in bed, visiting
"Almschi" Mahler, and risking "going down in history as
a terrible glutton," he wrote Helene on August 14. He
also looked into the procedures he and his wife would
have to follow for a second wedding ceremony, this time
in a Catholic church, and went about catching up on
Viennese social and musical gossip. Alma Mahler and
Oskar Kokoschka had been thinking of legitimating their
affair with a marriage license. Schoenberg had had a
heated quarrel with Alma's friend Lilly Lieser-Landau, his
summer hostess in Semmering, and a lesser tiff with
Alma herself. A performance of Mahler's Third Symphony, to take place in early fall, had been written on everybody's calendar.

As Berg described it to his wife, his first day in the
military — Monday, August 16 — was not at all unpleasant. He rose early and took his first breakfast back to
bed with him, then dressed and arrived at the barracks
thirty minutes early, in time to have a cup of coffee in a

nearby café and read the morning papers. He happened to be sitting next to a soldier who told him of something called the "artists' company" of the army, filled with writers, actors, and professional men. Berg found out how to join that elite group, then gathered with the other recruits, and, to his surprise and pleasure, met some old friends and was recognized by others. There were plenty of breaks for goulash and coffee, and plenty of people to talk to. Berg was offended that the uniform he was issued had an unpleasant smell and that the pants were too short; but his description made the military sound like a college reunion, and, though he claimed to be tired at the end of his first day as Private Berg, he still had the energy to visit Helene's family and model his uniform, which looked, he said, "quite nice."

The second day was filled with drills at the parade ground, with what Berg described to Helene as "a constant horse-dung zephyr," but there was still no shortage of companionship or food, and he had "nice educated people as my superiors." The beginnings of military life were not at all bad.

But what Berg had portrayed as a rather pleasant initial experience with the army came to a precipitous end. At the beginning of October 1915, he was sent to training camp at Brück an der Leitha, near the Hungarian border. The letter he wrote to his wife right after his arrival set a different scene:

> This is Hell in the true sense of the word . . . Each bad experience makes me forget the one before . . . Just imagine standing outside the train for a whole hour in the pouring rain, then being crammed into the compartment soaking wet . . . then seven hours to go a distance any local train would cover in an hour and a quarter . . . Then half an hour on the double to the camp, where they gave us black coffee for supper . . . [and] freezing to bed with half our clothes on.

Berg found a pleasant dairy restaurant where he could have a good breakfast in peaceful solitude and try to raise his sagging spirits. His friend and fellow composer Rudolf Ploderer was at the camp to keep him company. But beyond these things, there was little for him to enjoy: "The beds are like rock, the sanitary arrangements are highly primitive . . . The lavatories are revolting, but, as I said, these are external things, which one can easily get over."

The camp broke Berg's spirit and his health, as well. On October 12, he went to the sick parade, suffering from a pain in the back of his neck. He was given aspirin and told not to carry his pack, and, by the next day, was quite well again. But the physical exertion of regular six-hour routines of "marching, running, charging across hill and dale, through the swamps and marshes, down on the ground, up again, and so on" proved to be too much for him. He spent a weekend at home in Vienna later in October with Helene, who had returned from the country. On the way back to camp, he was grateful for the sandwiches Helene had given him; they allayed his hunger during the trip.

But at the beginning of November, he suffered a complete physical breakdown and was taken to the reserve hospital at Bruck. Helene hurried to visit him, found him completely exhausted, and consulted the doctor. A thorough examination followed, with x rays of Berg's heart and lungs. The diagnosis, dated November 15, 1915, reported "bronchial asthma, swelling of lungs . . . deadening of tips of lungs . . . Stomach also sore. Heart too small. Patient complains of shortage of breath during strenuous exercise. Has suffered from asthma since childhood, with violent expectoration. Non-smoker. [This was not true.] No prospects of cure. In hospital since

November 6. One sick parade. Suitable for orderly duties."

The decision was made to return Berg to Vienna and
guard duty there, though his rank as an officer-cadet
should have exempted him from the guard routine. He
was given time to regain his strength, then ordered to
report for guard duty on the third Monday of December.
He was disturbed by knowing that he would serve next
to some of the same men to whom he had previously
given orders, and by the uncertainty of whether he would
stay in Vienna or be transferred out of the city, perhaps
to Serbia, where, he had heard, guards were needed. He
wrote to his student Kassowitz on December 11, outlining the schedule he would face: "Report at 7:00 o'clock in
the morning, the usual duties (such as drills, exercise,
etc.), to the barracks then from 2:00 P.M until guard duty
begins, when I have to go somewhere or other and relieve someone every two hours as guard captain. That
lasts until 2:00 the next afternoon, even through the
night! Then I am free afternoon or evening until the
whole thing begins again at 7:00 the next morning! —
So, guard duty every other day for thirty-one hours
straight."

He did get to stay in Vienna, but that, he found, made
his life only slightly more bearable. On Christmas Day,
1915, he wrote a more dramatic letter to Kassowitz,
charging his student to help find a way to get him transferred. The younger man was to have been in touch with
an officer who might have been of some assistance, but
the man was away, and Berg grew testy and impatient.
He went over what was familiar ground to Kassowitz by
then, reminding him that it would be easy and within the
regulations to arrange for a transfer from guard duty to
auxiliary duty within the same company, and that the

guard duty was not the customary (or, Berg thought, the fair) assignment for a man of his one-year matriculated status in the military. Berg argued that an office appointment would help him regain his health, which had weakened and was continuing to deteriorate.

It has been impossible for me to get proper medical treatment, since more attention is paid to flat feet and broken limbs, etc., than to internal ailments. And my illness is such that I can carry out my duties by simple courage and necessity until I simply collapse . . . Recently the head medic, a dentist, simply declared me "serviceable" and threatened to give all the guards their commissions and declare them fit for field service! . . . Activity in the guardhouse equals zero. It means sitting around for twenty-four hours in a little room filled with smoke from ten or twelve recruits . . . In the night I can sleep for four hours, but this is effectively reduced to three since it doesn't get quiet until 10:00 P.M. . . . You can imagine how I feel, how I have to fight off sleep, drinking unconscionable amounts of black coffee in order not to fall asleep sitting up!

Finally, in January 1916, he was moved to a desk assignment, and in May he was promoted to an official post in the War Ministry (probably with help from his brother Charly), where he remained until the end of the war. He did not like it — he called it "imprisonment" and "slavery" — but it was much better than the guard duty. On August 5, 1916, he wrote to Helene in the country that he was looking and feeling well, eating "more than enough," and sleeping well in a life that was "splendidly simple and regular." His most serious immediate concern was that his uniform had begun to show signs of age but the tailor had not been in when Berg stopped by his shop, and some shoes he had purchased threatened to be uncomfortable. He also regretted that he would not be getting leave in order to see the room that had been redecorated for him at Trahuetten; rules of service in the War Ministry did not provide vacations for men who had served there for less than one year.

Life was not ideal, but neither was it intolerable. Berg could rejoin Vienna's musical circles, live in his own flat, and work in a civilized atmosphere, even if the situation was not one he would have chosen for himself. He remained in the War Ministry for two years and two months, until Austria surrendered, on August 4, 1918. His thoughts then were less on the outcome of the war than on the cheering prospect of regaining his freedom and rejoining civilian society.

It is difficult to pity the recruit who was pleased that he looked handsome in uniform, who so readily scorned the people he associated with in the army, who evidently expected the military food and accommodations to be as good as those at home, and who managed, in the end, to see virtually none of the worst parts of the war. Was he really as out of touch with reality as his letters would suggest? In 1965 the publication in Prague's *Miscellanea Musicologica* of a long letter from Berg to Erwin Schulhoff cast some light on this issue. Schulhoff was a pianist and composer who was influential in promoting Berg's music in Czechoslovakia, and who became an active Marxist and died in the Wuelzburg concentration camp in 1942. He had written to Berg exactly a year after the November 11 cease fire, shortly after Austria had been humiliated into signing the Treaty of Versailles. Perhaps Berg's remarks to Schulhoff should be read with Berg's own Austrian nationalism in mind, remembering how strongly he had looked forward to the potentially cleansing effects of war. His reply to Schulhoff was dated November 27, 1919:

You are very wrong if you imagine me to be an imperialist or a militarist . . . I asked myself in August, 1914, whether a people that treats its own greatest men in the way that the German people did and does, doesn't actually deserve to be defeated . . . Only Karl Kraus, my strongest support at that time and in the days to come, dared speak the truth about it . . . and in the midst of his own country's danger, as no Frenchman would have dared to do . . . In spite of all that, I still believe in the German people. Not in the people of today, or in the Viennese or the Berliners, but perhaps in the Thuringians, in the Alpine peoples. In the people who have produced Beethoven, and all the absolutely great ones up through Mahler and Schoenberg (names such as France — despite Debussy, Ravel and Satie — and other Entente nations cannot produce), yes, in the people who . . . in these filthy days still have a Karl Kraus . . .

Whether we shall ever again lift ourselves out of this filth depends on when the people recognize why they were abandoned thus by all good spirits, that is, whether this war and what has come of it have already been enough of a lesson and punishment for us and for our soul-searching . . . At least we know where we are, how newspapers, capitalism, Judaism (in other words: here, as there, the single God — the "God of the Jews," the "God of the Germans" — standing opposed to the Christian God . . . to the God of all humanity!) and militarism gained the upper hand . . .

Believe me, though I was never in the fighting, nor ever wounded, I suffered no less than you in my military service. (Kraus says somewhere: "More annoying than anything: to have to salute!") . . . All of these years I suffered as a corporal, humiliated, not a single note composed — oh, it was dreadful, and so today, when I am actually freezing and have nothing to live on, I am happy in comparison with those days, when life was at least physically endurable. I don't think you'll find such a fierce anti-militarist as I!

Berg went on to defend Germans and Austrians against the French, whom Schulhoff had cited for valor, and to defend Schoenberg in similarly glowing tones, although Schoenberg and the pianist were merely involved in an incidental, personal misunderstanding. Many of the sentiments Berg expressed on political subjects were typical of Austrians of the time, and Berg wanted more than anything to be a patriot. Throughout his life, he stressed that he was an *Austrian* composer. Sometimes he would admit himself into the larger German musical fraternity, but his primary allegiance always rested with his native land. Berg, Kraus, and other Austrians could criticize their country, but similarly harsh words from foreigners were not welcome. Berg's protestations in his letter to Schulhoff fail to convince any reader that he was as antimilitaristic as he claimed to be. When threatened, crossed, or challenged, he and his fellow Austrians would fight.

And, as he had done before, Berg was not above stretching a point here and there to prove his case. When time came to write to Schulhoff, the War Ministry evidently looked a lot worse than it had during the last two years of fighting. Fortunately, it was simply not true that, in his three and a half years of military service, Berg had got "not a single note composed."

Chapter 9

Discovering *Wozzeck*

JOHANN FRANZ WOZZECK, "thirty years and seven
months old, militiaman and fusilier, in the second
regiment, second battalion, fourth company, uneducated,
uncomprehending," is the servant to the captain of his
outfit and guinea pig to its doctor. As the curtain rises, he
is giving the captain his morning shave, hearing his superior's speculations on the nature of time and life. Wozzeck, says the captain, has no morals. Struggling to support himself, his woman, Marie, and their child,
Wozzeck answers, "Captain, sir, the good God will not
ask my poor little bastard whether the Amen was said
over him before he was made . . . No doubt if we got to
heaven we would have to lend a hand with the thunder!"
The captain concludes that Wozzeck thinks too much.

At sunset, Wozzeck and a soldier, Andres, are cutting
sticks for firewood. Wozzeck feels the place is haunted;
he sees eerie lights and imagines that a head is skimming
along the ground. Mumbling about the Freemasons and
fearing that the ground will open and swallow him up,
Wozzeck wildly begs Andres to flee.

In her room, Marie plays with the child. Soldiers march by; Marie and the drum major wave to one another. Margret, the neighbor, remarks sarcastically about Marie's interest in the soldiers, and the women argue. Marie shuts Margret out by slamming the window, takes the child, and sings a lullaby. Her reverie is broken when Wozzeck knocks on the window to say he is late to the barracks and cannot come to her. She holds up the child for his father to see, but Wozzeck is not interested. Disturbed, Marie puts the boy back in the cradle, saying, "Ah, we poor people . . . I cannot endure it much longer."

The next day, Wozzeck is hallucinating and, testing out a new dietetic theory, the doctor puts him on a different schedule of nourishment. Wozzeck is too confused to rebel. Warning that unless the soldier goes along with the treatment he will end up in a madhouse, the doctor rubs his hands in satisfaction: "Oh, my theory, my fame! I shall be immortal!"

In front of her house, Marie gazes at the drum major, who is even more handsome than he was at the Sunday parade. Flattered that he would look at her, she goes to him and throws herself into his arms. The two disappear into the house.

Admiring herself in the mirror, Marie wears new earrings, which she must hide from Wozzeck as he enters. She tells him she just happened to find the jewelry; he does not believe her, but turns to the child, whose forehead is moist. "We poor people — nothing under the sun but work, and even in our sleep we sweat!" He hands his earnings to Marie, then leaves, as she turns back to her mirror in a mixture of triumph and shame.

The captain and the doctor meet in the street, and the doctor warns his friend that he looks unwell and may be apoplectic. When Wozzeck walks by, the two superiors tease him about Marie's faithlessness. The soldier escapes, and the doctor gazes after him with curiosity: "A phenomenon, this Wozzeck."

In front of Marie's house, Wozzeck babbles about sin and asks if his rival, the drum major, stood in that same spot. Marie says the street is public; when Wozzeck seems ready to strike her, she says, "Better a knife in me than a hand on me!" She leaves him in confusion: "Better a knife! My head is swimming!"

In a beer garden crowded with drunken soldiers, Wozzeck sees Marie dancing with the drum major. He is about to charge at them when the music stops; Andres sings a lusty song and someone else delivers a mock sermon. As the band starts up again, a fool whispers to Wozzeck that he "smells blood." Wozzeck's fantasies become wilder.

That night, in the barracks, Wozzeck tosses restlessly to the sound of the soldiers' snoring. A knife flashes into his mind. The drum major comes in to brag of his conquests, insults Wozzeck, and suddenly assaults him. Wozzeck is badly beaten, but the others merely laugh cynically and go back to sleep.

By candlelight, Marie reads the Bible story of Mary Magdalen, reflecting on her own frailty, and, turning to her child, she prays.

Wozzeck and Marie walk to a pond in the woods, and he makes her sit down, promising that her feet won't hurt much longer. As darkness falls, he reminisces about the years they have spent together, growing less and less coherent. Marie notices the red of the moon; Wozzeck's mind turns to blood. He pulls a knife, plunges it into Marie's throat, waits until he is sure she is dead, and stumbles off.

In the tavern, Wozzeck tries to forget his horrible deed. He dances with Margret and would seduce her, but she sees blood on his hands and screams. A crowd gathers around Wozzeck, who tries to explain that he cut himself, then runs out screaming, "Am I a murderer?"

Wozzeck remembers that he left his knife at the pond, and goes back to find it. He tosses it into the water, but, fearing it has not gone far enough from the shore, he wades in to throw it again, loses his balance, and drowns. The captain and the doctor walk past. Hearing a moan coming from the water but not wanting to admit anything is wrong, they quickly walk on.

Back in front of Marie's house, Wozzeck's son is playing with his friends. One shouts that his mother is dead. The other children rush off to see the body, but the boy goes on playing with his hobby horse, going faster and faster until, finally, he follows the others, still saying, "Hop! Hop!"

Berg drew this plot for his opera *Wozzeck* from the drama by Georg Buechner, the first and most precocious offspring of a doctor in government service in the small German town of Goddelau, in Hesse. Born in 1813, the same year as Richard Wagner and Giuseppe Verdi, Buechner grew up hearing his father expound on rationalism and praise Napoleon. The young man decided to follow his parent in the study of medicine; his brother Karl went into government service and became a member of the Reichstag; Luise Buechner was a novelist and an early fighter for women's rights; Ludwig, also a physician, became widely known as a Darwinist and author of the controversial book *Kraft und Stoff* (*Power and Substance*); Alexander, a novelist, was a professor of literature.

Young Georg Buechner went to Strasbourg in 1831 to pursue scientific studies, then transferred to Giessen, where he concentrated on philosophy and history. There, perhaps under the influence of the literary group called Das junge Deutschland, whose members included Heinrich Heine and Karl Gutzkow, Buechner emerged as a revolutionary. In 1834, at the age of twenty-one, he founded the secret Society of Human Rights, drawing on the ideas that had spread into the narrow-minded German provinces in the aftermath of the French Revolution. His political pamphlet, *The Hessian Courier,* written in the same year, called for "peace to the humble dwellings, war on the palaces!" Buechner continued: "The life of the aristocrats is a long Sunday: they live in beautiful houses, they wear elegant clothes, they have fat faces, and they speak a language of their own; whereas the people lie at their feet like manure on the fields . . . The life of the farmer is a long workday. Strangers devour his fields before his very eyes, his body is a callus, his sweat the fare on the aristocrats' tables."

The pamphlet, with numbers and statistics to support its cries to arms, was clandestinely but widely distributed. It began with a warning: "This paper is meant to inform the Hessian people, yet whoever speaks the truth will be hanged; yes, even the man who reads the truth may be punished by some prejured judge." Buechner went on to list rules for those who read *The Hessian Courier:* hide it, or pass it on.

Thirteen years before Marx and Engels delivered the Communist manifesto, Buechner's words caused a storm in conservative Germany. In 1835, a warrant was put out for his arrest. He fled to Strasbourg, then to Zurich, where he despaired of the ineffectiveness of political activism and returned to the serious study of science. In Strasbourg, he wrote a dissertation in French on the nervous system of the gerbil. His command of the language was so firm that he translated Victor Hugo's *Lucrèce Borgia* and *Marie Tudor* into German soon after they were published. He was invited to give a guest lecture at Zurich University on the cranial nervous system, and his mastery of the subject so impressed the academics that he was immediately requested to join the faculty there. But his predictions that his own life would be short and tragic came true; he died on February 19, 1837, at the age of twenty-three.

Although Buechner had never seriously considered a literary career, he devoted much of his time in Strasbourg and Zurich to writing. *Danton's Death* (the subject of a 1947 opera by the Austrian composer Gottfried von Einem, who figures later in developments surrounding Berg's work) is an extraordinarily powerful first play. Buechner is said to have written it in a period of five weeks in 1835, for the real if not ideally noble purpose of making money. It sets forth his beliefs that there is no such thing as free will, that man is only a pawn, that action is futile, and boredom inevitable. Using the French Revolution as a point of departure and, indeed, preaching to his audience, Buechner tried to point out that "the word *must* is one of the curses with which mankind is baptized. The saying: 'It must needs be that offenses come; but woe to him by whom the offense cometh,' is terrifying. What is it in us that lies, murders, steals? I no longer care to pursue this thought."

His theory of dramatic art, set down in a letter to his parents, dated July 1835, foreshadows turn-of-the century Vienna and predicts the thoughts of Kraus, Schoenberg, and Berg:

The dramatic poet is . . . nothing but a writer of history, except that he stands above in that he creates history for the second time; he transplants us directly into the life of another era . . . His work may be neither more nor less moral than history itself; but history was not made by the Lord God to serve as proper reading matter for young ladies, and therefore I ought not to be blamed if my drama happens to be equally unsuited to that purpose . . . The poet is no teacher of morals; he invents and creates characters, he brings the past to life, and from this people may learn, as though from the study of history itself and the observation of it, what happens in human life around them . . . As regards the so-called Idealist poets, I find that they have given us nothing more than marionettes with sky-blue noses and affected pathos, but not human beings of flesh and blood, who make us feel the joy and sorrow with them, and whose deeds and actions fill me with revulsion or admiration . . . I have great fondness for Goethe and Shakespeare, but very little for Schiller.

Somewhat ironically, Buechner's second play, *Leonce und Lena,* was not peopled with flesh-and-blood characters; it was born of fantasy, a take-off on the *commedia dell'arte* tradition, and might at first seem to be a sentimental excursion into the pastures of German Romanticism, though it is in fact an indictment of that style. The characters flutter about, thinking they are exerting their freedom of choice, but, of course, there is no freedom, only predestination. Leonce and Lena might as well be as blind as Candide in his best of all possible worlds as they run off to escape marrying each other, meet in exile, fall in love, marry and then discover that they have done exactly what fate had ordained from the beginning.

Woyzeck was Buechner's third play; a manuscript of his fourth, *Pietro Aretino,* is lost. The only other bit of his work to have survived is *Lenz,* assumed to be the beginning of a novel (but probably meant to be complete in itself, which it essentially is). Jacob Michael Reinhold Lenz was a boyhood friend of Goethe, a poet and author of the play *Die Soldaten* which may have had a strong effect on Buechner and which also went to the operatic stage in 1965 in a version composed by Bernd Alois Zimmermann. Lenz, an eccentric if typical representative of the *Sturm und Drang* school, went mad and died in obscurity, near Moscow, in 1792.

Through the voice of Lenz, Buechner expounded his theory of art, decorating and embellishing the theme of organic growth and perpetual variation that Webern took as his credo from Goethe and that was of great import to all members and followers of the New Viennese School:

> I demand of art that it be life and that it represent potential reality — nothing else matters; we have no need then to ask whether it is beautiful or ugly. The sense that what has been created has life . . . is the only criterion of art . . . Idealism is the most humiliating of insults of human nature. Let them try just once to immerse themselves in the life of humble people and then reproduce this again in all its movements, its implications, in its subtle, scarcely discernible play of expression . . .
>
> The most beautiful pictures, the most swelling tones, form another group and then dissolve. Only one thing remains: an unending beauty which passes from one form to another, eternally revealed, eternally unchanged . . . One must love mankind in order to penetrate the particular existence of each thing; there must be nothing too common or too ugly. The most insignificant of faces can make a deeper impression than the mere sensation of beauty.

Like *Lenz, Woyzeck* was drawn from history. In June 1821, in Leipzig, a forty-one-year-old barber named Johann Christian Woyzeck stabbed his mistress, the widow Woost, in a fit of jealous rage. He was tried and condemned to death. However, for the first time in the his-

tory of German law (and twenty years before the
M'Naghten rule became part of the English criminal
code), the question of diminished responsibility on the
basis of insanity was raised. A forensic expert testified at
the trial that Woyzeck had been sane at the time of the
murder, and a date was set for the barber's execution, but
a private observer volunteered the information that the
defendant had been mentally unstable prior to commit-
ting the crime. A second examination by Dr. J. Ch. A.
Clarus failed to reverse the original medical decision, and
Woyzeck was beheaded on August 27, 1824. Dr. Clarus
wrote about his part in the trial in a medical journal,
where Georg Buechner found the subject for his greatest
drama.

Woyzeck, according to Clarus, had drifted from job to
job, showing signs of paranoia, depression, and even experiencing hallucinations. He imagined that he was persecuted by the Freemasons, and could turn aggressive and
violent; but he could also be a regular sort, a not-too-
bright but thoroughly reasonable person. He had had
several mistresses and had fathered a child by one of
them; he left because of her infidelities and had been
known to assault her, just as he finally attacked and killed
the widow Woost. He planned the murder, stabbed his
victim seven times, and told Dr. Clarus he had planned
to throw the murder weapon into a pond on the outskirts
of the city. He also contemplated suicide, not only to escape punishment but also to relieve himself of the visions
and of the awful poverty in which he lived and from
which he saw no way out.

This was the real-life model for Buechner's antihero.
The young scientist registered the facts of the doctor's
report; the political radical saw society victimizing its
poor; the playwright recognized the makings of outstand-

ing theater. To underline his credo that there is no such thing as free will, Buechner made Woyzeck a soldier, caught in the webs of the military. Woyzeck, in order to support the child he did not want and had never wanted, added to his meager income by submitting to physical contact with two male authorities, the captain and the doctor, both of them nameless, standing as prototypes in the *commedia dell'arte* manner. Each morning, Woyzeck had to shave the captain, who prattled about whatever came into his mind, insulting his servant whenever he realized that he was in the company of another human and was not merely talking to himself. For extra money, Woyzeck submitted his body to the most degrading experiments made in the name of science, subsisting on peas shelled out to him by the doctor in return for all his urine. (Berg in his opera made the fluid phlegm instead of urine.)

Woyzeck's only contact with human warmth came through Marie and their child, but the soldier had little time for his lover, and less for his son. As poor as Woyzeck and fully as downtrodden as he, Marie was neither whore nor saint, but a woman torn between loving her child and resenting him, between fidelity and desire, between honoring the commandments of the priests and selfishly ignoring them, in order to try to save herself and her son. She loved Woyzeck through poverty and suffering. She also loved the big, masculine drum major, who could literally sweep her off her feet and who brought her presents. Marie did not have the power to play a more important role in the drama or to offer salvation. Self-protection was all she had the strength for, and at the last she could not even find that.

Buechner's Woyzeck is not crazy. He is weak, a pawn, attacked emotionally by the captain and physically by the doctor. Losing Marie, he is bereft of the only person who had given reason to his life. Under the circumstances, his decline and his death were inevitable.

Woyzeck was left in a fragmentary state when Buechner died. As in the case of Berg's second opera, *Lulu,* the writing was very nearly finished, but final preparations for performance had not been made. Buechner's play took the form of a series of short scenes, some shorter than a printed page each, without an obvious sequence. Three drafts of the drama are known: first, a folio of twenty-one scenes; next, a short set of only two scenes; finally, a group of thirteen scenes. There is no way to be sure how the playwright intended *Woyzeck* to end; traditionally, and in Berg's opera, the soldier drowns while trying to bury the dagger in the muck at the bottom of the pond. The editors of some versions have Woyzeck brought back alive to face his son and his judges, on the assumption that Buechner would have added a trial scene to parallel history and reflect the famous trial sequence in *Danton's Death.*

Woyzeck was not included when Ludwig Buechner brought out his late brother's collected works in 1850, in part because the family did not approve of the play's extraordinary naturalism and also because key parts of the manuscripts were virtually illegible. In 1879, Karl Emil Franzos used a chemical preparation of distilled water and sulphuric ammonia to restore the faded script, which was, even then, difficult to decipher. A well-meaning amateur in the art of editing, Franzos was the one who changed "Woyzeck" to "Wozzeck" and added the stage direction for the soldier to drown. Though his work has been the object of a good deal of debate, he is to be credited for having brought the play to the attention of the public in a performable version and for having applied his scientific methods to a worthy work of art.

In May 1914, just before the war, Berg saw *Wozzeck* at the Residenz Theater in Vienna. Albert Steinrueck played the title role. The composer went more than once to see the eighty-year-old dramatic precursor of both the Naturalist movement and the Theater of the Absurd. Berg probably knew nothing about Buechner when he went to the theater that first night, and there is no way of knowing whether he saw the Franzos version of the play or an arrangement made in 1909 by Paul Landau, but it does not ultimately matter. What is important is that the composer decided, practically on the spot, that *Wozzeck* would be the subject of his first opera.

He had been heading in the direction of opera for a long time, ever since his childhood years of acting out homemade shows as well as dramas by Ibsen and Strindberg with young friends and relatives in Vienna and at the Berghof. As early as 1912, Schoenberg suggested that his former student think of writing something for the theater, "because I believe you could do it." Both men thought that a work by Strindberg would make an attractive and interesting libretto, but Berg found it hard to choose among the plays, and never made any appreciable progress. The Altenberg Songs of 1912 were obvious preliminary steps to a larger dramatic work. But Berg went somewhat off course with the Clarinet Pieces, Opus 5, and the Three Orchestral Pieces, Opus 6, before he, like so many of Vienna's artists, fell under the influence of the rediscovered *Wozzeck*.

The pairing of Alban Berg and Johann Franz Wozzeck is unlikely. As drawn as the composer was to the theater and as confident as he may have felt in his own sense of what might make a good opera, he was not, three months before the beginning of the war, particularly interested in things military, nor was he concerned in any active way with the fate of the underprivileged. Berg was

never particularly conscious of social issues as they affected members of the lower classes. Aware of the precarious financial positions of artists in general and Schoenberg in particular, he envisioned himself the *grand
seigneur*. He hated humanity as it crowded into the third-
class cars on trains, was repelled by the smells of other
bodies, had no use for peasant food or wares. However
slender his own means, he lived in a comfort that, by
Webern's and Schoenberg's standards, bordered on luxury. He was probably in the audience for the first night
of *Wozzeck* not out of any particular interest in a drama
that dealt with pressing social issues but because, on that
particular evening in Vienna, it was the place to see and
be seen.

Nevertheless, Berg responded to *Wozzeck* with zealous
determination, and instantly set about sketching and
planning an opera. The fragmentary nature of Buechner's
text was at once a liability and an asset. It called for a new
kind of music drama, which was exactly what Berg intended to provide. The last thing a composer or a libret-
tist needs to work with is a play with the seamless integrity of Shakespeare or the detail of Strindberg, no matter
how wonderful such dramas may be on their own terms.
Berg did have to face the problem of pruning Buechner's
scenes and putting them in a reasonable sequence, but at
least he did not have to break up the already subdivided
play. In fact, the very nature of Buechner's short scenes
was probably both inspiration and encouragement for the
inexperienced young composer of opera.

But there was a bigger issue for Berg to face. Schoenberg had suggested something for the theater, but, to
date, his own works for the stage had been limited to the
short and rather unorthodox *Die glueckliche Hand* and
Erwartung, both of which Berg knew well, and neither of

which would serve as a model for a work like *Wozzeck*. Nor, for obvious reasons, would Strauss's hothouse, late-Romantic *Salome,* which Berg had followed around Europe, nor the reactionary *Der Rosenkavalier,* which had appeared in 1911. (*Ariadne auf Naxos,* Strauss's latest opera, had had its première in Stuttgart in 1912, and *Die Frau ohne Schatten* was not to appear until 1919.) From the beginning, Berg intended his *Wozzeck* to be a full-scale work that would go on the same stages and play to the same audiences as Wagner's *Tristan und Isolde* and Verdi's *Il Trovatore;* that much of the old operatic tradition he intended to keep. Yet, in light of the new musical language, which did not allow scenes and acts of an opera to be built up around cornerstones of tonality, was opera still within the realm of possibility?

Lectures Berg later gave recalling the creative processes that led to his first opera show that he was thinking of precisely these questions as he began work on *Wozzeck*. He consistently denied that he had any intention of reforming the art form, as Gluck had done in eighteenth-century France, or of writing a work that would serve as a model for future efforts, either his own, or others'. He claimed that he had nothing else in mind except "to render unto the theater what is the theater's — and that means to shape the music in such a manner that it is aware in every moment of its duty to the drama . . . The music must produce everything that the play needs for its transposition into the reality of production . . . without prejudicing the music's own life, which may not be hindered by anything extra-musical."

Here, Berg gave the essence of his ideas about opera. He found ways to make the music and the drama work in such close conjunction that each is working to the advantage of the other at every moment. Both the music and the drama have private, independent powers, yet they are inseparable; the drama reveals the music, and the music contains important clues to the dramatic progress. There is no feeling in Berg's work that this is a play set to music, any more than there is the dubious impact of a symphony with costumes and words. *Wozzeck* fits Richard Wagner's ideal of music drama, the complete amalgamation of music and theater, in which the music cannot be explained without reference to the drama, and the drama gains its vitality through the support of musical forms.

As he began to think about the problems he would face in his opera and to experiment with possible solutions, Berg also had to defend himself against stern opposition. Schoenberg made it clear that he thought such a project was impossible; he wanted his student to write an opera, but not *this* opera. Tosca, Madama Butterfly, and Mimi were the belles of the international opera balls; how, then, could an antihero like Wozzeck ever move on the same stage as these heroines? On a more personal level, Schoenberg did not think that Berg was the right man to deal with the story; the composer, Schoenberg believed, was too meek and timid to confront the tragedy in its full depth. Schoenberg predicted that the opera was doomed, a preordained failure.

The difficulty of the task he had set for himself and his teacher's pessimism led Berg occasionally to think of putting aside *Wozzeck* for a few years, if not forever. But his mind kept returning to Buechner's soldier. Berg's first actual efforts in the composition of the work centered on the scene in which the doctor and the captain meet on the street and taunt the passing Wozzeck about Marie's affair with the drum major; this would eventually become Act II, Scene 2. But the work was brought to a halt, first by

Berg's other obligations, then by the war. His chances for concentrating on such a mammoth project as an opera — especially his first opera — while undergoing basic training, serving guard duty, tending his mother's property, working in the office of the War Ministry, and trying to keep his health were obviously limited.

But the opportunities were by no means nonexistent. During this period, fate let Berg see something of Wozzeck's life at firsthand. On August 7, 1918, Berg was visiting Trahuetten on a short leave. He wrote to his wife, who was staying with Alma Mahler, helping tend her children after birth of a son by the successful playwright, Franz Werfel (the child died when he was only a few weeks old). Berg had been enjoying the freedom of the country, thinking of Wozzeck. "There is a bit of me in his character," the composer wrote, "since I have been spending these war years just as dependent on people I hate, have been in chains, sick, captive, resigned, in fact, humiliated. Without this military service I should be as healthy as before . . . Still, perhaps but for this the musical expression (for *Wozzeck*) would not have occurred to me."

Berg was being somewhat dramatic in his mention of chains and humiliation, but army life had given him several very specific ideas for his opera. While he was in the training camp in Bruck an der Leitha, he lay awake at night listening to the "polyphonic breathing, gasping, and groaning" of his comrades-in-arms; this was to be the inspiration for the famous snoring chorus of Act II in *Wozzeck*. The doctor in the opera, too, may have been drawn on the character of one of the army medics who examined Berg at Bruck. (Buechner, in turn, is said to have modeled him after one of his professors at the University of Giessen.)

Of course, Berg's situation in the military was never
like Wozzeck's, and any direct comparison between the
composer and the soldier is impossible. The best Berg
could do was observe some of the same things that the
poor murderer experienced in the play; Berg heard the
sounds of the military, the singing and snoring of
drunken soldiers, and he witnessed the humiliation and
helplessness experienced by enlisted men less fortunate
than he.

Just as the war seemed endless, progress on *Wozzeck*
was annoyingly slow. There was a tinge of despair in his
words when Berg wrote to Schoenberg from Trahuetten
in mid-1917 that he was again at work on the opera, "already three years in the planning." A year later, however,
his time away from the army office and his confidence in
the creative project had increased to the point where he
could tell Kassowitz, on August 18, 1918, that he had
made significant progress on the opera. The next day,
Berg sent his friend Webern a full report. Early uncer-
tainties had kept Berg from even mentioning *Wozzeck* to
his old friend, but now he was sufficiently sure of the
opera's eventual emergence as one of his most important
works to bring Webern abreast of his activity:

> I fill as much time as possible with work, and have in fact
> managed to get a lot done. Whether I'll be satisfied with it, I
> can't say yet; I always feel good when I am writing music
> down, and it's also easier for me when I return to it after a
> long break . . . Do you know the drama? I saw a perfor-
> mance of *Wozzeck* before the war, and was so strongly im-
> pressed by it that I immediately . . . decided to set it to
> music. It's not only the universality of the work . . . that
> appealed to me, but also the unique atmosphere of the indi-
> vidual scenes. And, naturally, the possibility of binding four
> or five scenes into one act with orchestral interludes also

engaged me . . . To express the humanity of the characters in these scenes I have also come up with a major deviation from customary musical form. So, for instance, I use normal operatic scenes with thematic development next to scenes without this kind of thematic treatment . . . Understand, not a reversion in style, but only in form! So far I've completely finished one scene and hope to finish another major one while I'm here. Both are melodramas in the style of Schoenberg's *Pierrot Lunaire,* and this is an issue that has given me a lot of trouble. I'm wondering whether this kind of melodrama is practicable on the stage, whether the human speaking tones [*Sprechstimme*] will reach out in the theater over strong instrumentation . . . The *Sprechstimme* won't dominate the piece, however, just replace song in a few crucial scenes.

Berg had considered restricting his use of melodrama and *Sprechstimme* to one or two characters, but as *Wozzeck* took shape, he decided to sprinkle these expressive devices throughout the work for dramatic effect, and not to confine them to particular roles. He continued to be bothered by the whole question of *Sprechstimme* — in which the singer speaks in pitches that approximate the contour of a melody — through the years of work on the opera, and even afterward. He was drawn to speech-song as Schoenberg had used it in *Pierrot Lunaire,* but just as that particular opus continued to mystify him, so did the issues of how such lines could be accurately notated and how he could be sure that singers and conductors would correctly answer questions of pitch and questions of balance, as well. (*Sprechstimme* is still a troublesome device. Few composers have ever managed to use it to the precise ends they imagined, and even fewer performers have found ways to work with it comfortably, naturally, and in complete accordance with the score.)

Wozzeck continued to grow in Berg's imagination, but the composer's best hope of actually getting down to work on the opera came in the summer months, when he could be away from Vienna in the relative quiet of the country. In the city, he did his research, such as making a visit to Josef Leopold Pick's instrument factory to explore the potentials of the accordion, which was not one of the instruments included in the curriculum of Schoenberg's orchestration class. The accordion would sound in *Wozzeck*'s inn scene, Act III, Scene 3, which turned out to be the most difficult one for Berg to put on paper. It wouldn't come, as he complained to his wife in the early summer of 1921, so the hopes he had had of finishing the opera before fall were dashed, and some passing thoughts of following *Wozzeck* with a ballet score were dismissed. By the middle of August 1921, Berg had finished the second act and moved into the third; on September 28, he was beginning the opera's final scene. Finally, by the middle of October of that year, the major battles had all been fought and won: the complete opera was on paper, and only the orchestration remained. (This is not an unusual order for a composer to follow. Berg's sketches included very specific ideas and indications for orchestration, and what remained was for him to go back and fill in the blanks.)

All of the instrumental lines were, in fact, not drawn until April 1922, but that part was "child's play," in the phrase Berg used for everything that followed the solutions to the complicated problems that delayed him on the inn scene. Even before the orchestration was started, any sharp musical mind could have seen that Berg had produced a work of unquestionable value. Schoenberg saw the unorchestrated score just after Berg completed it, and was so impressed by his former student's accomplishments on the project that was supposedly doomed from the outset that he wrote immediately to Hertzka at Universal Edition, directing him to sign a contract with Berg that would give him enough money to be free of other obligations until *Wozzeck* was prepared for the stage. "I was always sure that Berg's talent would lead him in important directions," Schoenberg wrote, "but nevertheless doubted seriously that he would come up with a great theater work. But . . . this is an opera! Real theater music! . . . I'm certain that it will be a great theatrical success . . . It left me with a very strong impression. It works so well that one would think Berg had never done anything but write for the theater."

Schoenberg's enthusiasm did not convince Hertzka to take *Wozzeck* or Berg for Universal. And though Schoenberg had urged the publisher to action by saying that there was already great interest from conductors and impresarios who wanted to put on the opera, the truth was that no producers had even the slightest interest in *Wozzeck,* and those who knew of its existence feared that it would be so difficult as to disrupt their rehearsal and performance schedules for an entire season.

Yet Schoenberg's enthusiasm did serve a very important function. It gave Berg the courage to fight for his opera and to see it through the long journey from his writing table to the stage.

Chapter 10

The Success of *Wozzeck*

SEVEN YEARS after he went to the theater to see Buechner's *Wozzeck*, Berg had finished not just one of the
most important operas of the twentieth century, but one
that was to become among the most popular. If *Madama
Butterfly* and *Der Rosenkavalier* did not have to be counted
as twentieth-century works, *Wozzeck* would certainly be
the most important and popular. Just as Buechner had
written the first modern play, Berg had written the first
modern opera. What, exactly, had he done?

First, he trimmed eleven scenes from the Franzos edition of the play, leaving fifteen scenes to be divided sym-
metrically into the three acts of the opera. Some of the
cuts were easily made; others were the cause of great concern and reluctance on the part of the composer. Berg
was to regret for years that he could not find a way to
include the scene in the junk shop where Wozzeck buys
the murder weapon. Twenty-three speaking characters in
Buechner (Berg's number of fate again) were reduced to

eleven singing parts in the opera (plus chorus). And the composer cleaned up the text — whether to satisfy his own moral sensibilities or those of prospective audiences, we do not know — by, for instance, requiring Wozzeck to cough for the doctor, instead of calling for him to urinate, as in the play. This bit of censorship on the composer's part makes very little sense in the opera, since Berg allowed Wozzeck to go on to speak of heeding "nature's call," but the inconsistency bothered neither Berg nor his audiences.

The musical form was developing simultaneously with the dramatic one. Berg found that the music itself would be so revealing as to function in several different roles; he could let the music speak for minor characters and let the instruments report on the dramatic progress without any loss to the substance or subtleties of the play. He gave the form of his opera classical roots, with exposition-development-catastrophe over three acts. Not coincidentally, this design parallels the musical sonata form of exposition-development-recapitulation, so the broad outlines of the *Wozzeck* score were immediately suggested.

Difficult as it was to work with a play that was essentially a series of fragments not tied together, either by the writer's judgment or by obvious progression, the very flexibility of *Wozzeck* gave Berg freedom to adjust and to hold the pace of both musical and verbal development. On one level, the composer put the text together so that the drama would seem to sweep to an irrevocable conclusion. But it is, in fact, the music that brings the drama into focus, aiming with unfailing precision at theatrical effect.

The tried-and-true chart of musical forms used in the various scenes — a chart suggested by Berg himself — gives the most effective base for explanation:

Scene	Music

Act I — Exposition: Wozzeck in relation to
the world around him. Five character pieces:

1.	Wozzeck and the Captain	Suite
2.	Wozzeck and Andres	Rhapsody
3.	Wozzeck and Marie	March and Lullaby
4.	Wozzeck and the Doctor	Passacaglia
5.	Marie and the Drum Major	Quasi Rondo

Act II — Dramatic development: Symphony

1.	Marie, the Child, Wozzeck	Sonata movement
2.	Captain and Doctor, Wozzeck	Fantasy and Fugue
3.	Marie and Wozzeck	Largo
4.	Garden of an Inn	Scherzo
5.	Guard post, barracks	Rondo with introduction

Act III — Catastrophe and epilogue: Six inventions

1.	Marie and Child (Bible aria)	Invention on a theme
2.	Marie's death	Invention on a note
3.	Tavern	Invention on a rhythm
4.	Wozzeck's death	Invention on a chord of the 6th

Orchestral interlude

		Invention on a key
5.	Children playing	Invention in a perpetual motion

Berg stressed the primary relationships of the opera's sonata by drawing strong parallels between Act I and Act III. Both are short (compared with Act II, and even considered independently), and both rely on separate, self-contained musical forms, the "character pieces" and "inventions." For the central section, Berg wrote the long-awaited symphony. Act II is the longest and the heaviest, dramatically and structurally. Each scene relates to the others like movements in a symphony, and the five hold together in closed form. But there are also interesting parallels between Acts I and II; each ends with Wozzeck being beaten by the drum major, to the tunes of rondos.

At some point, too, Berg had to make a decision on a very practical issue: scene changes. He did not want to write the kind of opera in which intermissions would take more time than the music, but he was working with fifteen brief dramatic segments. He decided to tie each segment to the next within the three acts by means of instrumental interludes, which serve a variety of functions. They develop old material, introduce new musical issues, or do both, either simultaneously or in sequence. Not to be overlooked is that the interludes dictate exactly how much time is available for changing the sets.

The interludes also keep *Wozzeck* from turning into the music-applause-music-applause kind of opera that is really a series of set pieces — arias, duets, trios, sextets, and so on. But Berg's opera is still as far from Wagner's through-composed, unbroken style as it is from Donizetti's clap-happy set-piece parades. For analytical purposes, *Wozzeck* can be thought of in the old terms of recitative and aria, ensembles, and similar divisions. Marie's Lullaby is no less an aria than Senta's *Lied,* its close ancestor in Wagner's *Der fliegende Hollaender.* Similarly, the whole of *Wozzeck* can be analyzed (with a bit of imagination and limited stretching of the rules) in terms of traditional tonal systems. Each act ends on the same chord, which can be called the tonic, and many passages are clearly set in standard keys of the C Major variety. But it is the total effect and impact that are important, and *Wozzeck* does not seem like a chain of arias and recitatives any more than it does a tonality-bound composition. What the listener notices is the gripping drama and theatricality, and, again, the unbroken bond between music and word.

And yet all the time the music is serving the words with such exemplary propriety, it has a formal life of its own, and, of all the solutions Berg found in the process of composing *Wozzeck,* this is the most ingenious. A symphony, a series of inventions, a suite, and a passacaglia — the interior musical plan of the opera conjures memories of the Baroque and Classical eras and their characteristic forms. Berg, of course, was by no means the first man to incorporate such forms into a work for the theater. Think, for instance, of the fugue that ends Verdi's *Falstaff,* and the one at the end of Act II of Wagner's *Die Meistersinger von Nuernberg.* Furthermore, it must be pointed out that *Wozzeck* is in no way a back-to-Bach opera, nor does it resemble Stravinsky's Neoclassic *The Rake's Progress* in form, mood, or sound. As he had done in the Prelude, or Preludium, that began the Three Orchestral Pieces and in his implicit or explicit uses of Baroque binary or Classical ternary forms in the pre-*Wozzeck* works, Berg was calling on these forms for their logic, their musical drama, for their special character, and for the directions and developments they suggested.

No listener sits up in Act I, Scene 4, of *Wozzeck* and recognizes a passacaglia. Berg repeatedly stressed that such identification games were far from his purpose when he cast the scenes in the old forms. And yet because this scene (I,4) between Wozzeck and the doctor is a strict series of twenty-one variations above, below, and around a theme that is introduced in the cellos, it does have a psychological effect on even the most unsuspecting hearer. It underlines the fact that Wozzeck is tied to the doctor's continuing experiments, that Wozzeck must suffer a variety of humiliations at the doctor's hands and whims, and that the doctor himself keeps coming back to the theme: his crazed desire for immortality.

Similarly, the Act II symphony was what Berg needed to sustain and increase dramatic tension throughout the long expanse. The listener need not know he is hearing the fourth movement of a symphony when the scherzo arrives to lighten the mood in the garden of the inn (Scene 4), although at some level the connections between this section and all of the others of the act (and the whole opera) will be working and registering in his mind. The inventions in Act III, the devices that most strongly suggest Bach and his keyboard Inventions, in fact are some of the most daring music of the entire opera. The Invention on a Note (Act III, Scene 2) is both the most famous and the most compelling. The note is a B-natural; it comes into the fugal interlude between the first and second scenes of the act as a complete stranger, then insinuates itself into the action and into the witness's mind in every imaginable way as the scene progresses: as a top voice, a bass voice, in all registers of every instrument, in octaves, harmonically, melodically, as a pedal point, and, at the moment when Wozzeck stabs Marie, as a loud whack on the kettle drum. The curtain falls, and the interlude following this murder scene is one of the opera's most memorable, and also the shortest. Instruments sneak in barely perceptibly, playing the note B, which builds up into a deafening, breathtaking chord; then the same pitch enters quietly again, in octaves and unisons, to make a more gradual *crescendo* from *pianississimo* to *fortississimo,* from barely audible to overpowering.

There are other places, too, where Berg left signals that engage even the unsuspecting listener's unconscious. As Marie dies, her life flashes through her mind, in the forms of memories of previous themes (the Lullaby, the Jewel scene, and so on), distorted as they tumble over one another. In the longest interlude, which comes between Wozzeck's drowning and the children's final play scene and is, in effect, a full dramatic scene for composer and instruments without voices, Berg looks back to Siegfried's death in Wagner's *Goetterdaemmerung,* as he compiles and develops all of the opera's important motives and glues them together in D Minor (Invention on a Tonality). This technique of identifying certain themes with people and events extends through the opera and has as an ancestor Wagner's complex systems of *Leitmotiven,* in which one phrase represents Siegfried's sword, another characterizes the dragon, a third stands for Valhalla, and so forth. In *Wozzeck,* however, the *Leitmotiven* are not nearly as literal as they are in Wagner's music dramas. They are used here as connective tissue, as suggestions and representations, not as the motivating muscle of the music.

Actually, Berg seems to have had a thoroughly gleeful time in sneaking hidden references into *Wozzeck.* Throughout his life he loved to be the one who would hide phrases for others to seek, and one of the things that gives even his most abstract instrumental works the feeling of drama and theatricality is this kind of cross-referencing. There are twenty-one variations on the passacaglia theme in Act I, Scene 4; for people like Schoenberg and Berg (and Bach) who were fascinated by the powers of numbers, twenty-one — three times seven — had special significance. Furthermore, the chamber orchestra that dominates Act II, Scene 3 — the largo of Berg's second-act symphony, the centerpiece of the whole opera, and the first point at which actual thoughts of murder enter Wozzeck's imagination — corresponds precisely to the ensemble used by Schoenberg in his

Chamber Symphony. Thus, at the center of *Wozzeck,* Berg paid homage to his mentor. He also made reference to his own work, by incorporating quotations from his Opus 6 Orchestral Pieces, first in Act I, Scene 2, when Wozzeck says fearfully, "Something down there is moving with us."

When Marie tells her child an old folk tale in the fifth variation of Act III, Scene 1 (the Invention on a Theme), she does so in F Minor, for Berg thought the old-fashioned world of tonality was especially appropriate to the mood of a children's story. And the connection of the musical form of the rondo with the character of the drum major is especially fascinating; not only does the man's swagger fit perfectly into the rondo's manner of returning to a theme (in this case, sex), but it is the same form that later represented the composer Alwa Schoen in the opera *Lulu,* the character in that second theater work most closely identified with Berg.

The number of these correspondences and coincidences in *Wozzeck* is only slightly smaller than in *Lulu.* The use of reference and reminiscence enriches Berg's music immeasurably, often marking particularly dramatic moments or appearing when it is least expected. Again, it does not matter whether the listener understands every relationship; the existence of the reference is generally enough to cast an aura or to stir a deep, if vague, memory. Ultimately, such devices may be more important to the composer than to the hearer, because of the old feelings they stir in the creator's mind and the lines they cast to other ports found on his exploratory journeys.

The ways in which Berg dealt with the voices themselves are also central to *Wozzeck*'s powers of communication; this, after all, is the primary level of operatic presentation. The voices traverse the widest range of pos-

sibilities, from the old *bel canto* singing most closely identified with Bellini and Donizetti, who put great stock in
perfect tone production and coloratura display; on to
pitched screams, spoken melodrama, the difficult speech-
song (*Sprechstimme* and *Sprechgesang,* the second variation
being one step closer to actual singing than the first), the
pure-voiced folk-tune singing, rhythmic speech, choral
drinking tunes, and the light timbres of children's voices.
The effect, again, is not one of conscious distortion, radi-
calism, or even sudden shifts for the sake of effect, but,
rather, of lifelike variety of expression, smoothly and
carefully worked to dramatic ends.

Similarly, the instruments of the large orchestra are
called on to sound in ways that would never have occurred to Rossini or even to Wagner. Berg's use of a
primary orchestra with four flutes, four oboes, four clarinets, bass clarinet, three bassoons, contrabassoon, four
horns, four trumpets, four trombones, tuba, two pairs of
timpani, cymbals, bass drum, side drums, tam-tams, triangle, xylophone, celeste, harp, and strings would seem
to reinforce Schoenberg's thesis that post-Wagnerian
opera had turned into "a symphony for large orchestra
accompanied by a solo voice." Add to this Berg's military band, tavern group (fiddlers, clarinet, accordion,
guitar, and bombardon or bass tuba), upright piano, and
extra percussion — all of which show up for sundry
party and crowd scenes — and the risk is clearly present
that the deluge of instrumental sound will drown out the
solo voices. Berg did concede that it might be possible to
draw the chamber orchestra and the onstage ensembles
out of the large philharmonic in the pit. But even this
would not have solved problems of balance had Berg not
seen to it in his techniques of orchestration that at no
point in the opera does the orchestra run any serious risk

of covering up the voices, even when the conductor is less than perfectly sensitive to the acoustics or individual singers' powers of projection. He accomplished this balance by reserving the full orchestra almost exclusively for the interludes, which swell out and engulf the listener in sound. To accompany the voice, the instruments stifle themselves with mutes, play at low, lower, or lowest volume (Berg called *Wozzeck* a *piano* opera), sound in their quietest registers, and perform in sequence, rather than in unison.

Nevertheless, the score is complex enough to have fully warranted Berg's continued use of the signals for principal (*Hauptstimme*) and secondary (*Nebenstimme*) lines, which he had first incorporated into his Opus 6 Orchestral Pieces. In the opera, Berg added further designations to indicate the hierarchy of rhythms, a dramatic phenomenon that was to appear more and more frequently in his later works. Recurring rhythms can tell the witness just as much about what is happening or about to happen onstage as a long melody or a scene change. All of these significant recurring rhythms are carefully marked through the score, which is worth examining, if only to marvel at what must be the most painstakingly annotated music ever published for an opera. Buechner left very few stage directions in his manuscripts. Berg saw it as his duty to facilitate the stage director's job by adding the times of day at which each scene should take place (morning, noon, twilight, and so on), positions for the moon in the sky, detailed scenic plans, and more. He expected every direction to be faithfully observed (as did Wagner, though his never are).

Not one of *Wozzeck*'s 1926 measures is devoid of some kind of instruction — from when the curtain should fall (and at what speed or speeds) to how a new tempo should be arrived at in relation to the tempo, or tempos, that precedes it. Far from being overwhelming, however, the directions are fascinating in themselves; with the help of translations from the glossary that Universal Edition provides with the German-English edition of the score, almost anyone can experience *Wozzeck* in silence at home, just by reading it and imagining the stage.

The processes Berg had to follow in order to get anyone to read his annotated score and put *Wozzeck* to the test of performance were arduous. In December 1921, four months before the opera was fully orchestrated, Berg and the pianist Edward Steuermann went to Frankfurt and Darmstadt for the opera's first auditions. Berg did not have the keyboard skills to present the score on his own, but he joined in to help Steuermann at the most difficult spots. The rejections started with Ernst Lert's letter from the Frankfurt Opera, at the end of May 1922, saying that he had other commitments, financial obligations, and, essentially, no intention of taking such a chance on a modern work.

Berg also had disturbing news from newspapers and on the radio. During his last bout of work on *Wozzeck,* he had wanted to avoid both Schoenberg and Webern. He was beyond the point where he could welcome anyone's suggestions, and he was not ready to display his completed work. When he began to re-establish contact with his friends, he found that anti-Semitism had been dogging his former teacher; in June 1921, Vienna's *Neue Freie Presse* reported that Schoenberg had fled from the town of Mattsee, near Graz, after the town council asked him to show proof that he was not a Jew. Jews were officially banned from the town, and though Schoenberg had papers showing his Protestant affiliation, he did not want to stay in a place where freedom of religion was being so flagrantly violated.

Berg hoped that Schoenberg would be able to settle in Salzburg for the summer, which, in fact, he did. Webern, however, was in Vienna, very much a part of Berg's life, dropping into the flat on Trauttmansdorffgasse without notice, using the phone, staying for coffee, and, Berg felt, nosing about and interfering with his work. Berg was acting even more antisocial than usual, and the only person he actually looked forward to seeing was his student Fritz Klein, who was working out the piano score for *Wozzeck,* and who, with the help of Gustav Mahler's nephew Franz (another of Berg's students), worked through the vocal score, as well. Without prospects for a performance, Universal Edition would not publish *Wozzeck;* without a presentable score, there was no chance of convincing an opera house to take a serious look at the opera by a composer with such a minor reputation; without Universal's resources, all of the preparations fell to Berg and his small band of devoted students.

As long as he was obliged to do so much work, Berg decided to take the next logical step and assume responsibility for printing a limited edition of the score on his own initiative; copies would then be sold by subscription to members of the Schoenberg circle, conductors, and directors of important opera houses. (The most illustrious would get them free, of course.) To this end, Berg solicited loans from his friends, planning to repay the money from future sales. Of course, if anyone happened to offer, he was amenable to contributions and donations, and these he received from Alma Mahler and May Keller, a friend of Smaragda. Slowly, the printing was completed and approved, and in January 1923, Berg, acting as his own agent, sent out a printed notice offering the 230-page score for 150,000 Austrian kronen.

Orders were few, and Berg finally gave away most copies of the score to his friends and relatives. And this time, Schoenberg managed to squelch whatever enthusiasm Berg had reserved to fight further battles on *Wozzeck*'s behalf. On March 29, 1923, while Helene was again taking the cure at Carlsbad, Berg visited the Schoenbergs at their house in Moedling and caught the teacher on one of his more irritable days. "He kept on finding fault," Berg wrote to Helene, "all the time with advice, admonitions, warnings, and pouring cold water in general . . . And it all goes on with such an air of tutor to apprentice, even orders from a higher authority, that I feel annoyed."

Two weeks later, Schoenberg was still attacking. Berg wrote to his wife, "Schoenberg was again criticizing everything about me: that I'm still working on *Wozzeck* ('very Karl Kraus-ish, this eternal correction'), that I smoke, that I shouldn't even dream that *Wozzeck* will have any success, it's too difficult, and worst of all, that I've still not really started on the Chamber Concerto."

Schoenberg could not bring himself to be supportive, even as Berg asked his advice about publishers and negotiations for *Wozzeck*'s performance. Berg still considered the older man to be his closest friend and mentor. But he no longer needed or asked for Schoenberg's musical guidance, and this irked the teacher. Schoenberg sensed, correctly, that Berg was on the verge of international success, while he, Schoenberg, approaching his fiftieth birthday, was never likely to know more acclaim than he had already had. Furthermore, religious persecution was making Schoenberg's life even more unsettled than usual, and while it was beginning to be evident to the older man that his conversion to Protestantism was not going to be a satisfactory defense against the prevalent anti-Semitism, he saw Berg safe in his Catholicism, reasonably secure in his finances, and obviously settled into what appeared to be pleasant domesticity.

Alban Berg in 1904, age 19. Vienna.

Arnold Schoenberg, about 1910.

Helene Berg in 1916, age 31.

Alma Mahler as drawn by
Oskar Kokoschka, about 1915.

Smaragda Berg in 1935.
Charcoal sketch by Edith Stengel.

Helene Nahowski Berg's family home on Maxinggasse in Hietzing, photographed in March 1978.

The house at Trauttmansdorffgasse 47 where the Bergs spent their entire married life, and where Berg's widow lived until her death in August 1976. The gated windows are those of the Berg flat. Photographed in March 1978.

Berg at home, with a portrait of Mahler in the background, about 1930.

A caricature of Berg, drawn by the Viennese artist F. A. Dolbin.

Hanna Fuchs-Robettin, the inspiration for the Lyric Suite.

Evelyn Lear in the title role of the San Francisco Opera production of Lulu *(with Andrew Foldi as Schigolch),* 1965. BELOW: *Anja Silva as Lulu in the San Francisco Opera production,* 1971.

Scenes from the Royal Opera House, Covent Garden production of Wozzeck, starring Sir Geraint Evans.

Berg, about 1935.

So Schoenberg tried to undermine Berg's hopeful enthusiasm, repeating his original view that *Wozzeck* would bring only trouble, and trying to get the student out of the public gaze and back to his private, creative work. Schoenberg was correct in assuming that Berg had made no real progress on the Chamber Concerto, which he planned as the sequel to *Wozzeck;* the final bits of cleaning and preparation that had to be done on the large opera score had taken an unanticipated amount of time and, ever the perfectionist, Berg had worried so much over the printing of *Wozzeck* that even he had begun to lose patience. He described the process to his wife as a kind of "spring cleaning" of the large work, coming back to all the secondary points and indications that had been missed or shelved in the first heat of creation. These included instructions for the putting on or taking off of mutes, for the string players to switch from plucking the strings to bowing them, for the flutes to change to piccolos, or for the oboe to switch to English horn. This kind of detailed work extended through all thirty-five to forty instrumental parts in all three acts. But, as Berg and his assistant, Klein, knew, every addition made at that pre-performance point and every mistake caught before the score was actually disseminated meant time saved in rehearsals and, possibly, a more perfect realization of the opera.

While all this homework was being done, Alma Mahler was exerting her charms, and finally, on March 31, 1923, Berg could happily write to Helene that, thanks in large part to Almschi's hospitality and persistence, Hertzka had accepted *Wozzeck* for publication. At the beginning, the affiliation promised to be more prestigious than profitable; naturally, Hertzka was offering as little money as he could, and Berg calculated that anything short of an unprecedented success would mean that he

would see no income from his opera for at least several
years.

Universal Edition would assume responsibility not
only for printing *Wozzeck* (which was already engraved),
but for promoting performances of the opera and for
publishing the Three Orchestral Pieces, as well. Berg was
especially eager to let Hertzka take over the bargaining
with theaters — Munich was the first choice for the *Wozzeck* première — but he decided to consult with Schoenberg before presenting Hertzka with his own coun-
terproposals, and was not prepared to dismiss the
possibility that *Wozzeck* would go to G. Schirmer, in
America, with whom he had also had preliminary negotiations.

Schoenberg continued to be discouraging. As Berg related Hertzka's offer to him, he found it simply and completely unacceptable, and suggested that Berg give up
hope of joining Universal Edition. Berg felt that he was
floundering, with no one to turn to for help. He did not
know a lawyer; Alma Mahler had shown no interest in
his case since she had promoted the original contacts, and
Schoenberg was clearly not going to exert any influence.
He decided to wait, but every lost day meant fewer
chances for *Wozzeck* to receive its première in the
1923–1924 season. Finally, Berg went back to Almschi,
who advised him to go along with Hertzka's offer and
forget about Schirmer, and who promised, with Werfel
as witness, that she would personally make up to Berg
the money he had already lost by printing the limited edition of the opera score. With that settled, Alma arranged
another social evening for Berg and Hertzka on the eve of
the final negotiations, and on April 11, 1923, after only a
few hours of bargaining, Berg walked away from Universal's offices with the assurance of an advance payment,

a quick publication schedule for both the opera and the Orchestral Pieces, and a Universal-sponsored publicity campaign to announce the appearance of *Wozzeck*.

For her help, Almschi received the dedication of Berg's first opera. But her charms had not been the only thing responsible for selling Hertzka on his new client. Scores that Berg had sent out to critics and music journals began to bring in responses, as the writers read through the music and reported on Berg's achievements. An article appeared in *Die Musik* that April, and although the critic Ernst Viebig made note of the opera's difficulties, he went on to call Marie's Lullaby "one of the most powerful lyrical inspirations in recent operatic literature." This endorsement delighted Berg, as did Viebig's analysis of the opera as a whole. Berg reported to Helene that the writer had stressed "the purely human element . . . and not the individual fates . . . And everything is as true as if I had told it to him myself."

The article helped, but it did not put *Wozzeck* on the stage. Various conductors and general managers wrote to Universal Edition inquiring about the availability and difficulty of the score, but no one was willing to schedule the première. In the fall of 1923, one of the inquirers was Erich Kleiber, the general music director of the Berlin Opera (not today's West Berlin Opera, but the old one on Unter den Linden, now in East Berlin). Kleiber's was not idle curiosity; he had already seen the vocal score, liked it, and had a special admiration for Buechner. Berg did not restrain his excitement; he arranged for Schoenberg's student Ernst Bachrich, a capable pianist, to play through the work for Kleiber in January 1924, when the conductor visited Vienna. Again, Berg helped out in the more difficult passages, but it was Bachrich, not the composer, who overheard Kleiber say that the case was

closed: he would do *Wozzeck* in Berlin even if it cost him
his job — which it very nearly did.

A contract from Universal Edition that would, with
luck, make the future secure; growing interest from people who wanted to stage *Wozzeck* — and, in addition,
fame. For it was also in 1923, at the Salzburg Chamber
Music Festival in August, that Berg's Opus 3 String Quartet met with such enthusiastic acclaim. One of the
by-products of that success was his meeting with Hermann Scherchen, who was especially intrigued by the
new opera and suggested that Berg prepare passages from
it for concert performances. Berg liked the idea for two
reasons. *Wozzeck* lent itself to this kind of presentation
because of its combination of arias and interludes (had he
written *Lucia di Lammermoor,* his task would have been
much harder), and Scherchen was talking of putting the
proposed *Wozzeck* pieces on his program for September
29, in less than two months. As it happened, the première
of the Three Fragments from *Wozzeck* did not take place
until June 1924, when Scherchen conducted them at the
fifty-fourth festival of the Allgemeine Deutsche Musikverein. Berg reported to Webern that "all went well: the
performance itself, that of the singer especially, and the
success from rehearsal to rehearsal was greater and
greater so that, finally, the public performances were
triumphs with the audiences, the musicians, and the
press."

The Three Fragments from *Wozzeck* reveal only one
part of the opera — the story of Marie, beginning with
the interlude between Act I, Scene 2, and Act I, Scene 3,
and continuing with the entire third scene, the Lullaby.
The second section is Marie's Bible scene (III, 1), and the
third part opens in Act III, Scene 4, just after Wozzeck
has drowned, continues into the Invention on a Key, and

closes with Scene 5, giving the singer who takes Marie's lines the option of also singing the child's final "Hop! Hop!" The Three Fragments were lifted from the opera with only two or three insignificant changes from the full score.

The Frankfurt performances of the Three Fragments under Scherchen brought *Wozzeck* into the open, and even more inquiries arrived at Universal Edition's offices from those who wanted to perform the Fragments or the whole work. But there were still no signed contracts. Berg persuaded his publisher to release the Fragments in haste. Although he feared that the Fragments might take attention away from the opera in its entirety, he also knew that the more audiences heard of *Wozzeck* in concert halls, the more likely it was that they would want to see the work onstage. (In fact, the Fragments did receive more attention than the opera for some time. Now, however, they have taken their rightful position, well behind the complete stage version of *Wozzeck*.)

Finally, on August 28, 1924, an agreement was signed between Universal Edition and the Berlin State Opera for the first performances of the complete work. Berg, who had thought that he might be fortunate to get his opera produced in a town as large as Munich, was overjoyed that it would go to the big, exciting, culturally adventuresome capital. According to Kassowitz, Kleiber laid down two requirements: the material was to be on his desk by October 1, and Act I was to be completely clean and error-free in the vocal parts. Since the engraving of the material had already been overseen with such care by Berg and his student-helpers, neither stipulation was an obstacle.

But there was still no date for the première, and even when Kleiber passed through Vienna in December 1924,

he either could not or would not give Berg any details of
the schedule. In February 1925, the composer wrote a letter pleading with Kleiber to let him in on the plans,
which, he suspected, had been made without his knowledge. But Kleiber did not respond, and Berg tried again
by letter in March, when the conductor responded only
that there was still no definite date. Originally, he had
hoped to stage *Wozzeck* in May, but a new production of
Strauss's *Intermezzo* had impinged on the hours that
would have had to be allotted to the Berg work. So
Kleiber proposed that *Wozzeck* wait until the fall of 1925,
implying that Berg's opera might even open the new
season in Berlin and be played in repertory through
1925–1926. As an untried composer of operas, Berg was
in no position to say no to Kleiber; furthermore, the
honor of being the first new production of the fall would
help to assure *Wozzeck*'s success.

Looking back on the Berg-Kleiber dealings half a century later, one finds it impossible to imagine that plans
for the production of an opera could have been made in
such a casual manner. Now, singers are booked four or
five seasons in advance, and productions involve so many
people coming from so many different places that they
cannot be slipped in and out of the schedule. But then, in
1925, it seemed to Berg that he was being forced to wait
a lifetime for *Wozzeck* to appear in Berlin. Kleiber scheduled *Wozzeck* for the first half of his 1925–1926 season,
but did not tell Berg exactly when. Resigned to the delay,
the composer began detailed communications with the
conductor. In June, Berg asked for realistic sets for certain scenes (the garden of the inn; the field with the town
appearing in the distance), but agreed that the public
house in the last act could be merely suggested, with
backdrops and a few props. He also sent Kleiber some

pointers on teaching singers to deal with atonal music. His advice was undoubtedly superfluous; a conductor as distinguished as Kleiber needed no tips. Berg's unsolicited assistance served mostly to give away his nervousness and to reveal that, rather than being involved in other new projects, he was primarily interested in getting *Wozzeck* on the stage.

Berg assumed that the first performance of his opera would take place in November, and it was not until that very month that Kleiber informed him that December 14 would be the date of the première. In the meantime, other companies had been waiting to see what would happen to *Wozzeck* in Berlin. And agitation against the work had already begun, even in *Die Musik,* where early mention of the opera's existence and potential had had such positive effect. What Berg did not know was that there was dissension and intrigue in the Berlin Opera itself, and the entire production almost had to be canceled at the last minute. The director of the Opera was dismissed, and Kleiber's own position therefore became precarious. *Wozzeck* had been rumored to be so difficult that the extra rehearsal time it demanded would throw the whole rest of the season into chaos, if it did not, indeed, put the company out of business. Kleiber denied reports that he had planned more than one hundred rehearsals for the première by displaying his calendar, which showed only fifteen orchestral rehearsals for the new work, including sectional meetings for winds and strings. But even with that proof, the press was not convinced.

Finally Kleiber, Franz Ludwig Hoerth (who was the ineffectual stage director for *Wozzeck*), and Rolf Winter were named provisional codirectors of the Berlin State Opera, and Kleiber, whose position was the most powerful, rallied all forces around *Wozzeck*. Although the con-

ductor's influence would soon begin to fade, the Viennese
critic Ernst Mandowsky could report, after the new governing triumvirate began its work on Berg's behalf, that
"the whole orchestra, the soloists, the choir and everyone
from the Berlin Opera who had anything to do with the
production of this work . . . got more excited from rehearsal to rehearsal."

Berg went to Berlin on November 12 to make a preliminary check on the production, and reported to his
wife that the cast, with the possible exception of the man
portraying the doctor, was first-rate and that excitement
was running high throughout the city. On the next day,
which happened to be Friday the thirteenth (a fact that
did not escape the notice of the superstitious composer),
he went to his first rehearsal, happily spending the hours,
as he wrote to Helene, "under the megalomaniac impression that *Wozzeck* is really something great, and that, ac-
cordingly, the performance will also be something great.
I never dreamed that I could find such understanding as a
musician and dramatist as I am getting from Kleiber, and,
of course, this gets transmitted to the singers . . . The
sets . . . are magnificent . . . Everybody concerned is
enthusiastic in the highest degree. I can confidently leave
everything to Kleiber."

Reassured, Berg returned to Vienna, then went back to
Berlin on November 30 and stayed there through the
première, with Helene joining him a few days before the
opening night. This second stay began with anxieties;
Berg could not find a hotel room because Berlin was
filled with people attending a motor show, and he finally
had to establish himself in a small pension, which was not
up to the standards he would have set for himself on such
an important occasion. Then there were the inevitable
worries that seemed to multiply as the date for public
performance grew near.

Be glad you weren't at the first full rehearsal [Berg wrote to Helene late at night on December 1, 1925]. True, I had the joy of hearing the thing played by the orchestra at last, but I also had the torment of all the points which are still wrong. If I did not know one can't judge after such a rehearsal, I should be very apprehensive if not downright depressed. But from everybody's assurances, and above all from the terrific eagerness of all concerned, I'm sure that everything will be all right, and much as I imagined it. Quite a lot is wonderful for sound, almost the whole of Act I (one gem after another). Several things in the second act were good, too. The orchestra itself is really marvelous. But will Kleiber be able to follow my intentions, in light of the fact that he is not going to rehearse any more with the orchestra alone, but always with the singers onstage? . . . Please don't talk about my doubts too much, and also be careful on the telephone when you're reporting . . . Say it's going to be a tough nut to crack, but that we'll manage it.

Social obligations were mixed in with musical ones, and Berg finally witnessed a performance of Schreker's *Die ferne Klang,* the opera of which he had made the piano score and had grown so fond a decade earlier; now, he concluded, *Die ferne Klang* was "awful." Meanwhile, *Wozzeck* looked better and better, as the cast became accustomed to going straight through the work, with actions and movements, and in the presence of the designs by the Greek painter Panos Aravantinos. The proud composer wrote to his wife that his work was "terrific, overwhelmingly powerful . . . absolutely fantastic." Even the people who were not spending their days and nights in the theater preparing for the première knew about *Wozzeck* from photographs and interviews with Berg that appeared in newspapers. Critics and reporters arrived from across the Continent, friends came from Vienna and Prague, and despite some sniping from conservative factions and prejudiced writers, the world première of *Woz-*

zeck, on December 14, 1925, at the Berlin State Opera
Unter den Linden turned out to be one of the most important operatic evenings of the century.

Berg joined the singers and Kleiber onstage to accept
the applause; ironically, it was the public's loud acclaim
that troubled the forty-year-old composer. After a post-
première dinner with Helene, Kleiber, Alma Mahler, and
other friends and dignitaries from Berlin's music society,
Berg walked the streets with Theodor Adorno, trying to
calm his feelings of excitement and pride by insisting that
if the audience had been so pleased on first hearing, then
Wozzeck itself must be a weak and facile opus. His years
in the Schoenberg school had taught him to believe that
public acclaim did not go along with creative achievement; indeed, he suspected that the opposite was true, although he was soon to overcome his fears and modesty,
and learn to welcome fame.

More critics were willing to report what was right
with *Wozzeck* than what they found wrong with it, and
as Berg read the newspapers and periodicals that appeared
on the morning after the première and in the weeks that
followed, he recognized that *Wozzeck* had changed the
course of his life and his career. No composer in his circle
had ever attracted such attention; Schoenberg's most important works had not been written about by so many
critics at such length, and even in reviewing new works
by Mahler, the critics had tended to be more interested in
the composer's conducting and in his position in the cultural hierarchy than in his music.

There were, of course, the curmudgeons, who, for
reasons both musical and political, attacked *Wozzeck* as
"tortured, mistuned cackling," "a work of a Chinaman
from Vienna," "criminal . . . a capital offense," "a waste
of considerable quantity of brain fat," "rhythmically

complicated, harmonically queer and perverse," and "a dissonant orgy." Brickbats like these wounded neither the composer nor his representatives, however, and Universal Edition was so pleased by the volume of comment on *Wozzeck* that the publishers compiled a pamphlet called *Wozzeck and the Music Critics* shortly after the première. Hertzka also summoned Berg and signed him to an extended contract, which would prevail until 1932, and under which he was guaranteed a monthly retainer of six hundred revalued Austrian schillings.

Wozzeck was performed in Berlin ten times during the 1925–1926 season — an honorable number, but not enough for Berg. The composer hounded Kleiber, with whom he was now using the familiar *du,* for more and more. In retrospect, once he had recovered from opening night, Berg had some reservations about the Berlin production, especially regarding the designs and a few of the singers. And in spite of all the good things that came out of the première, it took several more productions to prove to both conductors and sponsors that *Wozzeck* was a lasting and feasible addition to the operatic repertory. The press and some gullible people kept repeating the rumor that the opera required an impossible number of rehearsals. As late as 1927, Berg sent an urgent letter to Kleiber, asking on behalf of Universal Edition that the conductor once again document his pre-première rehearsal schedule and prove that reports of 137 rehearsals were absurdly exaggerated.

The Prague première of *Wozzeck,* on November 11, 1926, conducted by Otakar Ostračil, had further damaged the opera's reputation, albeit once again for extramusical reasons. The day before the first Czech performance, Berg had been completely optimistic: "The best thing of all in this production is that when there is something to sing, it is really sung — and, for the most part, by splendid voices," he wrote to Schoenberg. "The sadness I felt since Berlin, thinking that in the vocal writing I had indeed made impossible demands, has now completely disappeared."

(Berg credited the musicality of the Czechs. Listeners in the 1970s who wish to experience the same kind of contrast Berg heard between the Berlin première and the subsequent Prague production need only compare two *Wozzeck* recordings. On the Columbia label — with Pierre Boulez conducting the orchestra and chorus of the Paris National Opera — they will hear that the singers' pitches are frequently only approximate. On the Deutsche Grammophon recording — with Karl Boehm conducting the chorus and orchestra of the German Opera, Berlin — they will note how the accuracy of the cast, led by Dietrich Fischer-Dieskau and Evelyn Lear, enhances the music's brilliance.)

Berg called the first two performances of *Wozzeck* in Prague "colossal successes," with "thirty or forty curtain calls" for the composer himself. But at the third performance, on November 16, with Alma and Franz Werfel in the audience, a well-organized protest reached riot proportions at the beginning of Act III, and the opera could not go on. The police were called in, and future scheduled performances were canceled. The press spoke of "Aaron Berg, the Jew from Berlin," and despite the protests of Prague's musical luminaries (including Leoš Janáček), *Wozzeck* was dismissed with nothing more than a meek letter from Ostračil, who explained to Berg that the scandal had been the responsibility of a group of reactionaries who had been trying to take over the National Theater and see that only works of native Czechs were presented there.

A Leningrad production came next, in June 1927, and though it could do little to restore *Wozzeck*'s shaky reputation in central Europe, Berg called it a "tumultuous success." He confessed to a Russian interviewer that he had come to Leningrad feeling apprehensive, and wondering how performers unaccustomed to the new musical idioms would make their way through the complex work. But to his pleasure he had found that the Russians had discovered the lyricism of his opera and were performing the music so smoothly and gracefully that Berg could make reference to his favorite comparison and again set the melodies of *Wozzeck* next to those of Verdi's *Il Trovatore*.

It was one thing, however, to have the opera performed on the big international stages, and quite another to ensure its continued life and financial success by proving that *Wozzeck* was also practical for smaller houses. When Johannes Schuler expressed interest in presenting the opera in the relatively small city of Oldenburg, Berg decided it would be advisable to make the score accessible to a smaller orchestra in a smaller pit. With the aid of Erwin Stein and, later, Hans Erich Apostel, the score was cut back to triple winds (instead of the original quadruples) and otherwise tightened. This was the version used for the Oldenburg première, on March 5, 1929; another, even smaller edition was also made, but was never used and was quickly forgotten. Conductor Schuler wrote to Universal Edition on March 14 that "the fairy tales about the impossible difficulty of *Wozzeck* have been put to rest once and for all." The reduced version accompanied Berg's growing conviction that he should do everything possible to accent the *bel canto* qualities of *Wozzeck,* and that many of the sections originally designated for *Sprechstimme* could, in fact, be sung, thereby pleasing the singers, increasing the likelihood of vocal accuracy, and underlining his original idea of a *piano* opera.

Berg called the Oldenburg performance simply "a wonder." And Josef Lex, the outstanding Wozzeck in this production, later wrote that "the unexpected success of the evening hit us singers like a flood." Lex had been particularly concerned, both because rumors of political protests had preceded the first performance and because the title role in Berg's new work was to be the debut vehicle of the baritone's new contract in Oldenburg. "I have never played a part with such sincere conviction as I played that first Wozzeck," Lex wrote. "I hadn't even dared hope for Berg's own praise, but he said, 'Isn't he a phenomenon, this Wozzeck?' "

When producers and conductors across Europe heard that the opera house in Oldenburg had undertaken *Wozzeck* and survived, the opera's reputation was assured. Productions were scheduled all around Germany, in Vienna (1930), Amsterdam (1930), Darmstadt (1931, with Karl Boehm conducting, not entirely to Berg's satisfaction), Philadelphia and New York (1931, with Leopold Stokowski; tremendous successes and the beginning of Berg's American reputation), Brussels (1932), London (1934, in a BBC concert under Adrian Boult; and 1935 at Covent Garden, with Kleiber conducting). At the time of the concert performance for the BBC in London, *Wozzeck* had been banned from German stages. Berg listened to the opera (performed in German) on the radio — it was the last time he would hear his first opera. A few days later, in March 1934, the composer received a letter from his friend from his years as a Schoenberg student, Heinrich Jalowetz, who had also heard the broadcast: "You know well how much I love this work, and know too that I've heard many performances . . . But I've never been as overpowered as I was yesterday . . . That was the highest recommendation for the music and for the people who performed it. And it means . . . that music in general, and your music in particular, is still a universal language, in spite of everything."

Chapter 11

Postwar Domesticity

THE SMALL MEMORIAL PLAQUE that the City of Vienna has affixed to the façade of the house at Trauttmansdorffgasse 27 honors Alban Berg, composer of *Wozzeck*. The opera was all Berg needed to ensure his fame.

But there were problems at home during the years just after the war when all Berg's available energy was needed to finish and promote *Wozzeck*. The severe inflation that eventually resulted in Austria's changing its currency from kronen to schillings (in 1923, one schilling equaled ten thousand kronen) necessitated strict budgets, where, in the past, only moderation had been necessary, and Berg even considered, briefly, curtailing his expensive tastes. He wrote to his wife on June 29, 1918, while she was in the country and he was in Vienna, that he was having to make a choice between "starving and spending madly, and nothing will induce me to adopt the first course!"

Although he did not admit it when he wanted to show how independent and self-sufficient he was, Berg was still receiving an allowance from his mother. Fortunately,

Johanna Berg increased the stipend in September 1918, to help keep pace with inflation. Berg called the money he received from family funds an allowance, but actually it was a kind of payment for the time he spent managing the seven houses in the city that still belonged to the Bergs. One by one, the houses were sold over the next eight years so that Johanna and Smaragda could live off the profits. The gradual divestiture did not upset Berg in the least; he found the tasks of management burdensome and time-consuming.

Nineteen eighteen also brought a development that helped Berg both financially and artistically. Following the demise of the various music societies as a result of both the turmoil of the war years and the scandals brought on by performances of works by Schoenberg and his students (for example, the Altenberg Songs' première), Schoenberg decided to start his own music society. The goals were self-serving, of course, but at least the style would be educational and not inflammatory. Berg wrote to Helene on July 1, 1918: "Schoenberg has a marvelous idea, to start another society next season, setting out to perform music of the period 'Mahler to the present' once a week for members only, and perhaps, in the case of difficult works, to perform them more than once. Players would be a specially-selected string quartet . . . male and female singers, pianists, and so on, not yet famous, but of good calibre."

The idea grew into the Society for Private Musical Performances (Verein fuer musikalische Privatauffuehrungen). Berg was entrusted with writing the group's lengthy prospectus, which appeared in February 1919. The society performed a tremendous service in focusing the attention of the Viennese avant-garde in the immediate postwar years and in encouraging not only composers trained in the Schoenberg school, but also talented outsiders. It was formed of the belief, true then and still the case today, that new music suffered from mediocre or inadequate performance. Insufficient rehearsal time or the inability of tradition-rooted instrumentalists to come to terms with new or unusual idioms detracted from the full realization of the music, and often the contexts in which modern works were performed worked against the audiences' appreciation.

The society intended to battle these forces of "unclarity" (one of Schoenberg's favorite terms) with virtually unlimited rehearsal time, with frequent repetitions of important pieces, and with "meetings" for members only, instead of regular concerts. Membership fees were charged on a graduated scale, from students up to sponsors. The purpose was not so much to support the society as to determine, through their financial commitment, which people were sincerely interested in new music.

The press was banned, guests were discouraged, and the evening's music was not announced in advance. (Indeed, it was sometimes not selected more than a few hours before the meeting.) The society's limited resources narrowed the repertory to some extent, but symphonic works were often performed in their reductions for one or two pianos, with the rationalization that such versions took away the frills of rich, colorful orchestration and pointed up the worth — or the worthlessness — of the music's essential ideas.

The society was highly organized, with Schoenberg as president, an archivist, a secretary, and five "directors of performance," including Berg and Webern. For Berg, who, unlike Webern, was not a traveling conductor and was, therefore, regularly in Vienna and available, this meant making piano arrangements, directing rehearsals

(Schoenberg usually did not appear to pass final judgment until the dress rehearsal), organizing the general operations of the membership, and four hundred kronen ($300, or £75) per month.

The first event sponsored by the society was held on December 29, 1918; the last took place on December 5, 1921, when funds ran out. Willi Reich calculated that during its three years, the society presented 117 concerts, including 154 works, from Mahler and Strauss to the most current music. The repertory list is fascinating, and not just because Schoenberg and his two star students were far from monopolizing the programming. Reger was performed more often than any other composer, followed by Debussy (due to Berg's influence), Bartók, and then Schoenberg, who decided not to allow any of his own music to be played until 1920. Berg was represented by performances of his Piano Sonata, Opus 1; his Four Songs, Opus 2; his String Quartet, Opus 3; his Clarinet Pieces, Opus 5; and segments from the Orchestral Pieces, Opus 6, in piano arrangements. The missing Opus 4 was the Altenberg Songs, which were still under a cloud because of the riot sparked by their performance a few years before; they had not yet been offered in their entirety.

If Berg had written more, he doubtless would have been represented more often on the society's programs. But the composer, now in his mid-thirties, remained relatively unproductive, and he was disturbed by the fact. Twice, once at the beginning of the organizational activities and again in August 1921, he tried to separate himself from Schoenberg's society in order to find more time to work on *Wozzeck,* but in neither case did he follow through with plans to break away. The composer was so embarrassed by the fact that he had so little to show for so many years of musical labor that after *Wozzeck,* which was only his Opus 7, he stopped using opus numbers entirely.

Once its activities fell into a routine, however irregular, the society also found ways to supplement its edifying purposes with nights of unadulterated entertainment. On May 27, 1921, the group staged a special waltz evening, with four waltzes by Johann Strauss arranged for string quintet, piano, and harmonium. Schoenberg arranged "Rosen aus dem Sueden" and the "Lagunenwalzer." Berg chose "Wein, Weib und Gesang," and Webern, the one of the three who cordially despised the schmaltzy music to begin with, chose the "Schatzwaltzer," from *Der Zigeunerbaron.* Schoenberg and Rudolf Kolisch played the first violin parts in turn; Karl Rankl was the second violinist; Steinbauer played viola and Webern played cello. Steuermann was at the piano, and Berg joined in on the harmonium. This in itself was enough to mark the evening as a rarity; though almost all other composers of his era made appearances as conductor or performer (usually in presenting their own works), Berg was neither inclined nor equipped to do anything from the stage except take a bow after someone else had presented his music — or to chime in on the harmonium, just for fun.

Twenty-five hours of rehearsal preceded the society's gala waltz evening, and at the end, the manuscripts of the arrangements were put up for auction to raise funds to allow Schoenberg to form and support a chamber orchestra. The full significance of this amount of preparation becomes clear when one realizes that a modern symphony orchestra usually devotes about nine hours of rehearsal to a standard program, with an extra hour or two added in the event of a particularly demanding work or a première.

Berg was devoting long hours to the cause and the business of the new society, teaching, and also tending to his precarious health. He wrote to Schoenberg that his three and a half years in the military had weakened him to such an extent that he had begun to take "narcotics" regularly; he never mentioned the nature of his complaint or the names of the medications. And then his relations with his family became troublesome, and demanded both time and energy. The Bergs had a history of treating one another coolly, especially since Smaragda had moved back in with her mother, and when problems arose regarding the property. Charly had been in charge of the Berghof while Alban oversaw the houses in Vienna. But in 1919, Charly decided to leave the country estate, which had been turned into a guest house, and Johanna Berg freely solicited further assistance from her youngest son, obviously in the belief that because she was, after all, contributing to the support of a musician who had no nine-to-five job tying him to Vienna, she was asking nothing out of the realm of possibility — and, in fact, might be doing Alban a favor by giving him the chance to enjoy life in the country.

Clearly upset, Berg responded to an eight-page letter from his mother on December 28, 1919, listing the duties of a property manager, which had kept him from answering sooner ("checking telephone accounts, increasing rents for fifty tenents, etc."), and practically ordering her to make it clear to the rest of the family that he would go to the Berghof only because he was needed there, not because he had any desire to do so. He was not going, he reiterated, because he had no work and needed the money. And in order to keep the arrangement temporary, he would leave Helene in Vienna, to await his return.

So from January until May 1920, Berg was away from
his wife, Schoenberg's society, and Vienna, tending to
the business of the Berghof, the home that he had loved
as a child but that was causing him so many problems
now that he was thirty-five years old. At first, the whole
family congregated there, with the others hoping they
could talk Alban into assuming permanent responsibility
for running the inn and tearoom and for maintaining the
grounds. Despite Berg's bad humor, the reunion was not
unpleasant; waiting for Hermann to arrive on January 11,
1920, Berg wrote to Helene that "today was a gossip
day." He was bothered by his mother's and sister's inability to understand that he had a career and a life in
Vienna and was in no way indigent or rootless. "Even
Hermann, who is really so touchingly concerned for my
welfare, seems quite convinced that it can only be my
greatest happiness to be steward of the Berghof," he
wrote, after his oldest brother had joined the circle.

From the family's point of view, it undoubtedly
seemed possible for Alban to live at the Berghof and continue his work; he would be in the country, of which he
was so fond — where he had always been able to work
most productively, by his own account — and the more
relaxed way of life could be a boon to his fragile health.
But as Berg wrote to Webern during his early weeks of
temporary employment as manager of the Berghof
(which meant doing everything from making sausage to
repairing the house, fetching groceries, and chopping
wood), "Here I am so far away from everything, so
abandoned by all good souls that . . . my senses, nerves
and spiritual forces are so blinded that I cannot even read
a good book . . . A hundred times a day I ask myself
what I am doing here . . . It is as though I had been 'detailed' to come here by some power just as questionable
as the militia in the war."

If he could not be at the Berghof on his own terms, then Berg did not want to be there at all. He was even ready to trade the peace of the country for the traffic and noise of Vienna's main thoroughfare, the Ringstrasse. Being at the Berghof, he felt, limited his personal freedom, and it brought out his most petulant side. An enthusiastic, young publisher from Vienna, E. P. Tal, wanted a monograph on Schoenberg, and Schoenberg suggested he get in touch with Berg. Ultimately, the task fell to Wellesz, another member of the circle. How Berg might have felt about writing the monograph had he still been living in Vienna, working on *Wozzeck,* teaching and participating in the activities of the Society for Private Musical Performances, can only be a matter for speculation, but there is every reason to believe that he would have jumped at the opportunity. As it was, however, he meekly and miserably declined the offer, protesting a bit too much when he wrote to Schoenberg, on January 15, "It has always been my greatest wish . . . to write something biographical about you, to take extra time, make every effort, and be advised on it by you. I would like nothing better — apart from composing — than writing guides, analyses, and articles about you, and making piano scores of your compositions. And now that the opportunity has come, I cannot take it."

Berg told Schoenberg that he was chained until the Berghof was either leased or sold, and that same day, the prospect of selling the estate was mentioned for the first time in the family circle. Mrs. Berg, Smaragda, and Smaragda's lover, May, all voted for a sale; Alban was also in favor of finding a new owner so that he would be rid of the responsibility for good.

Prospective buyers were not hard to find, especially as the value of the Austrian currency fell in relation to that of neighboring countries. On January 18, Berg wrote to

Helene that the wait would not be long; an Italian from Annenheim was interested in the property. But, of course, the negotiations dragged on. For fear that someone would discover the details of the "completely confidential" matter (it may have involved unreported exchanges of foreign currency), Berg wrote about the progress of the bargaining to Helene in a kind of code, which she may or may not have deciphered. While he waited for an agreement to be reached, Berg went out and broke ice, treated cider, smoked meat, and talked to other interested parties about the property, just in case the Italian backed out.

Except for lacking time to compose and missing the mainstream activities of musical life, Berg would have been enjoying himself tremendously — if only he had been able to relax and admit it. He mentioned to Helene that he was performing physical feats he had never imagined himself doing, and he finally reached the point where he could admire and report on the winter landscape. He ate good, fresh food, and sent his wife hard-to-get real butter, wrapped so that the package looked as if it contained a book. His dogs, Nero and Lulu, were playful companions in the snow. Perhaps Berg had second thoughts when the Italian returned and made an offer far below the Bergs' asking price for the property. But he lost patience when his mother would not accept less than 1.5 million kronen (over $1 million, or more than £250,000), and he wrote Helene in a tone of displeasure that, with that amount, "she could live, with Smaragda, just as luxuriously as they both hope," able to afford country vacations, and satisfy their appetites for expensive foods. According to her son, Johanna Berg ate "meat, eggs, fine vegetables, and all that in large quantities, plus alcohol" — no potatoes or milk. Smaragda, in

contrast, took "only the lightest (and finest) food . . .
white bread and butter." They expected to be able to afford the best seats for the theater and concerts. "How do
we paupers in Vienna live at all?" Berg asked impatiently.
"And yet we do have at least as fine nerves and senses
and tastes and inclinations. I don't begrudge them all this,
but can't see why I should sacrifice myself for it."

Still, Berg thought, his family was convinced that he
would agree to take over the permanent stewardship of
the Berghof. On February 28, he wrote to Helene that
Smaragda had had the temerity to suggest that it was
both thoughtless and unseemly for him to be spending all
that time away from his wife. Smaragda also blamed
Helene for letting her husband go off on his own. Berg
defended himself, then wrote that his relatives were acting both stupid and obstinate. He had no interest in any
future inheritance, he said, but was concerned only with
hurrying home to resume his composing and a normal
life.

Obviously, Berg was going to have to find some other
way to earn a living, and, knowing that he would not be
able to count on an allowance if he did not take over the
administration of the Berghof, he gave the matter much
serious thought during his Carinthian winter exile. He
wrote to Webern, on March 16, 1920, that he was thinking of devoting his life to writing about music, making
piano scores of larger works, and so on. "I think I can do
something in this line that would be on a higher level
than my work in the Society," he said. "In this way, it
would be possible — I think — to have a regular income
. . . Besides this I would give as many lessons as possible. Composing?? Yes, that would be very nice. Perhaps one or two months in the summer!!"

Berg did not really feel as casual about composing as he

apparently wanted Webern to believe. Nevertheless, he had rarely been completely free to compose except for "one or two [or perhaps three] months in the summer," and he also had no reason to believe that his compositions would ever earn him any substantial amounts. How devoted was he, really, to composition? Would he — could he — have given up composing, or turned it into a kind of warm-weather avocation? If *Wozzeck* had not been a success, would Berg have turned away from a creative career?

Fortunately, the crisis point was never reached. The Italian finally purchased the Berghof at Johanna Berg's price, and Berg was free to return to Vienna for good in May 1920. He rejoined his wife and concentrated on writing about music, something he did well and thoughtfully, but with no particular fluency. When he turned around Hans Pfitzner's *The New Aesthetic of Musical Impotence* (a tirade against the Schoenberg school) so that it became *The Musical Impotence of the New Aesthetic of Hans Pfitzner* and submitted it for publication in the June 1920 edition of Universal's house organ, *Musikblaetter des Anbruch,* the advisers found the article so interesting and controversial that Hertzka offered the composer-author the head editorial position on the biweekly paper. Berg accepted and agreed to begin his new job on September 1; he wanted to write, and the position was more important and lucrative than he had allowed himself to hope for. But even before his tenure began, he realized he had made a mistake.

> Believe me, I too regard the near future with fear and trembling [he wrote to Webern on August 14]. Will I be able to defy all resistance . . . avoiding clashes, making no enemies? . . . Will I be in a position to make absolutely no concessions? . . . Will I really be able to do what is needed? . . .

Believe me, I have spent many sleepless nights wishing I had never laid a hand on *Anbruch* . . . To take over the whole management in such a slippery — almost journalistic field. Truly, if I didn't have to do it, if I didn't stand before the necessity of scraping out some means of existence, I would write to Hertzka today and throw the whole thing over . . . But as it is, I have to stake my immediate future . . . on a "career" (horrible word) that means nothing to me but the bare possibility of existence.

The same letter to Webern gave further evidence of Berg's financial insecurity: he admitted to having sold several antiques in order to find the cash needed to publish his String Quartet, Opus 3, and the Four Pieces for Clarinet and Piano, Opus 5, and to pay to reprint the Piano Sonata, Opus 1, and the Four Songs, Opus 2, with corrections. He thought it urgent that his works be made available, especially as he embarked on a second career in editorial work. And he reassured Webern that he was not acting out of ambition, only from necessity.

As editor-elect of *Anbruch*, Berg did in fact have trouble balancing the various sensitivities and political interests. His own feuilleton, *Schoenberg and the Critics*, was withheld, lest the press take offense and strengthen its attacks not just against Schoenberg, but against all the composers represented by Universal Edition. Worried, upset, and angry at what he felt to be censorship from within the publishing house, Berg removed himself — or was removed — from the editorial fraternity even before he actually joined it. At the end of August 1920, his health broke again, and, suffering from weak lungs and nerves, he was sent to a sanitarium, where he stayed until November 8. When he was stronger, he returned to work for Schoenberg's Society for Private Musical Performances, but never to the *Anbruch*. He continued to write essays, but his enthusiasm for expressing himself on paper steadily diminished as the public's enthusiasm for *Wozzeck* grew. His articles were essentially limited to apologies for Schoenberg or introductory remarks to his own music. Much later, he offered a great deal of moral and editorial support to the beginnings of Willi Reich's *23 — Eine Wiener Musikzeitung,* which was issued thirty-three times between 1932 and 1937 as a musical counterpart to Kraus's *Die Fackel.* In Austrian law, paragraph number twenty-three of the criminal code deals with correcting erroneous statements made in the press, but in using the number twenty-three, Berg's *Schicksalszahl,* in the publication's title, Reich was also knowingly paying tribute to his teacher and friend.

Chapter 12

The Chamber Concerto

THE POSTWAR PROBLEMS at the Berghof and in musical journalism, Berg's financial troubles, the activity of Schoenberg's Society for Private Musical Performances, the concentrated work on composing *Wozzeck* and getting it performed, the unexpectedly acclaimed performances of the String Quartet, Opus 3, at the festival in Salzburg, the copying and completing and editing and correcting of scores — all these activities tended to overshadow the fact that, despite his frequent apologies for his lack of productivity, Berg had completed another major work before the première of *Wozzeck* in 1925.

The Chamber Concerto owed a great debt to yet another event that had taken place during the busy spring of 1923. Though Schoenberg had always felt free to prod Berg for his lack of ambition, the teacher had himself been going through a sterile period. After his Four Songs with Orchestra, Opus 22, Schoenberg worked on — but never finished — the oratorio *Die Jacobsleiter,* then released nothing until 1923. But then came a flood: the Five Pieces for Piano, Opus 23; the Serenade, Opus 24; and

the Piano Suite, Opus 25, and, with them, the definition
of a new direction in the art.

On Easter Sunday, April 1, 1923, Berg had dinner with
the Schoenbergs in Moedling, near Vienna. The younger
man had fretted a bit about the prospects for such a social
afternoon at a time when his relations with Schoenberg
had been strained. But the company was pleasant;
Schoenberg was in one of his friendly and confiding
moods; and, sometimes at the expense of the other
guests, he was intent on explaining to Berg "all the secrets in his new works."

Those secrets were the principles of twelve-tone composition, something that had been in the air for years, but
that Schoenberg had only now formulated to his satisfaction and was to present formally to his assembled students and associates only a few days later. In his new
formulations, each note of the chromatic scale had equal
rights with every other. To replace the old principles of
tonality, there was a new structural base: the row of
twelve tones, arranged in an order chosen by the composer. In theory, once this row was decided on, and once
all twelve notes of the chromatic scale were arranged in
place, the sequence of tones could not be changed — no
pitch would re-sound until all eleven others had been
played. The row could be changed in certain specified
ways — it could be turned upside down (in inversion),
played backward (in retrograde), or twisted both ways at
the same time (retrograde inversion). It could also be
transposed; that is, started on any pitch, from which the
original contour of the row would be followed. By using
these special sets of twelve notes each, Schoenberg had
found that he had more than ample material on which to
build his music. And, according to the theory, these
twelve-tone building blocks would provide the kind of

unification that music had been missing since the dissolution of tonality.

The twelve-tone techniques rely on variation. All music is variation, but in the case of Schoenberg's twelve-tone procedures, the original row is the theme and nucleus from which everything else develops. The methods are also close cousins of the old round — in the manner of "Row, Row, Row Your Boat" or "Frère Jacques" — in which the same tune is repeated again and again by the different voices. Another relative of twelve-tone composition is the Baroque fugue, with its staggered appearances of themes in either original or transposed forms. Schoenberg's new ideas were well grounded in music history.

The principles of composing with twelve tones all equal to one another, as Schoenberg told Berg on that Easter afternoon, governed both the melodic and harmonic aspects of a composition. The rules permitted the sounding of all twelve notes together; if a chord contained the first six notes of a row, the other six would have to follow separately or together; if all twelve notes of the scale were sounded simultaneously, the composer was obliged to begin all over with his original melodic pattern. And if, as the teacher himself had maintained, the test of creativity was knowing how and when to break the rules (Schoenberg never said whether that included breaking *his* rules), then the new methods allowed for a wide margin of creativity, especially when the composer took the original row and divided it in half or in thirds or into even smaller groups of notes, and worked with these fragments as primary building blocks, instead of with the whole twelve-note set. This kind of dissection was to become one of Webern's favorite methods.

This twelve-tone "set theory" is now history, having

served its purpose in much the same way as Cubism served to revolutionize paintings. Despite the stringent rules that Schoenberg laid down to his disciples, the new techniques aimed at providing a new freedom, and this they did do — to a degree dependent on the imagination of the craftsman — in a variety of ways. In order to prove the viability and accessibility of his ideas, for instance, Schoenberg showed Berg how the new rules could be applied to old forms, to dances such as the minuet, for example, or sonata schemes. Such applications are, on at least one level, redundant, since the old forms themselves had been closely tied to the old systems of tonality, and since composers had already proved that it was possible to use the old floor plans for music that was neither tonal nor twelve-tone, but lay in that nebulous area called "atonal."

Then the question arose as to what was twelve-tone, and what was not. Schoenberg, Berg, and Webern had all used lines that could be called twelve-tone rows in their works written well before 1923. Stretching the point, some have identified and analyzed and counted rows in Beethoven's late quartets and even the Ninth Symphony. Audiences like to ask if a work is "twelve-tone," and critics frequently make mention of the techniques in their reviews, but knowing whether a piece of music has been constructed on the particular principles that governed Schoenberg's twelve-tone methods tells one very little about the sound of the music, its formal integrity, or what effect it will have on even the most technically astute listener.

Nevertheless, Schoenberg's pronouncements were of great importance, not only because whatever the master announced influenced his friends and students, but also because so many years had passed since the search had begun to identify guidelines for the changes that were in

the air. When he assembled his disciples for the ceremo-
nial unveiling of the new directions, Schoenberg expected
his students to apply the rules to their own work at once,
and, in fact, some of them did adopt the twelve-tone
practices as soon as they were explained. Webern was already deeply involved by the time Schoenberg made his
discoveries public. Ernst Krenek was among the younger
men who, during the decades to come, were to deal with
the subtleties and implications of the principles.

Berg, however, was more resistant, and it is probable
that some of the bad temper shown by the master toward
one of his favorite (and, formerly, one of his most mal-
leable) disciples in and around 1923 had to do with his
knowing that, whether any words were actually exchanged on the subject, Berg did not immediately rejoice
and find salvation in Schoenberg's rules. His reservations
were probably twofold. First, his romanticism and his
strong technical and emotional ties with the past made it
difficult for him to make this particular kind of break,
especially when the twelve-tone principles carried with
them the tacit implication that they would be used to
avoid recourse to tonality (though, in fact, this did not
turn out to be an important aspect of their application).
And, second, Berg had just entered the world of opera
with *Wozzeck*. If the rules of twelve-tone writing were to
allow composers to work once again in the larger forms
that had theoretically been denied them during the era of
"atonality," it was quite another thing to imagine a
twelve-tone opera of an entire evening's duration, where
dramatic gesture and effect called for the use of a wide
range of styles and techniques, and in which singers
needed the support of instrumental accompaniments of a
less independent kind than twelve-tone composition in its
early stages would have allowed.

Not that Berg was, at this time, planning another

opera. The thought was in the back of his mind, but for the moment, he had decided to follow up on another old suggestion of Schoenberg's. The teacher had a friendly involvement with a wind ensemble in Copenhagen, and had once suggested that if Berg felt inclined to write for winds, that group might be prevailed on to perform whatever he might produce. Berg was also searching for a gift to present to Schoenberg on his fiftieth birthday, which would fall on September 13, 1924, so thoughts for a new project were on his mind early in 1923. A letter to his wife, dated March 29, showed that he had already made enough progress to announce that most of the basic questions of the early stages of composition had been answered.

There is no way to know exactly how long Berg had been delving into possibilities for a new work, but considering the fact that the instrumentation on *Wozzeck* had been finished early in 1922, he could have been pondering his next project (which would have been Opus 8, had he not given up numbering) for a full year. He lost a good deal of time while he corrected, prepared, and sold the opera, of course, but this was a relatively small obstacle compared with the one the composer faced when he realized how difficult it was going to be to write something worthy of being called *Wozzeck*'s successor.

Berg began with the idea of writing for winds, then added the concerto aspect to satisfy his urge for drama, letting the soloist or soloists substitute for the prima donna of the operatic stage. The decision to use winds was significant in itself; since wind players have to breathe, Berg was ruling out any possibility of drawn-out, seemingly endless phrases or cushions of sound. He would have to allow time for the instrumentalists to breathe, just as he had done for the singers in *Wozzeck*, only without the added dramatic impetus provided by words. And the man who had repeatedly reminded friends and followers that *Wozzeck* was a *piano* opera would have to raise his dynamic levels, because neither woodwinds nor brass instruments can fade their sounds as far into the distance as strings can.

The question, then, was which winds and how many. If Berg had made those decisions by the end of March 1923, he did not say so. He wrote to Helene to stress the concerto aspects of the work in progress and to complain about Schoenberg's tedious fault-finding. The teacher was distressed that Berg still did not have a firm start on the Chamber Concerto. But by July 12, good progress had been made, though slowly, and Berg could write to Schoenberg from Trahuetten that he was "at long last back at work, which does not flow easily. After all, I've composed almost nothing in the past twenty months; now it seems as if something will come of it."

Retracing the work's origins for Schoenberg, Berg admitted that he had once considered writing a piano conerto, or even a two-, three-, or four-piano concerto ("forgive my incurable elephantiasis," Berg begged), but that did not fit comfortably with his desire to write for winds; he needed a combination of instruments that would themselves act as inspiration, and heeded his teacher's old warnings against creating unnecessary difficulties for himself by writing for an ensemble he did not find immediately appealing. By July 12, he had written approximately fifty bars of the Chamber Concerto for solo piano and violin accompanied by ten wind instruments; he was planning to extend that beginning into a lengthy symphonic movement of as many as five hundred measures.

But progress was very slow, and Berg's plans changed

again. The accompaniment to the two solo instruments grew from an ensemble of ten to an ensemble of thirteen (Schoenberg's number of fate), and the sonata movement Berg had intended to put at the beginning turned into the sonata-rondo finale. Not surprisingly, Berg did not finish the Chamber Concerto in time to present it to Schoenberg for his fiftieth birthday.

Among other interruptions there was a disturbing period in November 1923, when Helene went to take a cure in Parsch, near Salzburg, and fell into the hands of a doctor of whom her husband did not approve. She was being treated according to the new and fashionable principles of psychoanalysis, and, somewhat resentfully, reported the diagnosis to her husband via express mail. He responded immediately, on November 26, 1923, urging her not to overreact, but to "pretend to obey the will of this Marquis de Sade. Accept the treatments you feel are helpful . . . and give the impression that you have changed your mind about resisting. He will imagine he has tamed you. Your revenge will come."

Whatever the treatments may have been, Berg called them "crimes," and three days later, he advised Helene to leave the spa, thus saving some money, and not to go to any more of the doctor's "sessions."

> Tell the doctor I have forbidden it, and say that if there had been any question of psychoanalytic treatment, we should have gone to Dr. Freud or Dr. Adler, both of whom we have known well for many years. . . . In a week's time, we shall be laughing about the crazy confidence game of this "psychoanalysis" and all these explanations of unfulfilled desires, sexuality, etc. A single day in the snow and woods . . . will wash away all the inner dirt which has been poured into your poor, clean little soul.

Berg had been intrigued by Freud's theories and by the doctor himself when, back in 1908, he had been consulted

about one of Berg's early attacks of asthma. But Karl
Kraus had decided that "psychoanalysis is the mental
illness of which it pretends to be the cure," and when
treatment for emotional disorders came too close to
home, Berg was evidently inclined to agree with the cynical writer. Yet Helene frequently went to "take the
cure," either for relief of specific aches and pains or to
calm her nerves. Why she went so often, and why she
stayed away so long, is hard to say. It is worth remembering, however, that this kind of rest and recuperation at
a medically supervised spa was, and still is, a not unusual
Viennese pastime, and is considered fashionable among
those who can afford the high daily or weekly fees.

Berg eventually forgot about the doctor's alleged
crimes and went back to his Chamber Concerto. The official date of completion is February 9, 1925, his own fortieth birthday; he finished the orchestration on July 23,
1925. Both of these dates are suspect; it would be remarkable that the last note of the short score happened to have
been written on the composer's birthday, and the last
note of the orchestration was filled in on the twenty-
third, his fate-day of the seventh month. Berg would not
have been the first composer to fudge dates and numbers;
Schoenberg had even stretched some opus numbers of
important works to make them more significant than
they would have been in their authentic order. In any
case, the Chamber Concerto was ready to be introduced
by Hermann Scherchen in March 1927, in both Zurich
and Berlin. It was performed in Vienna that same month,
with Webern conducting. The dedication to Schoenberg
was printed in the Viennese music magazine *Pult und
Taktstock* and was dated February 9, 1925. Berg called the
work "a little memorial to a friendship that is now
twenty years old," and revealed the source of his basic
melodic fragments:

In a musical motto that introduces the first movement, the letters of your name, Webern's, and mine have been captured — as far as it is possible in musical notation — in three themes or motives, which then take on important roles in the development of this music.

This already announces a trinity of events, and such a trinity is also important in the whole work. It is, after all, your birthday, all the good things that I wish you, and all good things come in threes.

Berg was speaking literally when he said he had taken the three motto themes for the Chamber Concerto from the letters of his own name, Schoenberg's, and Webern's. In English, musical notes are represented by only seven letters — A,B,C,D,E,F, and G — and accidentals are signified verbally with added words, as in F-sharp or B-flat. But the Germans have a different way of denoting and verbalizing musical pitches. The notes A,C,D,E,F, and G are the same, but the German *B* means B-flat, and the letter *H* stands for B (in English, B-natural). In addition, what is called E-flat in English is *"Es"* in German, so it can be represented by the letter *S*. Berg could, therefore, transfer into pitches more letters from the three names than an English-speaking composer could have done, and the themes as they appear in the names are ArnolD SCHo(e)nBErG, Anton wEBErn, and AlBAn BErG. Their first appearance acts as a signal that the Chamber Concerto is about to begin. Such translations from words and names to pitches was by no means original to Berg. Many composers have signed their compositions in a similar manner; the most famous examples are Bach's.

Berg carried his idea of "a trinity of events" to extremes throughout every facet of the work. The Chamber Concerto is to be performed in one long, uninterrupted sweep, but it divides clearly into three distinct

but connected sections: a theme with variations, an
adagio, and a rondo *ritmico* with an introduction in the
form of a cadenza, a brief passage meant to suggest im-
provisation. Berg gave each of the three large sections its
characteristic sound and its own instrumental combination. The basic instrumental ensemble of winds contains
piccolo, flute, oboe, English horn, clarinets in E-flat and
A, bass clarinet, bassoon, contrabassoon, two horns,
trumpet, and trombone. The solo piano is accompanied
by the wind band in the opening theme with variations;
the solo violin takes over from the piano in the adagio.
For the finale, both solo instruments, the piano and the
violin, join in virtuoso concerted display. The fact that
his instrumental resources, including the two solo
players, added up to fifteen was in itself significant to
Berg, not only because the number was a multiple of
three, but also because it matched the size of the ensemble
Schoenberg himself had used in his Opus 9.

The number three and its multiples continue to prevail;
in the opening movement, the variation theme divides
into three parts and lasts thirty measures, and with five
variations following the original statement, the section
divides into six parts of thirty or sixty measures each.
The central adagio is cast in the traditional ternary "song
form" (A-B-A), in which the second A is a variation of
the first, in this case the inversion; again, the number of
measures in each section is a multiple of three and, like
the theme and variations, the adagio lasts through a total
of 240 bars. The third movement, with its introductory
cadenza for the two soloists, runs 480 measures, as many
as the first two put together, in a marriage of sonata and
rondo forms. Berg's intention in the finale was to create
the sum of the first two movements in both musical and
numerical ways; his challenge, as he explained to Schoen-

berg, was to combine "on the one hand a variation
movement of about nine minutes duration . . . and on
the other a broadly sung, extended adagio lasting a
quarter of an hour." He used three basic methods to effect this musical mixture: he layered certain passages with
structural correspondences on top of one another, taking
certain freedoms to increase their compatibility; he let
small phrases and motives from the first movement answer their counterparts from the second, in a manner of a
duet; and he located certain lines and phrases from both
movements that would mesh together without any
changes at all. The additive processes were made even
more complicated than they might otherwise have been,
not merely because of the very different musical moods
of the first two movements, but also because the theme
and variations were written in triple time, and the adagio
moved primarily in duple meters. The rondo, then,
ended up as a pairing of the two, with constantly fluc-
tuating time signatures and some intentionally ambiguous
passages.

The rondo became *ritmico* when Berg applied a primary rhythm, a secondary rhythm, and another small
rhythmic motive to the two melodic lines that dominate
the movement. The rhythms themselves helped promote
cohesion, as Berg had found possible in *Wozzeck* and the
Orchestral Pieces, and they added measurably to the
overall dramatic effect. In the Chamber Concerto, the
composer took his ideas of rhythmic organization one
step further than he had previously, by exploring and
varying the basic patterns, elongating them, abbreviating,
turning them backward, changing the accents, and so on.
These techniques, ancestors of the later movement toward complete rhythmic serialization, turned out to have
wonderful powers that Berg himself could not have pre-

dicted. In the adagio, for example, the rhythmic stability and the strong support it offers enhanced the beauty of one of the most glowing melodies the composer ever wrote.

Berg was very aware of Schoenberg's techniques for composing with twelve tones of equal status when he wrote his Chamber Concerto, but instead of actually using the new methods, he chose only to refer to them, as if he were taking a respectful bow from several paces back. The rhythmic patterns and their reversals are comparable with Schoenberg's rules for melodic structuring. More directly connected to the twelve-tone techniques are the first movement's variations: variation number two presents the theme in inversion, or upside down; variation three turns the melody retrograde, running it back to front; variation four explores the retrograde inversion, and the last variation returns to the theme's original shape. In the second movement, while adhering to his three-part A-B-A form, Berg also divided his structure in half and made the second part a mirror of the first, sometimes freely reversing the thematic material and sometimes using the exact retrograde. Such horizontally oriented techniques clearly meant that the harmonies would have to be vague — Berg referred to "dissolved tonality" — but passages in both the first and second movements (and therefore also in the third) are distinctly tonal, furthering the impression that the Chamber Concerto does not just add up its first two movements to make the third, but adds up an amazing variety of ideas in an incredible display of compositional virtuosity and control.

Berg concluded his letter of dedication to Schoenberg with a paragraph hinting that there was more to the Chamber Concerto than would ever meet the eye or the ear:

If in this analysis I have spoken almost exclusively of things connected with the number three, this is because, first, it is just those aspects that will be ignored by everybody who looks for other, more musical aspects; second, because as an author it is much easier for an author to speak about such external matters than about internal processes . . . I can tell you, dear friend, that if it became known how much friendship, love, and how many spiritual references I have smuggled into these three movements, the adherents of program music . . . would go mad with joy, and the representatives and defenders of "Neoclassicism" and "new matter-of-factness," the "linearists" and "physiologists," the "counterpointists" and "formalists" would rush to attack me, outraged by my "romantic" language . . . And the concerto is the very art form in which not only the soloists and their conductor have the opportunity to show off their brilliance and virtuosity, but the author can, too, for once.

As Berg suggested, the Chamber Concerto contains more cross-references, puzzles, riddles, inside jokes, and hidden patterns than anyone has ever come close to cataloguing; the composer took the opportunity to display his own virtuosity as he wrote music to challenge the most brilliant and facile of soloists. The Chamber Concerto filled the order Schoenberg had placed years before for his student to write a happy, good-natured piece. No matter how difficult and treacherous the work is to perform, nor how artificial some facets of the work may seem (especially in written descriptions), the first impression the music leaves is one of joviality, and it spreads out with a kind of welcoming eagerness to be explored.

Wozzeck was an antihero, but the Chamber Concerto is filled with heroes. It is chamber music in that only one musician plays each part; by the customary definition, however, it is not chamber music, for there is no way the work can be presented without a conductor's guiding

Tabular general survey for the Chamber Concerto (prepared by Berg)

	Theme basic shape	Var. 1	2 retrograde	3 inversion	4 retrograde inversion	5 basic shape		Number of bars
I Theme with variations	(Exposition)		(Development)			(Second reprise)		
	Bars: 30	30	60	30	30	60		240
II Adagio	Ternary A₁ B	A₂	A₂	B	A₁ Retrograde			
		(inversion of A₁)			(mirror from preceding B)			
	Bars: 30 12 36	12 30 30	30 12	36 12	30			240	480
III (=I+II) Rondo ritmico con Introduzione	Introduction (cadenza for violin and piano)	Exposition	Development	Coda				
			(da capo)					
	bars: 54	96	79	76				305 175	480
		repeat: 175						960

hand. Next to its good humor, the second feeling the
Chamber Concerto leaves with listeners is one of virtuosity in the old-fashioned manner. Members of the wind
ensemble are more than accompanists; they are second-
string soloists acting in support of the piano and the violin. The musical heroics, well accomplished, can be exciting for performers and listeners alike, but the Chamber
Concerto is extremely difficult — perhaps the most difficult music Berg ever wrote — because of the clarity and
the precision it requires from each player, and because the
tautness of the writing and the amount of activity means
that even the smallest slip can lead to disaster. The whole
structure can easily collapse.

Pierre Boulez has called the Chamber Concerto
"Berg's strongest work," and Adorno said that the work
was the archetype for everything Berg wrote after it. It is
fascinating in this context to notice how boldly the composer began to present himself in his music, and the flair
with which he took his bows. He made himself a character in the drama of the Chamber Concerto — a commen-
tator and master of ceremonies, not merely the compiler
and absentee note-writer.

After the short, tight scenes of *Wozzeck* — scenes that
stay in the memory like richly detailed still photographs
rather than extended moving-picture takes — the
Chamber Concerto lays itself out quite leisurely, almost
voluptuously, seeming to have all the time in the world
yet wasting none of it. A frequent cinema-goer, Berg was
enthralled and influenced by cinematic methods and
movement; he wanted to exercise his composer's control
over time just as a film director and cinematographer
might exercise theirs. One direct parallel is the composer's use of retrograde, which is most easily thought of
as running the music backward — a sure guarantee of
formal cohesion.

The use of retrograde is a kind of musical game composers play, just as Berg's $A + B = C$ formula for the Chamber Concerto's three movements represents the challenges he set for himself, a kind of solitary daring. By this time, it was not at all surprising for Berg to rest his strongest musical arguments in a work's last movement; in the Opus 2 Songs, the Opus 5 Clarinet Pieces, and the Opus 6 Orchestral Pieces the final sections served to do much more than simply bring the pieces to satisfying conclusions, and the Orchestral Pieces, like the Chamber Concerto, end with a section longer than the preceding two put together. In tipping the balance toward his finale, Berg gave his works cumulative effects quite different from those carried by the old sonata form, when after the serious presentations and developments of the first movement the rest could seem anticlimactic.

Like all alert dramatists, Berg thought very specifically about how his music might affect, move, and involve its audiences. Even more than his other works, the Chamber Concerto simultaneously challenges the intellect and the emotions. After the signal intonations of the three motto themes, the English horn introduces the first-movement variation set gradually, first playing two notes, then three, then four, and finally giving the impression that the summit has been reached by spilling over into a statement of the complete theme. The process of adding the notes one by one may be seen as a hint of additive procedures to come; it is no less important, however, to recognize that the English horn is beginning a lilting waltz in a manner very reminiscent of that of the Viennese hero Johann Strauss.

Similarly, Berg's use of quarter tones — smaller intervals than those used in the common chromatic scale — in the violin solos of the middle movement can lead to a discussion of the various theories of microtonal writing, which was becoming popular in those years. In the context of the Chamber Concerto, however, the microtones do not function theoretically; they are colorful bonuses that enrich the already romantic melodies.

The question remains, however, of the value that can be placed on the seemingly gratuitous elements of the score that are hidden from the listener's ear, or that must be noticed by reading the score. There are a number of such instances in the Chamber Concerto; indeed, two of the work's most famous moments are at least partly made of inaudible musical gestures. When the violin enters with a whispered *ppp* at the end of the first movement, to take over the starring role from the piano, the audience will see the bow moving on the string before the violin's sound is actually heard; the effect is theatrical. And at the beginning of the adagio the soloist is already poised, waiting only for the others to finish their more frenetic activity so that he can settle into the new, sweeter melodies.

And the twelve low C-sharps that chime out in the middle of the adagio from down at the bottom of the keyboard of the piano, which is otherwise silent in this movement (or from the contrabassoon in the event that the movements are played individually and no piano is available — an alternative Berg reluctantly sanctioned), are all but completely hidden in even the best recorded performances of the Chamber Concerto. For the listener lucky enough to catch these fleeting notes, however, or for the observer who sees that the pianist is suddenly, though temporarily, back at attention, the chimes seem to ring in a mysterious musical moment when everything turns in on itself, when the music moves into retrograde and comes back as if reflected in eerie mirrors of a room forgotten by everyone save the ghosts.

Berg was, in effect, writing in the realm of both the heard and the unheard, the known and the unknown, writing music of dramatic implication. Everything he did after the Chamber Concerto would expand on these ideas. *Wozzeck* was not to be imitated or rediscovered. In the new works there would be nothing stark or hard; the contours were rounded, soft, sexy, and suggestive. With *Wozzeck,* and especially with the Chamber Concerto, Berg seemed to have discovered that, for him, writing music meant not crossing out all possibilities except one, but generously filling his forms as full as they could be, to the point where they seemed ready to burst with energy and imagination.

Chapter 13

The Secrets of the Lyric Suite

ALBAN CALLED HELENE "my golden one," "my angel," "my proud little girl," "a piece of me," "my life." They had pet names — she was "Pferscherl" (a variation of "Little Pear") and "Schnude." He worried about her constantly, as, for example, in his letter of March 10, 1914:

> If only this would change. You must try to get your nerves straightened out, and simply live for once, instead of worrying so much about living . . .
>
> Believe one thing: You must do everything, everything, my Pferscherl, my Life, to get well, so that you can really live. You must put on some weight . . . Don't be too "modern," my darling . . . The natural loveliness of your body has nothing to do with fashion, and your soul is eternal.

Helene's pet names for him were "Blinus" and "Schribi." She relied on him for advice, obeyed him, was a stylish and practical wife, tried to give him space and freedom to work, and worried about him. Although a good number of Alban's letters to Helene are available either in libraries or in published collections, her letters to him are not, and many have probably been lost or destroyed. But neither in person, according to people who knew her at the time, nor in what is known of her writing was she given to the same kinds of romantic flights her husband was. Two years before their marriage, while Alban was suffering and struggling through a period of *Sturm und Drang,* she sent him a very matter-of-fact letter with apologies for having been unduly harsh and with strict orders that he take better care of himself:

> I'm sure [your health] must have suffered a good deal from the effects of your not living in a more sensible way. Look, it's all right for Smaragda to drag you off with her carousing all night, and Hermann does the same thing when he's in Europe. But Smaragda has a good long sleep the next day, while you get up without enough sleep and try to work, fighting your tiredness by drinking all those cups of strong tea. And what with these nights in smoky places, with alcohol and no food, you've reached the point of being over six feet tall and weighing only one hundred thirty-five pounds . . .
>
> You are always writing of your great love for me, but you don't seem to care that our future depends on your health's improving. From their point of view, my parents aren't entirely wrong to turn you down. They think I would be worrying about you all the time, and wouldn't be happy with you. Any woman who loves is bound to wonder whether her love is going to bring her suffering, even though it may be her destiny to suffer. But won't you, Alban, have one more try to get well? . . .
>
> But no, I am not giving you up. Perhaps you will still achieve something great someday and I want to help you with it, so that you can do your work unhampered by physical frailty, and can also enjoy life.

It is strange to hear the reservations in Helene's words "perhaps you will still achieve something great someday," as if, despite the trust they shared, she had serious doubts. It seems strange, too, for twenty-four-year-olds to be fretting so much over each other's health, like two crotchety grandparents. To be sure, neither was hale and hearty in the style of the families one can still see perched on spindly chairs at Dehmel's or the Café Aïda, gobbling the cream-filled pastries that even now are so much a part of Viennese afternoons. Alban had asthma, and doctors said his heart was too small (in German, a *Kinderherz*) and his thorax too narrow in proportion to his height. So he was warned against participating in sports, though he was a regular and devoted fan of Austria's championship soccer team, and would drag his friends and students out to the park whenever there was a home game. And he was a very strong swimmer; when he had to, he found that he was able to perform all the muscle-building chores required to maintain the Berghof and actually felt better for having done so.

He loved to eat, but stayed thin without much effort; he hated obesity in those around him, and was lucky that he never needed to worry over his own waistline. Helene, too, was thin, for the sake of style rather than of health. She nibbled and abstained, and her husband thought she might really be undernourished. She was also nervous — perhaps even more "sensitive" than the nail-biting Alban, who could give vent to his trials and suffering in letters, conversation, and music, then return to his even ways. Some measure of instability ran in Helene's family; whatever might be said about her mother's alleged affair with the emperor, there was also the well-substantiated case of her brother, Frank, who was repeatedly institutionalized for schizophrenia and who, as Mosco Carner put it, "committed a Van Gogh-like act" by cutting off his little finger in an inexplicable sacrifice.

Neither Helene nor Alban came from the strongest or most solid of stocks. Allowing for their "artistic natures," so fashionable among the upper classes, allowing for the careful selection and heavy editing of the available letters — even allowing for the fact that the couple, naturally, exchanged letters only when they were separated from each other — their correspondence is strangely full of references to illnesses and cures, to nourishment or lack thereof, to real or imagined worries about their fates and conditions.

Ironically, however, the people who remember the Bergs from Vienna and the country do not recall that they were ill any more often than anyone else in their circle. What they remember is the images of beauty, the picture of the loving, well-dressed, smiling couple, ever so much — and ever so publicly — in love. They do not seem to remember the stories that have been passed down about how Berg and a companion or two would go out into the Vienna nights in search of prostitutes who would beat them.

What kind of life did Alban and Helene live? Much as they might have liked to be, they were not actively social. They made their appearances at concerts and the theater, but when they received dinner invitations, more often than not he would accept and she would decline; that way, they reasoned, they would not be expected to reciprocate. Eventually, they earned the reputation of being aloof. They were self-consciously sensitive; they could make a theatrical production out of stopping on the street to give a child a piece of candy. Worse, Helene thought it might be her "destiny" to suffer. What had happened to the naturalness and happiness of those early summers at the Berghof?

Their marriage was not as ideal as Helene, in particu-

lar, wanted it to appear. Having agonized and apologized
to his future wife in the early days of their courtship for
having been "unfaithful" to her during a performance of
a Mahler symphony because he thought only of the
music and not of her, Berg spent the last ten years of his
life in love with another woman.

The infatuation must have started in May 1925, when
Berg traveled, by himself (as usual), to Prague, where his
Three Fragments from *Wozzeck* were to be conducted by
Alexander von Zemlinsky at the Third Festival of the In-
ternational Society for Contemporary Music. It was
probably Alma Mahler Werfel who arranged for the
composer to be the house guest of her sister-in-law,
Hanna, and her industrialist husband, Herbert Fuchs-
Robettin. Berg was impressed, first by the musical life of
Prague and then by his host and hostess. He wrote to
Helene on May 15 that he was comfortably ensconced in
the Fuchses' villa while "the musical life of the world is
surging around me, so that my brain is on fire." Kleiber
was there to talk about *Wozzeck;* the Opus 3 String
Quartet was to be performed in Moscow, and Berg felt
"pretty respected and distinguished," especially since the
music magazine *Auftakt* had just featured his picture.

And, apart from the music, he had a car at his disposal,
compliments of Fuchs, and a "room with hot water,
glorious view, Roger & Gallet soap, Venetian blinds,"
and breakfast served in his room every morning at seven,
with fresh crusty rolls. At eight on his first morning in
Prague, the two Fuchs children (a girl three and a half
and a boy seven) were allowed to knock on the door to
visit the "famous composer"; Berg found them "very
sweet" and "refreshing." He visited the theater and was
received by Mrs. Werfel, the mother of Hanna and Franz,
before he was picked up and driven back to the suburban
villa for lunch and a rest.

Berg called it "the simple life," but it was not simple at all, and Helene may have been able to read guilt between the lines of her husband's letter. She considered joining him in Prague; on May 18 Berg wrote to her that it was really too late for her to make the trip without having to turn right around and go home, but that, of course, if she decided to come she would be a welcome guest of either the Fuchs family or Mrs. Werfel. With hindsight, it is clear that Berg did not want his wife to join him. He did remark that he had left Helene's passport out at home, just in case she decided to make the trip. But she would have to get a visa and pick up the tickets herself — and, not so incidentally, she would have to pay full fare for the train because she had not planned the trip in advance.

Helene did not come, and Berg was free to enjoy the music festival and the Fuchses. Herbert Fuchs had one of the most celebrated wine cellars on the Continent (Berg was convinced that it was "the most wonderful wine in the world"), and the guest became increasingly comfortable around the children. He was reluctant to leave Czechoslovakia and eager to return.

Six months later, Berg was on his way back to Prague, stopping off there en route to Berlin for *Wozzeck* rehearsals. This time, on November 11, 1925, his letter to Helene had a slightly different tone, and Hanna Fuchs-Robettin was already known familiarly as "Mopinka":

> The taxi ride to the station consisted in my banging the door of the wretched cab shut about seventeen times, and holding it closed with my hand for the rest of the ride. I only just got to the station on time. I'm so sad that I didn't leave you a few chocolates . . . Promise you'll be a very good girl and eat plenty while I'm gone! Come to think of it, I promise I'll be a good boy!
>
>   It goes against my grain, really, to have to reassure you about me and Mopinka. Perhaps I should just say that faith-

fulness is one of my best qualities (I'm sure I must have been
a dog in a previous incarnation, and perhaps shall be in a
later one, but . . . may I die of distemper if I ever sin against
faithfulness!). Faithfulness towards you, and also towards
myself, music, Schoenberg (and *he* really makes it hard for
one), even towards Trahuetten . . .

So, being of such a conservative disposition, how could I
help, my darling, being anything but faithful to you and
remaining faithful forever? Believe me, as I believe the same
of you.

Herbert Fuchs-Robettin met Berg at the train station in
Prague and immediately invited him to be their guest on
his way back to Vienna from Berlin. At the villa, they
rested, then met for coffee. Berg reported to his wife:

Mopinka also appeared then, with the children. The boy is
growing fast, the girl is sickly, though, and looks ill — not
even pretty because of that. But still such a dear that you
would certainly like her. Altogether, once you meet these
people, you'll like them just as much as I do. It's really a
friendliness and warm-heartedness, without any holding
back. That's why — that's the only reason why I'm so fond
of them. And you will feel the same.

You know, darling, why I'm making so much of this. Not
because it's so terrific here (my thoughts are already in Berlin), but to stop you from worrying about Mopinka's
charms!

Dinner with the Fuchses consisted of lobster eggs,
grouse, potatoes, applesauce, cheese, fruit and wine, then
brandy. Afterward, Berg retired to his room, enchanted
by the peace and beauty around him.

Helene did stop for a night in Prague when she finally
went to meet her husband in Berlin just before the *Wozzeck* première; Berg sent word to her when she was with
the Fuchses and warned them all to be sure to arrive in

plenty of time for the dress rehearsal. Everyone was then together in Berlin for the final preparations, performance, and celebration: Berg and Helene, Alma and Franz Werfel, Hanna and Herbert Fuchs-Robettin. They were a close-knit group, dedicated primarily to Berg and to music. Almschi, in addition to being the dedicatee of *Wozzeck,* had cast herself in the role of Helene's confidante.

Berg had seen Mopinka for a few days in May 1925, then again in November and December in Prague and Berlin. They may have been together on other occasions, too; perhaps when *Wozzeck* was performed in Prague in November 1926 (and censored after the third performance), or for other premières and festivals in Prague or when Berg was en route to Berlin. Prague was so close to Vienna that it would have been normal for Berg to have gone there whenever one of his works or something by one of his colleagues was being offered; Prague was also the convenient stopping place between Vienna and Berlin. No one would have suspected that there were other than musical reasons for Berg to travel to Prague. And naturally, while he was there he would visit the relatives of his close friends the Werfels.

Alban Berg and Hanna Fuchs-Robettin stayed in close touch with each other until his death, in 1935. Her letters to him were sent through Berg's student Fritz Klein. They reportedly have been burned.

But Berg's letters to Hanna were preserved, at least in part, and one of them, written in October 1931, reads like a confession:

> Not a day passes, not half a day, not a night, when I do not think of you, not a week when I am not suddenly flooded by yearning, which submerges all my thoughts and feelings and wishes in an ardor which is not weaker by a breath than that

of May, 1925 — only still shadowed by a grief which, since then, rules me more and more, and which for a long time, now, has made me into a . . . play-acting person. For you must know: everything that you may hear of me, and perhaps even read of me, pertains, insofar as it is not completely false (as, for example, this, which I read today by chance in a Zurich program: "a completely happy domesticity, with which his wife surrounds him, allows him to create without disturbance") — pertains to what is only peripheral. But it pertains only to a person who constitutes a completely exterior layer of myself, to a part of me which in the course of recent years has separated itself (ah, how painfully!) from my real existence, and has formed a detached being, the one I seem to my surroundings and to the world . . .

But believe me, Hanna (and now I can finally address you properly: *one and only eternal love*), all this pertains only to this exterior person, the one I have been forced to present myself as to my fellow human beings and whom you, thank God, have never known, and who (only in order to characterize him some way) might for a time be fulfilled with the joys of motoring, but would never be able to compose *Lulu* . . . When I work and take hold of your pen, at that moment I am here, and am also with you, as I am with myself when I am with you in thought.

Alban Berg's love affair with Hanna Werfel Fuchs-Robettin began in May 1925, when he was forty and she was in her early thirties. It continued until he died, ten years and seven months later. There is nothing to suggest that they ever seriously intended to break up their homes and leave their spouses in order to be with one another. Berg's love for Hanna did not alienate him from Helene, and probably had no noticeable effect on his married life.

The affair had to be kept secret. Reich, who did not meet the Bergs until November 1928, but who observed them with the care of a prospective biographer, was con-

vinced of his accuracy when he wrote of Helene's role as
her husband's adviser and the provider of a peaceful and
comfortable home in which he could work productively.
The truth is, however, that Helene did not accompany
her husband on many of his trips. She was not the critical
adviser of the working composer; as the letters indicate,
he rarely discussed his music with her, she carefully observed his privacy, and she was not even fond of a good
number of the compositions. If her homemaking and her
organization gave "the artist the peace and comfort of a
relaxed home life," why did Berg worry so regularly
about his wife's health and nerves, and why was she so
often gone to take the cure at spas? The most surprising
thing is that the façade of the happy marriage could have
been maintained for so long and that there was not more
speculation about Berg's relationships with other women.

Surely members of Berg's circle knew that he was involved with Hanna Fuchs; Alma Mahler Werfel would
have been aware of it, and the letter-receiver Klein, and
perhaps some other students who were also friends. It is
possible, though, that they did not know the real nature
of the liaison, or how important it was to Berg, or any of
the details surrounding it. Berg expressed his love in the
most passionate and lasting way he knew how: through
his music.

It took fifty years for anyone to notice. The story of
the love affair in music finally provided the clue to some
of the most tantalizing and important works of twentieth-century music, with scholars cast in the unlikely
roles of detectives. Musicologists and students of Berg's
music had long been suggesting that there was more to
the Lyric Suite than immediately met either the eye or the
ear. Adorno called the string quartet Berg started to write
in November 1925 a "latent opera." Did Berg's student

and biographer know that his description of the music
was fully correct, or was he, like others, speculating, on
the basis of the sounds' suggestiveness? George Perle, the
eminent American specialist on Berg and his music,
guessed that parts of the work were "literally programmatic" long before he knew the actual program, and concluded that the Lyric Suite was "a wholly subjective psychological drama."

Perle and Adorno may have suspected that Berg had
had an actual program in mind for the Lyric Suite, but
the possibility also had to be considered that the string
quartet was simply so rich in associations that it tempted
its hearers to jump to conclusions, whereas, in fact, Berg
had written no more secrets into the music than he had
put into the Chamber Concerto. (Or, perhaps, there is
more in the Chamber Concerto than anyone has yet discovered.)

Scholarly curiosity, persistence, and luck led to the re-
opening of the mystery of the Lyric Suite. The chief de-
tective was Perle, though Hans Ferdinand Redlich, one of
Berg's biographers, had, for the most part unwittingly,
laid the early groundwork, and Douglass M. Green, a
British musicologist, uncovered a myriad of clues at the
same time Perle was moving to complete his investiga-
tion and close the case. Perle's report was first printed in
the June 1977 issue of the Newsletter of the International
Alban Berg Society.

After Redlich's death, in 1968, the letters and documents in his library pertaining to his studies of Berg's life
and music were turned over to Perle, representing the International Alban Berg Society. Among the papers were
letters indicating that the manuscript of the Lyric Suite
was not, as Redlich had originally assumed in his biography of the composer, in the possession of the heirs of the
dedicatee, Zemlinsky. It was, rather, totally unaccounted

for, lost. Attempting to answer questions that had arisen about possible errors in the published version of the score, Redlich pursued the trail of the manuscript; he remembered Mrs. Zemlinsky's once having mentioned to him over the phone something about a woman named Hanna Werfel-Robettin in connection with the Lyric Suite. But the name meant nothing to Redlich and, since he did not suspect that there was a mystery, he did not follow the clue. Mrs. Zemlinsky informed Universal Edition, in January 1962, that neither she nor her husband had ever been in possession of the original score of the Lyric Suite. Helene Berg and Universal asked Redlich to take up the search, but after ten months no progress had been made, and the urgency diminished.

The loss of a manuscript is, unfortunately, not unusual. Several of Berg's major manuscripts, including the original of the Piano Sonata, are on the list of the missing. Often, composers' handwritten copies of their works are lost to fire or flood, auctioned off (sometimes, tragically, page by page), or stored in attics and even libraries or vaults, where they remain, forgotten. The confusion among the principal parties involved in the story of the Lyric Suite manuscript is highly unusual, though, since this valuable relic would have been either carefully accounted for or definitely determined as lost by one among the many who knew of it.

Though Berg had publicly dedicated the Lyric Suite to Zemlinsky, he had given the score to Hanna Fuchs-Robettin, the woman for whom the music had been written. Shortly after Berg died, Alma Mahler Werfel had tried to convince her sister-in-law to return the score to Helene Berg, and had even sent a priest, Johannes Holinsteiner, to act as messenger and protector of the manuscript on its return trip to Vienna.

Hanna could safely display the handwritten version of

the Lyric Suite, for the large manuscript itself had no tales
to tell. The most personal and important of her souvenirs
was a small, printed score of the quartet, which Berg had
prepared especially for her, with the secrets of the Lyric
Suite carefully described on each page. When Perle first
heard of the existence of this annotated score, he thought
nothing of it. Having no reason to suppose that the relationship between Berg and Franz Werfel's sister went
beyond friendship, and, indeed, with no suspicion that
the composer had ever been less than completely faithful
to his wife, there seemed to be nothing intriguing in the
fact that a rich society woman who had been the composer's hostess in Prague had possessed a miniature score.
What could Berg have written in it, beyond his best
wishes?

But when Mrs. Zemlinsky mentioned again in 1976
that she had once heard about a miniature score of the
Lyric Suite which Berg had prepared and annotated for
"Mrs. Werfel-Robettin," Perle could make some important connections. By that time, he had concluded that the
"Mopinka" referred to in Berg's letters to his wife was
actually Hanna Fuchs-Robettin, even though this was not
at all obvious in the unannotated German edition of Helene's collected letters, where, of course, nicknames had
been used without the writer's specifying to whom each
belonged. Perle learned that Hanna Fuchs had died in
1964, and concluded that the score, along with her other
possessions, had probably fallen into the possession of her
daughter, Dorothea. Finally located in New Jersey,
Dorothea did indeed have the small copy of the Lyric
Suite, and was happy to show it off and provide whatever explanations she was able to. She had not paid any
attention to the score, was not concerned with its importance to musical studies, and had never mentioned it because no one had ever inquired about it.

The pocket-sized score showed Berg's complete program for the Lyric Suite, addressed to the woman who was the music's heroine. It was this small edition that divulged the secrets of the music, told of the connections that put Berg, Hanna, and her two children into every phrase and every line of the string quartet, and made Adorno's "latent opera" into one of the most fully explained pieces of program music in the literature — complete with suggested but unsung words.

The ninety-page first edition of the Lyric Suite in small score dates from 1927; Hanna and, later, Dorothea had kept the annotated copy in excellent condition. Berg wrote on eighty-two of the ninety pages and underlined passages in the preface written by Erwin Stein. The composer's flair for fine graphic detailing made his annotations particularly striking to the eye; he used three different colored pencils and inks to distinguish among the various lines — mainly red (for himself and Hanna), but sometimes blue, and, in the second movement, where both children figure as characters, some green. Over his name, which is printed beneath his picture on the inside of the score, Berg signed simply "Alban"; at the top of the title page, he wrote his own dedication, "For my Hanna." In Stein's remarks to the effect that Berg's use of the twelve-tone systems of composition in the Lyric Suite were far from limiting or restricting, but, in contrast, allowed the composer "the freedom to quote from the opening bars of *Tristan und Isolde*" in his string-quartet score, Berg underlined "allowed the freedom" and drew an arrow from those words to the open space below, where he wrote:

It has also, my Hanna, allowed me further freedoms! For instance, I have secretly inserted our initials, H.F. and A.B., into the music, and have related every movement and every section of every movement to our numbers of fate, ten and twenty-three.

I have written these letters and numbers, and much that has other significance, into this score for you, for whom, and only for whom — in spite of the official dedication on the following page — every note of this music was written.

May it be a small monument to a great love.

The "official" dedication to Schoenberg's teacher, Zemlinsky, might seem odd, were it not for several important connections. Berg used a quotation from Zemlinsky's Lyric Symphony in the Lyric Suite's fourth movement, an "impassioned adagio." The line from Berg through Zemlinsky to Mahler's *Das Lied von der Erde* is important, for the Lyric Symphony, like *Das Lied,* is a symphony of songs for voice and orchestra. The phrase Berg borrowed for the Lyric Suite originally carried, in Zemlinsky's version, the words *"Du bist mein Eigen, mein Eigen"* (You are my own, my own). The use of the word "Lyric" in both titles is no coincidence. Zemlinsky's importance as the man Schoenberg called his own mentor cannot be minimized, nor can Zemlinsky's participation in helping Schoenberg set up his school in 1904, or the older man's continuing interest in the work of Schoenberg's students, especially Berg. But the crucial point, the inspiration for the dedication, was probably the fact that it had been Zemlinsky who conducted the Three Fragments from *Wozzeck* at the International Society for Contemporary Music Festival. It was this concert that had led Berg to Prague in May 1925, when he met Hanna Fuchs-Robettin.

The first references that Berg pointed out to his "one eternal love" in the annotated score involved certain aspects of the music of which analysts had long been aware but were unable to explain with accuracy, as well as other details that the composer himself had alluded to or explained specifically in his own writings on the Lyric Suite. The use of Berg's number of fate as a governing force behind both the formal plan of the work (including the number of measures in several of the six movements) as well as the choice of tempos (even though numerical considerations occasionally made it necessary for Berg to use metronome markings that do not reflect the custom-ary sequence of speeds) had long been evident; so was the realization that another number had been at work in the score, acting with equal strength. But it had been impos-sible to tell whether that second important number in the Lyric Suite was a five or a ten, and there was virtually no possibility that anyone would ever guess that number's significance.

It is surprising, however, that no student ever hap-pened to come across the truth behind the use of the ini-tials. There was a precedent for this kind of reference, of course, in the Arnold Schoenberg–Anton Webern–Alban Berg motives from the Chamber Concerto. In the Lyric Suite, it had long been obvious that the central pitches, the signposts that supported the twelve-tone rows, were A,B,H, and F (again using the German notation system, in which a *B* is the English B-flat, and *H* is the English B).

The analytical notes Berg wrote for the violinist Rudolf Kolisch when the latter's string quartet was preparing the work for performance do not attempt to hide this impor-tant four-note cell. Berg said that he had altered the twelve-tone row in four of the movements (the alle-gretto, allegro, the trios of the presto, and the largo) by changing the positions of certain important pitches. "The change is not important to the line, but is important to the character — 'suffering destiny' [*Schicksal erlei-*

dend]," the composer wrote. He had connected each movement to the next not just by using closely related tone rows, but by repeating one element — a theme or an idea — from the preceding movement in its successor, even if that necessitated changing the mood of the musical fragment; the last movement, then, specifically refers back to the first. Such references, Berg told Kolisch, were not mechanical; they occurred in respect to the "larger development (mood intensification) in the Suite as a whole ('suffering destiny')." Here again, the composer left hints to an inner meaning, but nothing more specific than the recurring phrase "suffering destiny."

In the miniature score, however, Berg drew vivid pictures of the key roles played by the initials. On the page facing the first of the six movements, a "jovial allegro," the composer wrote, "This first movement, whose almost inconsequential mood gives no hint of the tragedy to follow, continually touches on the keys of H and F Major. The principal theme [the twelve-tone row that, with variations, governs the whole work] is likewise enclosed by your initials, F and H." The basic row also leaves no doubt as to its affinities to special keys; the first half outlines the F Major triad, and the second half moves into H or B Major.

The second movement, an "amorous andante" (even the titles Berg wrote into the score for the six movements suggest a dramatic plot), is the most fully annotated in Hanna's dedication copy. First, "To you and your children I have dedicated this rondo — a musical form in which the themes (specifically your theme), closing the charming circle, continually recur." The very fact that this movement is a rondo is significant, since Berg associated the form first with the manly drum major in *Wozzeck* and then with the composer Alwa Schoen (who

represents Berg himself) in *Lulu*. Perhaps Berg envisioned himself watching over the play of the Lyric
Suite's rondo, which is dominated by Hanna's principal
subject, charmingly interrupted by the themes identified
with her two children. The boy, Munzo, arrives first in
the music, his theme marked somewhat vaguely with the
words "not unintentionally, but with a gentle Czech
touch." For decades, string players read and honored the
composer's instructions without fully understanding that
the Czech accent was to reflect the fact that Munzo was
enrolled in a Czech school and spoke the language more
fluently than he did his parents' German.

And it seems perfectly obvious now, with all the clues
laid out, that Hanna's daughter, Dorothea, known by her
friends and family as "Dodo," would be represented musically by repeated C's — do-do. Dodo appears in the
rondo, according to the score, "threateningly, but she
isn't to be taken too seriously . . . on the contrary, *dolcis-
simo.*" Dodo and Munzo play, but soon the children
begin an argument that has to be mediated by their
mother. The second movement evidently ends with
Dodo's running away, since her "do-do" call in the last
bar must come, Berg said, "as from a distance." There
are 150 measures in the rondo-andante, fifteen times
Hanna's number ten, and sixty-nine in the opening alle-
gretto, or three times Berg's own twenty-three.

At the beginning of the third movement, Berg wrote a
date to spur Hanna's memory: "May 20, 1925," five days
after he arrived in Prague to be the Fuchses' house guest
during the festival week, a day or two after he realized
that Helene was indeed not going to join him there, and
doubtless the day he and Hanna admitted that there was
something special between them. The movement begins
as an *allegro misterioso,* "because," Berg wrote, "every-

thing was still a mystery — a mystery to *us*." Here the
four initials intermingle in a recurring cell; Berg marked
the four notes H-F-A-B for Hanna every time they appear. The *allegro misterioso*, with its whispering passages,
explodes into a *trio estatico*, "suddenly breaking out,"
"always as loudly as possible" — but, Berg reminded
Hanna, "repressed, still with mutes" on the strings to
dull and reduce the sound. In this trio, which serves as
the contrasting section of the traditional scherzo movement, the first violin recalls the final line of Marie's Lullaby from *Wozzeck,* where she sings the words *"Lauter
kuehle Wein muss es sein"* (It must be pure, cool wine) —
the clearest reference in the quartet to Hanna's husband,
by way of his wine cellar, which had so impressed Berg.

After their first encounter, the couple had to separate
and face the world as though nothing had happened;
when the *allegro misterioso* music reappeared at the end of
the third movement, Berg wrote only, "Forget it — !"

They could not forget, however, and the fourth movement, which takes place on the following day, according
to the composer, is an *adagio appassionato* in which A.B.
and H.F. engage in canonic, round-robin musical play.
The lyrical references begin then, first in small bits that
only suggest *Tristan,* and soon, in the viola and the second violin, in the clear quotation of the phrase from
Zemlinsky's Lyric Symphony, which Berg marked so
that Hanna would be sure to realize who was speaking;
first he "sang" the line "You are my own, my own," and
then, a few measures later, she "sang" it back to him. At
the climax of the movement, Berg instructed the players
in the quartet to let their music sound *pesante e ritenuto*
(peasantlike, and holding back), then he added for Hanna,
"and fading — into — the wholly, ethereal, spiritual,
transcendental — " with his words carefully spaced over
the musical lines.

The last two movements of the Lyric Suite for string quartet, the fifth and sixth, held even more remarkable and revealing secrets. The fifth is a *presto delirando* with tragic *tenebroso* interruptions; here, Berg wrote in words that run through the whole movement, with special graphic significance, and with exactly twenty-three words in the first section of the original German (ending with "days," before the four instruments in succession introduce the motive of the "racing pulses"):

> This *presto delirando* can be understood only by one who has the foreboding of the horrors and pains which are to come — Of the horrors of the days, with their racing pulses . . . of the painful *tenebroso* of the nights, with their darkening decline into what can hardly be called sleep — and again the day with its insane, rapid heartbeat . . . As though the heart would rest itself — *di nuovo tenebroso* with its heavy breathing which can barely conceal the painful unrest . . . as though for moments the sweet comfort of a true, all-forgetful slumber sank over one — . . . But already the heart makes itself felt . . . and again day and — so — forth — without ceasing — this delirium — without end.

Berg needed the dots and dashes of punctuation to string his words out under the music in Hanna's score. The feeling of sinking into forgetful sleep for eternity recalls the last movement of Mahler's *Das Lied von der Erde* once again.

The mystery of the sixth movement had been discovered even before Perle unearthed the annotated score, though its significance became clearer in the context of the Lyric Suite's complete story. Working among the vast collection of papers from the Berg estate in the Austrian National Library in Vienna in 1976, Douglass M. Green studied several sets of preliminary sketches for the Lyric Suite and an early manuscript of the entire work, which, according to the composer's widow, had been

the music Berg had frequently used when he coached rehearsals of the piece. As he had done in making the annotations for Hanna, Berg worked in this score with a variety of pencils and inks, using the visual contrasts to trace
his use of the tone row in its various versions, evidently
to satisfy a private urge to make sure that every appearance of the row was complete and accounted for. Berg's
study score was not complete; the first, second, fourth,
and fifth movements were nearly finished in this draft,
but the third movement and the finale had not yet assumed their final shapes.

Green wrote that he had spent several hours studying
the composer's maps of his twelve-tone rows before he
realized that words had been written below various lines
in the last movement. The handwriting, definitely Berg's
own, was hard to read (as the composer's always had
been), and, to increase the challenge, the text was
sketchy, with some words abbreviated and some omitted
completely, giving the impression that the composer had
been experimenting and that the words, at that point, at
least, were meant for no other eyes but his.

Nevertheless, the text fitted the melodic lines precisely,
and, by making out what words he could and searching
through books of poetry, Green finally identified the
words as the sonnet "De Profundis Clamavi" from Baudelaire's *Fleurs du Mal,* in the Stefan George translation
into German. George's poem, which is more than translation but less than an adaptation of the Baudelaire, can
be rendered in English as follows:

> To you, my only dear one, my cry rises
> Out of the deepest abyss in which my heart has fallen
> There the landscape is dead, the air like lead
> And in the dark, curse and terror will rise.
> Six moons the sun stands without warmth.

Through the other six, darkness covers the earth.
Even the polar lands are not so barren
No brook or tree, nor field nor flock.
But no terror born of man's brain can approach
The cold horror of this icy star
And of this night, a gigantic chaos!
I envy the lot of the most common animal
Which can plunge into the dizziness of a senseless sleep . . .
So slowly does the spindle of time unwind!

These are the words than run through nearly all of the finale of Berg's Lyric Suite, the "suffering destiny," *largo desolato*. This is not a suggested text, not merely an idea, but a design that was actually realized to fit syllable by syllable into the quartet. In the instrumental score there is no line that can actually be sung (the singer would have to have a range of nearly four octaves), but one could easily be extrapolated. It was Perle's guess that Berg would have had nothing against a performance of the finale with the vocal solos, but that he knew it was out of the question because of the necessity of keeping secret both the program itself and his relationship to Hanna.

Somewhat more skeptically, Green hypothesized that Berg had merely been "toying" with the possibilities of adding a voice to the quartet, and that if he had ever been serious about including the text in the final version, mention of the possibility or plans would have been found in his letters of the period. It is, however, important to remember that Schoenberg had added a singer at the end of his own String Quartet Number 2, and the Lyric Suite is Berg's own second quartet. Furthermore, the odds against Berg's rhythms and melodies' having happened by chance to fit George's translation of the Baudelaire poem are overwhelming; the correspondence had to be of the composer's own doing, and it would have had to be

in Berg's mind from the beginning of this work on the finale. The sonnet could even have been the impetus for
the whole work, even though he probably realized all the
while that the music could never be performed with the
words. In Hanna's copy of the score, Berg wrote the
name of the poem, its author, and its translator, called attention to the crucial placement of their initials, and
pointed to the integral use of the *Tristan* motive. Only at
the very end of the movement, and thus at the end of the
whole work, does Berg fail to identify the A-B-H-F cell.
The "spindle of time" had unwound; Berg wrote that the
viola line, which trails the Lyric Suite off into eternity
(again in the manner of *Das Lied von der Erde*), was "dying
away in love, yearning and grief — "

The discovery of the Baudelaire poem also helped to
explain the use of the quotation from *Tristan*. Although
there was nothing unorthodox or suspect about Berg's
paying tribute to Wagner in this manner, the full meaning of the reference is revealed in the combination of the
opening motive from the opera and the eighth line of the
poem, "No brook or tree, nor field nor flock," and the
accompanying feelings of loneliness and desolation and
hopelessness.

There are only a few other things that need to be said
about the Lyric Suite. It was the first major work in
which Berg used Schoenberg's method of composing
with twelve equal tones, and it was based on a peculiar
series discovered by Berg's student Fritz Klein (who received Hanna's letters to Berg), which incorporates all
possible intervals; the chord made from stacking up all
these notes came to be called the "mother chord." Berg
was working on the Suite during the summer of 1926,
not entirely happily, because the whole Nahowski clan
was about to turn up at Trahuetten, and Alban and He-

lene would have to return to Vienna earlier than they
otherwise might have in order to make their rooms available to the other visitors. Berg told Schoenberg that this
imminent return to the city had put him under great pressure to get the Lyric Suite sketched in full so that he
would only have to fill in certain portions when he was
back in Vienna, where creative work was difficult for
him.

He documented at length the experiences he had had in
his first lengthy excursion into the methods of composing
with twelve tones: "Slowly I am finding my way into
this mode of composition, which is a great consolation
for me. It would have grieved me immensely if I had
been denied the possibility of expressing myself in such a
manner. For I know that, apart from personal ambition
(and idealism), one will compose in this style after all the
piping and doodling of the (international) composers
have long disappeared into limbo."

On a separate sheet of paper, with a number of musical
examples, Berg outlined for Schoenberg the twelve-tone
workings of the Lyric Suite. He had started out in the
first movement using Klein's series, but, as he worked,
he found it difficult to manipulate the row because of its
symmetrical nature: the second six notes are the retrograde of the first six, transposed down a diminished fifth.
In order to give himself more possibilities and variety,
Berg switched the fourth and tenth notes of the series
beginning in the quartet's second movement, and discovered a particularly inspiring group of four pitches at the
beginning of the altered row, which, along with the "initial" sequence, became an important kernel throughout
the rest of the piece. He also took the time to write out all
the possible canons (seventeen of them) that would make
use of this seminal four-note group. "That's why in order

not to lose hope [I've done some] occasional backsliding
into my tried and true free style."

Why did Berg use a row that presented him with problems? It could have had to do with a desire to include
Klein in the Lyric Suite in some way, to thank him for
the use of his post box, whether or not Klein was actually
aware of what use Berg and Mrs. Fuchs-Robettin were
making of his mail service. The seventeen four-part
canons were also a mystery of the Lyric Suite until 1972,
when Dr. Jan Maegaard, a member of the faculty of the
University of Copenhagen, found and documented them
in an article printed in the *Zeitschrift fuer Musiktheorie*.
Having isolated all of the four-voice canons that avoid
parallel motion of voices, Maegaard found that Berg had
decided to use only eleven of them. There are no further
program notes or secrets that have been unearthed from
the canons.

A half-century proved that audiences did not have to
know the inner secrets of the Lyric Suite, or even to understand the use of the twelve-tone row and its subtle, internal alterations, to love the work. The intense lyricism
of the music engages the listener on a level that has nothing to do with counting and ordering pitches; what Berg
called the "mood intensification" (*Stimmungsteigerung*),
achieved by arranging the movements so that the odd-
numbered ones become faster and faster while the even-
numbered ones get slower and slower through the course
of the work, served as the most compelling kind of musical argument, even without text or historical characters.

Berg's second string quartet had its first performance
on January 8, 1927, in Vienna. The composer used the
penciled early version of the score to help the Kolisch
Quartet prepare for the première. Beyond the fact that
the music was "suffering destiny," Berg did not reveal
any personal details when he talked to Kolisch and his

colleagues. He never mentioned that the music he was looking at had words written underneath, never remarked that the *M* which everyone assumed stood for "Motive" also stood for Mopinka.

The Lyric Suite was an immediate success, and when the Kolisch Quartet took it on the road and stopped with the piece in Baden-Baden in July 1927, the response was so warm and vigorous that the work had to be repeated later in the program. At the suggestion of Hertzka at Universal, Berg arranged the Suite's three middle movements — *andante amoroso, allegro misterioso* with *trio ecstatico, adagio appassionato* — for string orchestra. Jascha Horenstein conducted the first performance of these Three Pieces from the Lyric Suite on January 31, 1929, in Berlin. Erich Kleiber took them and the Fragments from *Wozzeck* with him when he introduced Berg's music to America in 1930 and 1931. The excerpts from the Lyric Suite were the first and only work of Berg that appeared on the programs of the elite Vienna Philharmonic during his lifetime. To many, it was the Lyric Suite that proved that there was nothing to fear in music written with the aid of twelve-tone rows.

The intriguing question that remains is how Berg would feel if he knew that the secrets of his Lyric Suite were no longer secret. Most likely, he would be relieved and amused. The composer took pride in the cleverness of his accomplishments, and had to bite his lip to keep himself from bragging. Berg left so many clues that it was only a matter of years until the truth was uncovered; by that time, only the secondary characters in the drama were still alive to see their ancestors' secrets become public.

It was fortunate that the complete story of the Lyric Suite remained shrouded until after Hanna's death, in 1964, and Helene's, in 1976, for not only had Berg con-

spicuously *not* dedicated his emotion-filled quartet to his
wife, but he had also engaged in a degree of musical-
romantic subterfuge. Berg had discovered Baudelaire
for the first time in August 1910, during his days of high
longing for Helene, while waiting nervously and impatiently for her father to consent to their engagement and
marriage. Shortly before he read the prose poem *Le Con-
fiteor de l'Artiste* for the first time, Berg wrote to his future wife about the depth of his reactions to nature, how
he could be overwhelmed and even frightened by it:

> This fear of nature still clings to me, the knowledge that
> great beauty in the natural scene drives me into restlessness
> and dissatisfaction instead of joy. I shun these frightening ec-
> stacies, as I shun sexual or drunken orgies or morphia
> dreams. I escape to my room, to my books and music. I feel
> here that I am in my own element, my own realm; anywhere
> else I might fall ill, and in nature I should disintegrate and be
> submerged . . .
>
> Yet I know that while other pleasures . . . are bad for the
> health and for the soul, those who can enjoy fully the beau-
> ties of nature are benefitting their bodies and their souls. So
> there is one hope I cherish, and that is this: a man, intox-
> icated by delicious wine, leaning in rapture on the breast of
> his beloved, with vine leaves in his hair, is transformed from
> a drunken beast into a sublime singer. A man shattered by
> Mahler's Third Symphony recovers his strength sobbing in
> the lap of his beloved. A rake obsessed with his need for sex-
> ual indulgence looks into the eyes of his beloved and sinks
> back in holy adoration. The morphia addict tormented by
> wild dreams falls into a deep and dreamless sleep when the
> beloved lays her hand on his brow, and from then on experi-
> ences only the good effects of the drug. And I shall one day
> feel the same . . . with Helene, my beloved, at my side.

Only a few hours after he wrote this letter, Berg began
to read Baudelaire's prose poems, a "precious volume,"

and he was struck by the parallels to his own thoughts. Through Stefan George's translations, he was transported into the poet's world, and found that he could not only share the Frenchman's romantic visions, but had actually anticipated them.

He shared his thoughts, his fantasies, and his discovery of Baudelaire with Helene, writing to her frequently in those anxious days while they both waited for her father to announce his decision and bless their marriage. Then, fifteen years later, Berg went back to Baudelaire's words, in George's translations, for the Lyric Suite he wrote to his new love, Hanna Fuchs. And that was not the only occasion on which he recited the same poetry to the two women. In the spring of 1907, just after their first meeting, Berg had sent Helene the letter quoting the Theodor Storm poem that begins, "Schliesse mir die Augen beide." The twenty-two-year-old composer had just set Storm's verse to music in honor of his new love. Eighteen years later, thinking of another woman, Berg went back and reset the same text. Some of the emotional impact of this double setting has been lost by a long-standing confusion as to the date of composition of the first "Schliesse mir" songs. Berg himself contributed to the confusion, probably as a result of carelessness, and not in an attempt to hide the facts or protect his privacy.

The occasion for the joint publication of the two settings of Storm's poem was the twenty-fifth anniversary of Universal Edition, which was celebrated by a special supplement to the journal *Die Musik* in February 1930, the month of Berg's forty-fifth birthday. The composer wrote in the preface:

The twenty-five years of Universal Edition's activity have seen the tremendous development in music from tonal composition to the "method of composing with twelve tones

related only to one another," and from the C major triad to
the "mother chord." It is to the lasting credit of Emil
Hertzka, the director of Universal Edition, that he has followed that musical development from the very start. To him
are dedicated these two songs, settings of the same poem by
Theodor Storm. They are intended to give an example of
that musical transformation, and are published here for the
first time. One of them was composed at the beginning of
the century, the other at the end of the first twenty-five years
(1900–1925).

One of Berg's dates was not accurate. The first setting
of "Schliesse mir" has been traced to 1907, not 1900; on
this point, the composer's memory could simply have
failed him. On another issue, though, there could have
been no memory lapse. The two settings of the same
poem were dedicated to Hertzka and his Universal Edition, but there is no doubt that the second, the 1925 version, was meant as a tribute to Hanna Fuchs and was the
first music Berg ever wrote for her.

The later "Schliesse mir" is, in effect, a study for the
first movement of the Lyric Suite, and it is Berg's first
known excursion into twelve-tone composition. In mid-
1925, after the call went out for works to celebrate Universal's silver anniversary, Berg wrote to Webern that he
had submitted two love songs, "the words of which have
no connection at all with the jubilee . . . The second I
composed up here [in Trahuetten] — my first attempt at
strict twelve-tone composition."

Berg had been seeking, consciously or not, to give the
new twelve-tone techniques his own personal stamp, to
find a way to imbue them with drama. And once Hanna's
appearance introduced new emotional heights and complexities into his life, the use of the novel methods did the
same in his compositions. The 1907 setting of the Storm

poem is old-fashioned and unremittingly tonal. The 1925 version, like the first movement of the Lyric Suite, uses the twelve-tone row associated with Klein, complete with all eleven intervals. The second "Schliesse mir" lasts twenty measures, two times Hanna's fate number. And in the middle, the basic row takes a form outlined by the notes F and H, Hanna's initials.

The influence of Hanna "Mopinka" Werfel Fuchs-Robettin continued to work on Berg and his music, perhaps more than anyone will ever know. From the spring of 1925 until the composer's death, everything he wrote had a connection with Hanna or her family, and she was always in his thoughts, if not actively a part of his life. Another lady had taken Helene's place in Berg's imagination.

Chapter 14

Pandora's Box

BENJAMIN FRANKLIN WEDEKIND (1864–1918), named for a statesman of the country where his parents met and married, grew up with ambivalent feelings about morality. Sex is nature, and nature is truth, he reasoned. But he also knew that sex could mean destruction, disillusionment, and death. The trained, channeled, bourgeois mind, he felt, could not survive against the force of sexuality. Yet that same force which had the power to liberate the human being from the repressions of a hypocritical society would inevitably drag him down. Wedekind saw no satisfactory middle ground, no way to win. He concluded that we all lead ourselves toward doom.

The son of a rich, liberal doctor and an actress, Frank Wedekind was born on July 24, 1864, in Hanover, Germany, after his father decided to return to his native country from wanderings through Constantinople, Palermo, Rome, Paris, and San Francisco. In California, the elder Wedekind had met and married a young member of a German-speaking theater company. Frank was eight when the family moved again, to Switzerland, to protest

Bismarck's policies of postrevolutionary unification in Germany. Private tutors and boarding schools prepared the young man for the University of Lausanne. At the age of twenty, he moved to Munich. Two years later, he was working as a publicist for a soup company near Zurich. He was a wanderer, and it looked as if his life was going to be anything but extraordinary.

But in Zurich, Wedekind began associating with a group of young socialist-naturalist writers, including Carl and Gerhart Hauptmann. Frank told Gerhart the details of his privileged but unhappy early years, which had been marked by family fights of notorious proportions. When Hauptmann indelicately broke the confidence and worked the Wedekind family saga into his early drama *Das Friedenfest,* Frank retaliated with a bitterly antinaturalist tract. Perhaps the rupture was inevitable. Nothing about the fashionable naturalists appealed to Wedekind, whose imagination drew him into the legions of artists, itinerants, adventurers, castoffs, and, especially, children. Until their parents and teachers had the chance to spoil them, children were pure; they lived in a world that had balance. Wedekind coveted that balance and envied the children's world. But, he believed, the rites of puberty always destroyed the balance. Adults, he concluded, used sex as a weapon against youth.

Wedekind exchanged the exaggerations of salesmanship for the artifices of the theater. Lame from birth, he was drawn to athletes and acrobats; he spent six months traveling with a circus troupe through England, Germany, Switzerland, and Austria. With his father's wanderlust and his mother's theatricality, he became a popular star of the first German literary cabaret in Munich, *Die elf Scharfrichter* (The Eleven Executioners), where he sang his own stinging, cynical ballads, accompanying himself on the lute. He found he had a natural talent for acting, and married one of his leading ladies, Tilly Newes.

Wedekind read Strindberg, Krafft-Ebing, Nietzsche, Goethe, and newspaper reports of the exploits in London's East End of a murderer known as Jack the Ripper. Through Hauptmann, he had been introduced to the works of the then-obscure Georg Buechner; Wedekind absorbed Buechner's style and ideas and advanced them toward what we know as the Theater of the Absurd. It was Wedekind who linked Buechner to the twentieth-century avant-garde. The two men's dramas share the feelings of slide shows and side shows. The audience senses isolation: characters talk at each other, to themselves.

Wedekind's first published play, *Spring's Awakening,* appeared in 1891 and disappeared instantly from public sight. Censors prohibited the staging of the play until 1906, and even then its story of children's sexuality had to be diluted and its message adulterated. German audiences at the turn of the century did not want to hear impudent indictments of the ways in which they hid sex from their naturally curious children, no matter how gracefully and lyrically these indictments were delivered. The children's wondrous combination of fear and elation was something that the elders felt they had to squelch. Wedekind's play showed the adults denying nature as they watched the youthful characters die at the hands of abortionists or by suicide, in shame and disgrace.

The thesis of *Spring's Awakening* was naïve. Wedekind had innocently endorsed pure and unashamed sexuality; in 1891 he went to Paris to find and experience what he thought would be an ideal life. He stayed there for two years, following Baudelaire, Verlaine, and Oscar Wilde down the paths of excess and debauchery. Enervated to such a point that he often escaped into periods of extended sleep, Wedekind saw and lived the life of the depraved; he was struck less by the sexual perversions than by the spiritual ones, the living of lies that seemed to accompany physical freedoms. Many years later, in the play *Death and the Devil*, Wedekind had Lisiska, a prostitute, explain what the backstairs life had done to her:

> For God's sake, you must never trust my love! My duty here is to pretend at love. Consider for a moment what it means when suddenly the door is torn open and all at once you must scrape your love together . . . To all who gather here, love is eternal torment, insatiable greed . . . How long my dream of highest bliss has been a land of undisturbed, eternal rest!

And Casti-Piani, the romantic moralist who is a white-slave trader in several of Wedekind's dramas, including the Lulu plays, has found hell:

> What is there left for me when sensual pleasure is only hellish human slaughter . . . like all the rest of the earth! So this is that ray of divine light that penetrates the dreadful midnight of our martyr's existence. I wish I had put a bullet through my head fifty years ago! Then I'd have been spared admitting this miserable bankruptcy of my swindling, stolen-together spirituality.

Wedekind had come to the end of his search, the ultimate in disillusionment and despair, which is worked out on an almost chillingly personal basis through the course of the plays. Even when he successfully managed to fight whatever remnants he harbored of bourgeois conscience, he found that his own sense of self-preservation was working against his desires for self-fulfillment. The forces of sexuality had to be quelled, and only death

was strong enough to confront them. Wedekind named
these forces "Lulu."

During his debauch in Paris, Wedekind had gone to see
a pantomime entitled *Lulu, Clownesse danseuse,* by Felicien
Champsaur. One of its characters was Arthur Schopen-
hauer, coldly and abstractly trying to analyze something
that would not be dissected, but could only be experienced. To make the philosopher look like a total fool,
Lulu merely had to stand up and dance.

Wedekind grasped this idea of sensual lure and ex-
panded it. He saw connections with such contemporary
events as the raids of Jack the Ripper and the cholera epi-
demic that swept Hamburg in 1892. The result was his
"Monster Tragedy in Five Acts" called *Die Buechse der
Pandora (Pandora's Box),* begun in 1892 and finished in
1895. The mythic and sexual implications of the title
were not lost on either author or publisher, and the latter
refused to release the work in its entirety, issuing instead
only the first three acts, under the title *Der Erdgeist (Earth
Spirit),* in 1895. In 1903, a complete edition was prepared,
but, again, only Part I was distributed. The next year,
another publisher risked releasing the second part, Acts
IV and V, of Wedekind's "Monster Tragedy," giving it
the title of the original, *Pandora's Box,* and including a
new opening act, which the playwright provided to make
Part II of his work complete in itself. At once, the courageous publisher and the author were hopelessly entangled
in court battles, all of which were decided against them.

Pandora's Box was banned from public stages, but not
from private ones. And so it was that, on May 29, 1905,
the twenty-year-old Alban Berg was a member of an invited audience in the pea-sized Trianon Theater for the
private Vienna première of the notorious drama, with
Tilly Newes (Mrs. Wedekind) as Lulu, Wedekind himself

as Jack the Ripper, and Karl Kraus playing the role of the black Prince Kungu Poti. Berg already knew the play that had been published as *Earth Spirit,* having read it a few summers before, at the Berghof. But the Kraus-Wedekind production of *Pandora's Box* introduced the young musician to wholly new material in the life of the heroine of the "Monster Tragedy," Lulu.

As fascinated as Berg had been by *Earth Spirit* and the first part of Lulu's story, he was even more engrossed when *Pandora's Box* completed her saga. To begin with, the second part of the "Monster Tragedy" is more interesting than the first; *Earth Spirit,* despite the sexual frankness and social criticism that Berg recognized as being both important and revealing of his era when he read the play in 1903, is only the beginning of Lulu's story, introductory material without crisis or conclusion. Furthermore, Berg matured a great deal between his *Earth Spirit* summer and the night in May 1905 when he saw Lulu's drama played onstage by the playwright, his wife, and the cultural hero Kraus. And though *Wozzeck* had presented itself to the composer immediately as a libretto for an opera, Berg took almost twenty years before deciding to set Lulu's story to music. It was experience, the guilt he doubtless felt as a result of his relationship with Hanna Fuchs, and also the secret passion he felt for the woman who was not his wife and would therefore always be denied to him that, combined, made it possible for Berg finally to deal with Lulu in his second opera, the work that would become his mysterious masterpiece.

And Lulu was irresistible. The plays and the lurid detailing of Wedekind's style presented problems for the composer-librettist, but Lulu herself begged to be set to music as strongly as *Wozzeck* had defied similar treatment. She is still an enigma. Who *is* she, this fascinating character whose stepson-lover will write an opera about her? She has no mother, father, or name; she is called Nellie, Mignon, Eve, and Lulu, and admits to being both all and none of these. She is at the same time pure, unspoiled nature, and the ultimate in degeneracy — a murderess with no remorse, no morals, no feeling for right and wrong, good and evil. She is a snake who lurks, pulsing with venom, lacking any rational comprehension of her own lethal powers. She is a naïve, innocent, comely child, centuries old and newborn, with no past and no future. She is totally free and completely enslaved, victim and victimizer, always the same and always different. She lives for love, but she does not have any sense of love. She is the embodiment of instinct, irrationality, and self-fulfillment. She is beauty; she says she wants to be like nothing else in the world, so she is the epitome of beauty in all its forms — transient, everlasting, delightful, saddening, destructive, and redeeming. There is nothing that can be done to her or about her. She is inevitable. It is not the flame's fault that the moth flies into it and is annihilated.

From Wedekind's "Monster Tragedy" Berg was to draw a libretto that begins with the circus's brawny animal trainer striding out to introduce his players to the audience; this is theater, clear artifice. He deals not in house pets, but in beasts "tamed by superior force of human power": the tiger, the bear, the monkey, camel, earthworms, maggots, crocodile — and, finally, Lulu, the serpent, carried out in front of the curtain dressed as Pierrot.

This is the outfit she has chosen in which to have her portrait done by the painter; as the curtain rises (Act I of the opera), artist and model are alone in his studio. Ludwig Schoen, tiger from the circus menagerie and editor of a newspaper, arrives to deliver his fondest regards to

Lulu, in the company of his son, Alwa, a composer. When they leave, the painter makes a pass at his seductive subject. She tries, playfully, to evade him, then submits, just as her elderly husband, a medical authority named Doctor Goll, forces in the door, sees the lusty pair, and dies of a stroke.

Lulu marries the painter, and her Pierrot portrait hangs in a position of honor in their elegant drawing room, which has been financed through the aid and influence of Dr. Ludwig Schoen (whose title is honorary, not medical). A letter arrives announcing the engagement of Schoen to a rich young woman of society; Lulu had been warned of the impending betrothal, but she is surprised to see it made formal. The doorbell signals a visitor; the painter sees a raggedy beggar and leaves Lulu to receive Schigolch, an aged figure who may or may not be her real father, may or may not be one of her ex-lovers, but is her friend and knows her well. As he leaves, Schoen arrives, and the strength and inevitability of the relationship between Lulu and the editor is made clear. Schoen begs Lulu to stay away from him: "Through me," he says, "you made a good marriage, then another good marriage. Your life is easy. Your husband is doing well, thanks again to my contriving. And if there's more you want, unknown to him, go and take it! But kindly leave me out of your game . . . My wishes are coming true. I am engaged . . . My bride must be brought home to a house without scandal."

Lulu insists that they continue to meet, and, having already claimed never to lie, goes on: "If I belong to one man in this world, then I belong to you. Without you, I should be — I shall not say where. You took me by the hand and led me, you gave me food, you gave me clothing . . . Can you think I would forget all this? Who ex-

cept you in all the wide world has ever paid any real attention to me?"

The painter returns and makes the mistake of asking
what is going on. When Lulu leaves, Schoen tells him —
tells him where his money is coming from and where his
wife spends her free hours. Neither man knows what is
true about Lulu and what is not. They even call her by
different names. But the painter, ruined by Schoen's rev-
elations, shakes hands, excuses himself, and goes into
another room to kill himself.

Another ring of the bell brings Alwa, announcing that
revolution has broken out in Paris. Schoen, worried
about his own future, calls Lulu a monster. "You'll
marry me in the end! Wait and see, Herr Doctor," she
replies.

Backstage at a theater where Lulu is working as a
dancer, she and Alwa share champagne; the poster hang-
ing on the wall is a copy of Lulu's Pierrot portrait. Lulu
wants to see Schoen but also has her mind on the prince,
who wants to marry her and take her away to Africa. As
Lulu emerges from behind the screen where she has
changed into her dancing costume, Alwa is stunned by
her beauty. "I feel something like an icy shiver running
up to my brow, and then downward," she says seduc-
tively on her way to the stage. "Someone could write an
interesting opera about her," muses Alwa the composer.

The prince arrives while Lulu is performing and waits
for her backstage, with Alwa, telling the musician that
Lulu's "body incarnates the joy of life." But the men's
discussion is interrupted as Lulu races in. She has spotted
Schoen and his fiancée in the audience, and cannot go on
with her dance. The editor stomps backstage and orders
Lulu to go on with the show. Left alone with each other,
Lulu and Schoen argue intimately; he is tied to her, un-

able to go back to sit beside the lady he has pledged to marry. Lulu takes advantage of the moment and forces him to write a letter, which she dictates: "I give you my word that I am not worthy . . . of your love . . . Three whole years I have fought to be free to love you, but I have not got the strength of will. I am writing to you at the side of her whom I obey. Forget me from now on."

The parlor in the home of Lulu and Ludwig Schoen (beginning the opera's second act) is more lavish than her previous drawing rooms, decorated in German Renaissance style, with gleaming furniture, flowers, a Chinese folding screen, and, of course, Lulu's portrait, prominently displayed. The first visitor of the day is the Countess Geschwitz, a lesbian in love with Lulu. She appears to leave before Schoen enters, but after Lulu guides her husband into the bedroom, the countess returns — followed surreptitiously by Schigolch, Rodrigo the athlete, and a schoolboy, all of whom have been hiding behind draperies and screens or under tables. The lovers and would-be lovers make themselves at home until Lulu rejoins them; they then have to hide again as Alwa Schoen's arrival is announced by a servant. Alwa has fallen deeply in love with his new stepmother; Ludwig sneaks into the room, to see his son kneeling reverently beside his wife, taking no notice as she smiles at him with contentment and says, "I was the one who poisoned your mother."

Schoen reveals himself and orders Alwa to leave, then moves toward Lulu with a gun in his hand. He insists that she shoot herself, but she tears away from him, saying decisively:

Although for my sake a man may kill himself or others, my value still remains as it was. You know the reasons why you wanted to be my husband, and I know my reasons for hoping we would be married. You let your dearest friends be cheated and robbed by what you made me, yet you cannot think yourself caught in your own deception. Though you have given me your later and riper years, from me you've had youth in flower, as fair exchange. I have not in my life asked to appear in any color other than the one which I am known to have. Nor has any man in my life been led to look on me as anything other than what I am.

Schoen tries to force her hand. She takes the gun, fires five shots into his back, and, as her husband dies, offers herself to Alwa, who was waiting to step in.

Lulu is arrested for murder and sentenced to prison. A year passes, and the richly appointed parlor has turned dusty and grim. Finally, her devotees plot to rescue her from the prison's isolation ward, where she is being treated for cholera. The Countess Geschwitz will trade places with Lulu; she has deliberately infected herself with the disease. Schigolch will lead Lulu over the frontier into exile. Rodrigo intends to marry her then, and train her to become an athlete. But when Lulu stumbles into her house, leaning on Schigolch's frail arm, Rodrigo sees that she has become too weak and thin from her ordeals in prison ever to be of use to his circus act. Since he will not be able to earn money through Lulu, Rodrigo decides to turn her in, perhaps for a reward. He runs off to the police — and suddenly Lulu is her old self, leading Alwa to intone a hymn of praise to her body:

If it were not for your two childlike eyes I look into, I should say you were the most designing of whores and bitches who ever inveigled a man to his doom . . . But under this dress I feel you as a musical form. These two ankles — *grazioso;* this enchanting roundness — a *cantabile.* Then your knees, *misterioso;* and then the powerful *andante* of love's desire. How peaceable and calm the two slender rivals! I feel them nesting, confidently knowing that neither can equal the other's beauty 'til the wild and moody queen of both awakes and the two competitors shoot apart like opposing magnets. I'll sing only in your praises — until your senses grow faint.

It takes no guile for Lulu to convince him to escape with her at once, and as Alwa buries his head in her lap, Lulu asks, "Isn't this the sofa on which your father bled to death?"

Lulu's Pierrot portrait looks down from the wall of a glittery, golden salon in Paris (the opera's Act III), where Lulu, Alwa, Schigolch, the Countess Geschwitz, and Rodrigo are together again, celebrating Lulu's birthday with a nervously gala party; she is now about thirty, definitely aging. Lulu would like to escape from the clutches of her former lovers and start anew, but she is still living with Alwa, who does little more than pimp for her, and she has also fallen into the web of the slave-trading "Marquis" Casti-Piani. The fake nobleman has given her venereal disease and has tricked her out of what money she had left. He is through with her, and plans to sell her to an Egyptian brothel. "I'll go to America with you, or to China," she says, "but I will not let myself be sold. That's worse than prison . . . I cannot sell the only thing I've ever owned." Casti-Piani, Rodrigo, and Schigolch are all trying to live off Lulu, but suddenly word spreads through the room that she has nothing left for them to steal — the shares she bought in the Jungfrau Railway are worthless. Lulu is terrified and talks Schigolch into killing Rodrigo when he keeps a rendezvous Lulu has arranged for him with the Countess Geschwitz at a sleazy hotel. With this accomplished, Lulu can flee to London, followed by Alwa, Schigolch, and the countess, utterly bankrupt, wearing the clothes of the latest servant to become her slave, a young Parisian groom. The crowd

chants, "The whole world loses." The stupidly grinning
groom, wearing Lulu's gown, is arrested.

There is nothing left for Lulu and her retinue except a
squalid attic flat in London's East End, where they cere-
moniously unroll the wrinkled canvas of Lulu's Pierrot
portrait and tack it to the crumbling wall, with the heel
of a shoe as hammer. With a lamp and a bottle, Lulu
begins her career as a prostitute, pimped by Alwa and
Schigolch. Her first client is a silent, poor professor (very
reminiscent in the opera of her first husband). The second
is the Negro, who smashes Alwa's head in rather than
pay money for Lulu's services. Finally, Lulu goes into the
street, looking for another customer. The Countess Geschwitz looks after her, distraught. "From the first day,
she detested me with the depths of her soul. I was nothing more to her than an adaptable instrument, one which
could be used for the basest tasks. I curse my life! I'll
jump off the bridge — what could be colder, the water or
her heart? I could dream until I went under. How often I
have dreamed that she kissed me! I curse my life!"

Lulu returns to the miserable flat with a new client. He
turns his attention curiously to the countess. "She's my
sister," Lulu explains. "She's crazy. I don't know how I'll
get rid of her." They turn toward the bedroom. "Why
are you looking at me like that," Lulu asks anxiously, as
they go into the room. A moment later, a horrible
scream is heard, and on his way out, Jack the Ripper —
whom Berg was to have bear an uncanny resemblance to
Ludwig Schoen — stops to stab the countess, bemoaning
that "people never seem to have a towel about." The
dying Geschwitz calls, "Lulu! My angel! Let me look at
you again! I am near you, I'll always be near you . . .
Eternally!"

Alwa Schoen calls Lulu *"Eine Seele, die sich im Jenseits*

den Schlaf aus den Augen reibt" (a soul rubbing the sleep from her eyes in paradise). It was that description from which Karl Kraus departed in the remarkable speech he made on the night of the drama's Vienna première, which he subsequently adapted for publication in the June 9, 1905, issue of *Die Fackel:*

Eine Seele, die sich im Jenseits . . . A poet and lover, vacillating between love and the artistic design of the beauty of women, holds Lulu's hand in his and utters these words, which are the key to this maze of femininity, to this labyrinth in which many a man lost track of his reason . . . And then, when he has drunk himself full at this sweet spring of corruption, when his fate has been fulfilled, he will find his words . . . in delirium before the portrait of Lulu: "In front of this portrait I retrieve my self-respect. It makes my doom comprehensible to me. All we have been through is so natural, so obvious, as clear as sunlight. Whoever feels secure in his respectability in the face of these blooming, swelling lips, these great child's eyes, full of innocence, this rosy white, exuberant body, let him throw the first stone at us." These words, spoken before the picture of the woman who became the destroyer of all because everyone destroyed her, encompass the world of the poet Frank Wedekind.

And then the mighty double tragedy . . . the tragedy of the hounded grace of woman, eternally misunderstood, who is permitted to climb into the Procrustean bed of the moral concepts of a stingy world. Woman is made to run the gauntlet; woman who was never intended by her creator to serve the egoism of her proprietors, and who can rise to her higher values only in freedom . . .

One of the dramatic conflicts between feminine nature and some male blockhead placed Lulu in the hands of terrestrial justice, and she would have had nine years in prison in which to reflect that beauty is a punishment from God, had not her devoted slaves of love hatched a romantic plan for her liberation, a plan that could never ripen in the real world even in

the most fanatical brain, and that the most fanatical will
could never bring to fruition . . . Now more than before it
becomes apparent that it is Lulu's grace that is the actual suffering heroine of the drama; her portrait, the image of her
best days, now plays a larger part than she herself, and
whereas earlier it was her active charm that motivated the action, now . . . it is the discrepancy between her former
magnificence and her present woe that arouses our feelings.
The great retribution has begun, the revenge of a world of
men that makes bold to avenge itself for its own guilt.

In a loose series of events such as might have been invented by some cheap thriller-writer, the clear eye sees the
construction of a world of perspectives, moods, and jolting
emotions; and "backstairs poetry" becomes the real poetry of
the backstairs, which can only be condemned by that sort of
official weak-mindedness which prefers a badly painted palace to a well-painted gutter . . . In Wedekind's world,
where men live for the sake of thought, there is little room
for circumstantial realism . . . The whole whimsy of naturalism is blown away. What lies above and below a man is
more important than what dialect he speaks . . .

But it is impossible in all seriousness to believe that anyone
could be so short-sighted as to mistake — on account of the
"embarrassing" stuff of the drama — the greatness of the
treatment and the inner necessity in the choice of this
"stuff." To overlook — blinded by truncheons, revolvers,
and daggers — the fact that this sex-murder is like a doom
brought up from the deepest depths of Woman's nature; to
forget, on account of the Countess Geschwitz's lesbian disposition, that she has greatness and is not just any patholog-
ical creature, but stalks through the tragedy like a demon of
un-pleasure . . .

What happens in this drama can be brought to bear as
much on our aesthetic attitude as . . . on our moralistic attitude to Woman. **The question as to whether the poet is more
concerned with the joy of her blooming or with the con-
templation of her ruinous career is one that each can answer
as he pleases.**

Wedekind had made his own personal search for the answer to this question, but he found that the solution, like Lulu, was at once too simple and too complex. In creating the character of Dr. Ludwig Schoen, whose name coincidentally carried such meaning for the composer Berg, the playwright wanted to give him "a spiritually robust and inflexible energy and brutality which . . . comes to grief through the exceptional nature of a primitive woman. I wanted to show how conscious thought, which is always and in all circumstances over-estimating itself, loses in the battle against the instinctive." And yet the matter would not be so easily settled, for it is Schoen, in the figure of Jack the Ripper, who returns and kills Lulu at the drama's end.

And at the opening of *Pandora's Box,* Alwa, the Wedekind–Berg figure, says, "The curse of our young literature is that we are all far too literary . . . Our horizon does not extend beyond the boundaries of our professional interests. In order to get back again on the path to great, imposing art, we would have to move as much as possible among people who have never read a book in all their lives and who are guided in their actions by the simplest animal instincts." Yet Wedekind had tried that very course in Paris, and ended up sick and disillusioned. And Alwa has his skull smashed in by the Negro.

The strange figure of Countess Geschwitz looms large. How does one deal with this woman who is not a woman, this lover who continually offers herself in sacrifice, a person of nobility who is at once above and still inferior to the other characters? Wedekind made her the play's most human and compassionate character, in spite of — or because of — the lesbianism, which was, at the time, considered to be a perversion, to be pitied, feared, despised, but never accepted in polite society. The countess possessed what Wedekind called a "superhu-

man" capacity for self-sacrifice in a context where fools
rushed into the den of egoism. She is, in one sense, freer
than any of the other characters. Lulu rails at her, "For a
man there is not enough in you, and for a woman you
have too much brain in your head. That's why you are
mad."

Just before her death in the play, the countess considers
the possibility of going off to study law so that she can
better help her sisters. Familiar as this may sound, the
issue is not one of women's liberation in the late-twen-
tieth-century sense of the term. Kraus launched an active
defense of prostitutes and homosexuals against the hypocritical forces of law and order. Wedekind might have
agreed with the journalist on a pragmatic level, but his
writings indicate that he considered prostitution to be a
savage kind of moral destitution, and homosexuality to
be an unworkable alternative. When Kraus analyzed the
Lulu drama, he did so from his own viewpoint of woman
as a sex-ruled being, motivated only by desire. He sub-
scribed in part to Otto Weininger's controversial theory
that the Platonic "masculine idea" carried with it perfect
rationality and creativity, but the "feminine idea" was a
wanton and ultimately unfulfillable urge toward sex. But
though Weininger wanted to blame all that was nihilistic
on the "feminine idea," Kraus viewed its accompanying
emptiness and nothingness as a source for creativity in the
masculine mind.

Wedekind's reactions to these much-discussed issues
were more emotional. Where, he argued, was Goethe's
"eternal feminine" and the salvation it had promised to
Faust? What exactly was the distinction between angel
and demon? On the one side, Wedekind envisioned Lulu
as a female counterpart to Faust; on the other side, she
was Don Juan. She could be dealt with only as myth.

Chapter 15

The Studies for *Lulu*

EVEN BEFORE *Wozzeck* brought him fame, Berg had been casting about for a subject for a second opera. He had thought about *Rebels of the Rhine,* by Arnolt Bronnen, and about the famous *Dybbuk* by S. Ansky, which, he decided, would better be set by a musician more intimately acquainted with the Hasidic life than he. He lingered a while on the possibilities offered by *The Grave of the Unknown Soldiers,* by Paul Raynal, obviously tempted to deal once again with war and the military. He told Schoenberg, on January 10, 1927, that he found the Raynal play "real theater and full of poetry. For some time it tempted me very much to make an opera out of it. What do you think?"

Neither Schoenberg nor anyone else thought much of the idea, and Berg became involved in another operatic plan, a setting of *And Pippa Dances,* by Wedekind's old enemy Gerhart Hauptmann. Berg went so far as to make some sketches for a possible *Pippa* opera, but then Lulu came back to haunt him. He could not decide, and wrote to Adorno, on November 30, 1927, that he wanted to begin writing another opera in the coming spring and had narrowed the field of possible subjects down to two, but could not make the final decision between *Pippa* and *Lulu;* he was so taken by both, in fact, that for a time he wanted to plan two operas, and was most concerned about which he would tackle first. Less than enthusiastic about the *Pippa* idea, Adorno cast his vote for *Lulu,* and also suggested another subject based on Hofmannsthal, which Berg vetoed because of his stylish scorn for that author. Yet the composer was still unable to decide in favor of either operatic heroine. The resemblances between Pippa and Lulu are notable; both are crazed, hunted women surrounded by grabbing men. Pippa, the embodiment of beauty, must dance with each of her suitors, and is eventually killed by one of them. She is more of a fairy-tale character than Lulu, though neither is taken directly from life. Like Wozzeck, Pippa exists out of time; Lulu, influenced by historical events, is a prisoner of the late nineteenth century in Germany, and this is at once a strength and a weakness of the Wedekind plays and, therefore, of the opera as well.

Actually, Berg first went after Pippa, and entered into discussions for the rights with Hauptmann's publishers as early as 1926. But after much back-and-forth, the writer's representatives made what Berg and Universal Edition considered to be unreasonable demands: 50 percent of the royalties, 20 percent of the sale of the libretto, and 5 percent of the vocal score.

It was then that Berg looked into obtaining the rights to the *Lulu* plays; and the talks with Tilly Newes Wedekind, the widow of the playwright-actor, who had died in 1918, were much more pleasant. Berg met her in Berlin on October 26, 1928, and was struck by her "completely natural manner, nothing histrionic about her.

She's almost lady-like, in fact, as far as that is possible in these artistic circles!" Berg fervently hoped that he could negotiate for the same very low terms the composer Max Ettinger had got when he had written an opera on Wedekind's *Spring's Awakening* a few years before, and the initial meeting with Mrs. Wedekind ended with the understanding that the arrangements would be made in correspondence between her lawyers and Hertzka at Universal.

After the *Wozzeck* revival performance, Berg had more to report to his wife. He had gone backstage to congratulate Kleiber, who joined the composer and Tilly Wedekind at dinner. The widow's attorney had advised her to ask for 40 percent of the profits on any *Lulu* opera. With a pained expression, Berg made it known that he considered this figure out of the question, and he left, believing that he had aroused Mrs. Wedekind's sympathy and would eventually secure an agreement on his terms.

His optimism turned out to be justified. Tilly Wedekind lowered her initial demand; and she, Berg, and Universal were all pleased with the signed contract. Even during the negotiations, Berg had begun working out a libretto for a new opera called *Lulu,* most likely basing it on the one-play, five-act version that had finally been published in 1913, under the title *Lulu.* But in the final months of 1928, the composer's work went slowly; he had been away from this kind of concentrated work for a long time, and other projects were also on his mind. He had decided to compile the set of Seven Early Songs and orchestrate them for quick presentation. And the success of *Wozzeck* meant continued work and obligations.

From Trahuetten, on June 17, 1928, Berg wrote to his wife that the weather had been dreadful; Helene was lucky to have stayed on in Vienna for a few extra days.

Berg was anticipating a long, hard siege of summer work; the libretto for *Lulu* was progressing very slowly.

The Bergs were to meet in Trahuetten and then go on to the Berghof, which had since been purchased from the Italian by a Doctor Loewe, who knew Berg by reputation. Loewe had put rooms at the disposal of the estate's now-famous former owner. But Helene took ill and went back to Vienna early. Nor was Berg entirely well; his asthma had recurred, as it always seemed to do at the beginning of his stays in the country. He was thinking of Hanna Fuchs-Robettin when he wrote out the words to *Lulu;* his hesitations in dealing with the Wedekind drama had to do with his own heightened sense of morality, of the power of women, of what love could lead one to do. He may have wondered whether he could deal with such a potentially inflammatory subject without arousing public wrath and, perhaps, stirring up the gossipmongers, who would want to dig up everything about him they could find. Deciding to write another opera meant a great commitment of time, effort, and emotion. Deciding to write *Lulu* meant much more: it meant revealing things about himself that might better have gone unrevealed.

But by the end of the summer he had started to compose, and was working out the libretto from an outline, filling in the details as he went along. On September 1, 1928, he wrote to Schoenberg that even though three hundred bars were on paper, he was still less than one-tenth finished, and no amount of self-discipline or satisfaction could make him believe that his plans would not change in the course of creation.

But Berg could look beyond the drama itself for inspiration, and it is not unlikely that Wedekind and Berg both saw Lulu before they heard her voice. The artists of Vienna, Paris, and all the urban centers of Europe had created her image during the first decades of the twentieth century, depicting the elusive "eternal feminine" in the luring guises of dance-hall girls, bedizened madames, murderesses of innocence and men.

The new style had a number of different names; Berg and his associates spoke of *Jugendstil* and then of Expressionism. The visions ranged wildly, from floral chintz curtains to writhing, macabre figures, but they engaged the imaginations of everyone from seamstresses to chiefs of police who were called in to quiet enraged viewers and to calm defensive creators. The artists never did agree among themselves as to what they wanted, but they knew what they were fighting. They shared an overwhelming urge to infuriate the people, organizations, and dictators of fashion who filled Neoclassic palaces with objects whose forms not only hid, but contradicted their functions.

Everyday life in Vienna was riddled with *Kitsch*. According to Egon Friedell, in his *Cultural History of the Modern Age,* the tastes of the bourgeois were worse than eccentric:

Theirs were not living rooms, but pawn-shops and curiosity shows . . . [suffering from] a craze for totally meaningless articles of decoration . . . a craze for satin-like surfaces . . . for silk, satin and shining leather; for gilt frames, gilt stucco and gilt edges; for tortoise shell, ivory and mother-of-pearl, as also for totally meaningless articles of decoration, such as Rococo mirrors in several pieces, multi-colored Venetian vases, fat-bellied old German pots, a skin rug on the floor, complete with terrifying jaws, and, in the hall, a life-sized wooden Negro.

Everything was mixed, too, without rhyme or reason . . . The more twists and scrolls and arabesques there were in the designs, the louder and cruder the color, the greater the success. In this connection, there was a conspicuous absence of any idea of usefulness or purpose; it was all purely for show . . .

Every material used tries to look like more than it is. Whitewashed tin masquerades as marble, papier mâché as rosewood, plaster as gleaming alabaster, glass as costly onyx . . . The butter knife is a Turkish dagger, the ash tray a Prussian helmet, the umbrella stand a knight in armor, and the thermometer a pistol.

The artist Klimt fought this in his own bohemian way; the architect Loos fought more formally and in print, especially in his essay "Ornament and Crime." Loos hated the golden dresses of Klimt's society women, and hated, too, the thousands of ceramic tiles that formed a floral pattern, with stems tracing up and out in parallel motion around the windows, onto the balconies and inside to the wrought-iron elevator gates on the apartment building decorated by Otto Wagner on Linke Weinzeile, the street in Vienna where Johanna Berg lived from 1915 until her death, on December 19, 1926. Loos chose to put his considerable influence behind Oskar Kokoschka, and helped to build his career as a portraitist in prewar Vienna. "My early black portraits arise in Vienna before the World War," Kokoschka later wrote. "The people lived in security, yet they were all afraid. I felt this through their cultivated form of living, which was still derived from the Baroque; I painted them in their anxiety and pain."

Kokoschka painted the intellectuals; Klimt painted socialites. The young Egon Schiele painted himself, narcissistically and masochistically, his figures so thin that the veins seem to leak blood out onto the skin. The images are painful, tortured; bodies are racked, elongated, so that joints no longer fit together. Where Klimt's quickly sketched *Self-Portrait as Genitalia* is amusing, the genitals on Schiele's long-lined images are gaping and red. Eroticism is the focal point, but in Klimt's works it is presented relatively discreetly, and in Schiele's it is uncovered, waiting, almost begging to be abused.

The great changes that took place in the visual arts between the founding of the Secession, in 1897, and Schiele's early death, in 1918, took Vienna out of Hapsburg artificiality and into the hard realism of war. The same kind of pattern had been going on for centuries and would be repeated. In the 1950s, David Riesman called it the switch from other-directedness to inner-directedness; it is what distinguishes the 1970s from the 1960s. Schiele, the 1970s, Lulu — all bound up in images of themselves, pitiless and cold, yet, in a way, sweet and naïve. Complete isolation was impossible; the social circles were too small and too tightly knit for that, not only in Vienna, but all over Europe.

In 1893, the year Wedekind ended his life of debauchery in Paris, Henri de Toulouse-Lautrec produced the poster for Jane Avril, with the aging dance-hall girl kicking up her skirts, her black-stockinged legs repeating the curve of the bass violin in the pit band. The dramatist must have remembered the picture when he thought of Lulu in her dancing costume.

And in Vienna, it is safe to assume, everyone knew everyone else. Alban and Helene Berg were acquainted with Freud, Adler, Loos, Kraus, Klimt, Kokoschka (though after his relationship with Alma Mahler ended, he was less often seen in musical circles). No one who traveled in Vienna's artistic mileux — even someone without Berg's continuing interest in the visual arts — had to look far to find pictures of Lulu. She was Toulouse-Lautrec's dance-hall girl. She was one of Schiele's tormented figures.

Klimt probably came closest to catching the essence of Lulu in his *Judith I*, which was just as rich in implications, as confusing, and infuriating when it appeared in 1901 as Berg's opera *Lulu* was to be more than three decades later.

Haughty and erotic, with her eyes half-closed and her mouth half-open, Klimt's Judith is all flesh and gold, not quite of this world. In the lower right-hand corner, next to her white skin, she holds the head of a dark-haired man — a head that is quite obviously no longer attached to a body. This, of course, led everyone to relate *Judith* to *Salome,* who held the head of John the Baptist; Salome, Oscar Wilde, and Richard Strauss were a fashionable trio of the decade. There is certainly something of the heroine of Wilde's play and Strauss's opera in Klimt's woman, even though the artist made it exceedingly clear that this was indeed Judith by putting her in a gold frame with the large legend "Judith and Holofernes," and by painting in a cone-shaped mountain landscape, fig trees, and grape-vines as site references. This is the Judith of the Apocry-pha, the pious Jewish widow who rid the commander of the Assyrian army of his head. Legend says that Judith took no pleasure in her mission, and Klimt saw to it that she, too, would be decapitated, at least figuratively, by a tight, thick gold collar. But the artist blurred his own vision and seems to have combined Judith's image with the popular Salome's by leaving the impression that this was one of Freud's "castrating females," who was any-thing but destroyed by the horrors she had committed and witnessed.

Judith is older than Lulu, and their circumstances are extremely different. Yet the men who made them sym-bols in their art shared certain concerns about woman's roles in society and mythology and, therefore, their own roles as well. The *Lulu* play runs from the Paris Commune uprisings of 1871 to the siege of Jack the Ripper, in 1888–1889. But Lulu is also a mythic figure; she takes the imagination back to Faust, Don Juan, and the Bible. And she is able — especially with the aid of Berg's music — to transcend the events and the people of whom she was so oblivious up to the moment of her death.

Despite all these ways in which he could see Lulu, then, Berg still had to wait to hear her voice. To this end, he received a push from circumstance and fate. Most of the time, he had written on suggestion, not on commission. He took Schoenberg's suggestions for "character pieces," symphonic works, sonata movements, and the like, all of which he could adjust to his own purposes. Until he was forty-four, however, Berg had never written a work to order.

This undoubtedly had something to do with there having been few, if any, offers of commissions. It took the successes of *Wozzeck,* the String Quartet, and the Lyric Suite to build his reputation to a point where the presence of his name on a program would promise its success. Nevertheless, he was determined to be only a composer — not a performer or a conductor or a peddler of his own music in any public way. Hard as it was from time to time, he was able to support himself in his preferred style by his inheritance, teaching, and the income from Universal, both royalties and payment for small tasks well done. Furthermore, he was temperamentally ill suited to compose to order. He worked too slowly, and his style evolved too quickly, with major changes from one piece to the next. People who commission music expect to have some idea of what they will receive for their money. Imagine the surprise of a patron who had placed an order on the strength of the String Quartet, Opus 3,

only to have the Altenberg Songs arrive in the mail. Who
would have expected the Chamber Concerto to come
from the man who had just finished *Wozzeck?*

Still, with *Wozzeck* came a new sense of ambition.
Berg himself was somewhat ashamed of it; he seemed to
spit out the word whenever he used it in letters to
Schoenberg or Webern, neither of whom had experienced
the kind of success that might have spurred them in comparable ways. Slowly, *Wozzeck* proved to Berg that he
was indeed good, perhaps even great. He went out to sell
the opera, partly because it was his only hope — if he did
not sell it himself, no one would — and partly because he
enjoyed it, loved the applause and the acclaim. Finally,
not without a touch of irony, there came his first commission.

The early months of 1929 were marked by triumphs —
first for the Lyric Suite, then for *Wozzeck* in Oldenburg.
The soprano Ruzena Herlinger heard of Berg's rise and
asked the composer for a concert aria along the lines of
those by Mozart; she wanted a showpiece in several sections of varied characters, designed to leave the audience
breathless at the end, and scored to let her shine above the
accompanying instruments. A Czech-born resident of
Vienna, Herlinger knew Berg's work; she had already
sung the Four Songs, Opus 2, and Marie's Lullaby from
Wozzeck at a private concert in Paris in 1928, accompanied at the piano by the composer himself. And for the
aria, she was prepared to pay 5000 schillings, an amount
that, with no end to *Lulu* in sight, Berg was prepared to
put to good use.

So he moved away from *Lulu* in fact if not in spirit,
and ran through arias and songs by Schubert, Reger,
Mahler, Verdi, and Puccini with Herlinger to get a thorough feel for the character and range of her particular

voice. The soprano sent the composer a volume of Mozart's concert arias to serve as inspiration. But it was Berg himself who suggested the texts for the new aria: poems from Baudelaire's cycle *Le Vin,* which appear as numbers 104 to 108 in the complete *Fleurs du Mal.* From the five poems in the complete group called *Le Vin,* Berg chose three: "The Soul of the Wine," "The Wine of the Solitary Figure," and "The Wine of the Lover," numbers 1, 4, and 5, leaving out the two poems that introduce elements of ugliness and evil. As usual, Berg was working from Stefan George's popularly accepted German translations of the poems, so *Le Vin* became *Der Wein.* The public dedication of the concert aria, which was composed with uncharacteristic speed between late May and mid-August 1929, was to Ruzena Herlinger, who sang the first performance on June 4, 1930, and who retained the sole performing rights for two years afterward. Privately, though, *Der Wein* must have been meant once again for Hanna Fuchs-Robettin. The Baudelaire who was never illuminated for the public in the Lyric Suite had full command in the concert aria, with compliments paid through the poems to the Fuchs family's famous wine cellar.

Berg enjoyed *Der Wein* because he could use both the aria and its soprano as studies for *Lulu.* The opera was to be written using the twelve-tone techniques. So far, no one had tried to use these techniques for such a huge undertaking as a full-length music drama. Berg had investigated Schoenberg's methods in the little second setting of "Schliesse mir die Augen beide" and in the Lyric Suite, but he still was not sufficiently comfortable to be able to apply them to a whole opera. More study was in order, especially because the work would involve a full orchestra, dramatic expanse, and a soprano voice akin to Lulu's own. A close relationship to the wine in "Der Trunkene

im Fruehling," from Mahler's *Das Lied von der Erde,* gave
Der Wein a useful tie to history. But, more important, the
mood of the text was to be youthful and vigorous. Lulu
herself might not have used the same words, but she
could easily have uttered some of the same sentiments. So
the commission gave Berg a chance to find out how his
new heroine might sound.

The composer reversed the order of the last two poems
so that he could build a three-part structure with a return
to the opening mood, in a kind of limited recapitulation.
Concerned about the problems of maintaining a balance
between voice and orchestra while still adhering to the
twelve-tone methods (however casually in places), he
used a large instrumental assemblage with the lightest
possible touch, in ways reminiscent of the Altenberg
Songs and, of course, in anticipation of *Lulu.* The chiming, delicate sounds of the percussion, harp, glockenspiel,
and piano easily suggest the chinoiserie that was so fashionable in Impressionist circles, so even in sound *Der
Wein* is linked to the French and *Le Vin.* More control,
though, is exerted by the basic row itself, in one of the
clearest examples of the way in which Berg could make
the new methods embrace history. All twelve notes have
been dutifully employed and need to be related to nothing but one another, yet they are, in fact, strongly related to the key of D Major or D Minor, and the first five
notes trace, very singably, the do-re-mi-fa-sol of a D
Minor scale.

Berg had successfully incorporated folk- and folklike
tones into the atonal scheme of *Wozzeck,* and quotations
from Wagner and Zemlinsky into the twelve-tone
scheme of the Lyric Suite. As if to prove that he could
still find room for the popular in a plan as formidable as
that of a twelve-tone opera, he tried his hand at jazz in

Der Wein and was sufficiently satisfied with his success to be assured that something similar would be possible in *Lulu*. Stravinsky, Hindemith, Milhaud, Krenek, and Schoenberg himself had already been attracted to the indigenous American sounds that were coming to dominate Parisian night life, and had put them to use, more or less convincingly, in their music long before Berg was converted. It was probably George Gershwin who finally convinced Berg that jazz could be moved out of smoky back rooms; in 1928, the Austrian presented the American with an inscribed copy of the Lyric Suite. Yet Berg was really never totally convinced; in *Lulu,* jazz would play a less than admirable role, representing the sham and low life of the theater. The tango in *Der Wein* is less accusing, but it is also so old-fashioned and stylized a form that it can hardly count as a full endorsement or an attempt to elevate jazz to concert-hall status. Berg did enjoy listening to jazz broadcasts on his radio. But, aside from the problems of timeliness he would have faced had he used something like blues or a Charleston in either *Der Wein* or *Lulu,* he, like Stravinsky, never departed from such standard, even obsolete, jazz forms as the English waltz, tango, and ragtime for his orchestral combos of saxophone, trumpet, trombones (with jazz mutes), side drum, piano, and strings plucked as if they were banjos.

Without trying to take into account the Americanisms hinted at in his references to jazz, language is an issue in *Der Wein,* and one of the major factors responsible for limiting both the success and the acceptance of the work. George's translations from the French, free and generally effective as they are, lack the subtle brilliance of Baudelaire's originals. (A mood much closer to Baudelaire, in fact, can be found in Wedekind's plays.) And although Berg obviously worked from George's versions, he was

also reproducing the French originals. The first printed
versions of the score contained two vocal lines — one for
the German setting of the text, and another to accommodate a French version, which Berg prepared with some
difficulty. Though he knew the language well and usually
enjoyed the challenge of expressing himself in foreign
phrases (with which he could be quite playful), Berg was
not secure enough in his French to master *Le Vin*. After
he had worked on the first setting of the French for *Der
Wein,* he had the opportunity to consult with the conductor Ernest Ansermet during a stay in Winterthur in preparation for the Zurich première of *Wozzeck,* in November 1931, and, as he told Helene, discovered that he "had
composed it quite wrongly, but have now put it right."

Some people think Berg never put it right, and there is
a strange feeling of homelessness in the combination of
words and music in *Der Wein*. Adorno has called the
whole aria "one big *ossia,*" speaking mainly of the significantly different effects of the French and German settings,
as well as of the various times Berg gave the soprano
Herlinger *ossias,* or alternative lines that would suit her
rather limited coloratura better than the principal vocal
melodies, which Berg had designed with an imaginary
Lulu in mind.

In its unbroken span of about fifteen minutes, *Der Wein*
gives only a teasing introduction to Lulu's world, as the
tango sequences hint both at Sunday strollers and sexy
gamblers; and the central scherzo rises to a floating plane
of erotic visions. *Der Wein* may have seemed originally
like a moneymaking diversion from serious work, but it
turned out to be the kind of interruption any composer
can well use. The result was not a success in artistic terms
or with the public, but Berg's work on *Der Wein* made
his return to more important business both easier and less

filled with anxiety. He had reminded audiences that he was still active. He had had a chance to communicate once again with Hanna Fuchs-Robettin through his music — talking, of course, about things he never mentioned to his wife. In *Der Wein,* Ruzena Herlinger was always present. But the more important characters were Hanna and another woman, one who had come much closer to revealing herself by the time the work was done: Lulu.

Chapter 16

The Composition of *Lulu*

As close as Berg was coming to the character of Lulu, he was still not making much progress on the opera. And primarily, it was *Wozzeck* that kept him from work on his next music drama. After a series of appearances at premières of, and lectures on, his first opera, Berg despaired that he would ever manage to complete his second. "I hope I still remember how to compose," he complained in a letter to Schoenberg written in May 1930. "These long interruptions are the cause of terrible doubts in me!"

By the end of the first week in August, however, Berg had a complete idea of *Lulu*'s progress. He outlined it for Schoenberg even though he was still working on the first act. His progress had been slow, he felt, more because of the difficulties he encountered in cutting Wedekind's often wordy detailing than by any problems posed by the twelve-tone techniques. The pruning of the drama into a libretto was, he wrote, going "hand in hand with the composition. As I have to cut four fifths of Wedekind's original, the selection of the remaining one-fifth is caus-

ing me enough trouble. How much more trouble will I
have when I try to adapt what I have selected to the
musical structures (large and small) and to avoid destroy-
ing Wedekind's particular language in the process! . . .
In spite of this clinging to detail, the libretto as a whole
has, of course, been clear to me for a long time."

Berg outlined his scenario, explaining to Schoenberg
how his three acts and seven scenes related to Wedekind,
and showing how, with the help of a long interlude between the two scenes of the opera's second act, he would
give his work symmetry, with Lulu's arrest, imprisonment, and release symphonically represented at its very
center. "The interlude," Berg explained, ". . . is also
the focal point of the whole tragedy. In it begins, after
the ascent of the preceding acts and scenes, the descent of
the scenes that follow, the inversion." Berg had also
firmly decided that the men who visited Lulu in her London attic were to be represented by the same singers who
had been her husbands and victims in the first half of the
opera, in inverted order. At the time of his letter to
Schoenberg he was planning for Lulu to have four visitors in the last scene; later he reduced the number to
three, so the final layout has the Act I doctor (a speaking
role) doubling as the silent professor in Act III, the
painter as the Negro, and Dr. Schoen as Jack the Ripper.
Because of Schoen's prominence in the story, he is the
only one who has the power to end Lulu; he murders her
at her weakest moment, just as she had shot him, off his
guard, in the back.

This was Berg's own contribution to the Wedekind
drama; the playwright had left no indication that actors
should double any roles. These should not be confused
with the other correspondences in the opera, however,
such as the composer's indication that the same singer can

serve as the prince, the manservant, and the marquis; the principal reason here was economic. The only other doubling that is crucial is that of the animal trainer, who sings and speaks the Prologue to the opera, and Rodrigo, both circus performers (as Wedekind had been) and cousins of the strutting drum major in *Wozzeck*. It is interesting to note that Berg specified and adopted a variety of male characteristics, good and bad, when he identified the animal trainer with the composer Alwa and thus with himself through musical quotation. In no way is the author's own role only a high-and-mighty one in this drama. At the beginning of the opera, the animal trainer is the manipulator and the order-giver, but later, as Rodrigo, he is a mass of brainless brawn, a bother to civilized society, and the victim of a plot carried out by the Countess Geschwitz and the weak old Schigolch. And Alwa himself is one of Lulu's more despicable victims, falling prey to his father's wife — who says she was also the murderer of his mother — and lacking the will or the courage to save himself.

The overlapping of identities is only one of the ways in which Berg made changes in the process of cutting down the Wedekind play. The composer's problems here were very different from those posed by *Wozzeck*. The very fragmentation of Buechner's play was an asset; the expanse of the *Lulu* drama presented a problem, and Wedekind had not given any cues to a solution even when he combined into an evening's entertainment the two dramas that had been made out of his "Monster Tragedy." On one level, Berg's challenge was just one of cutting out words, but the difficulties were compounded by Wedekind's details and the melodramatic nature of the story. In *Wozzeck,* the action of each scene could be described in a phrase or two, and the drama depended on

presenting the characters and then moving them into a
critical situation. *Lulu* went from crisis to crisis, the characters changed and developed, the action was consistent
and ever more complicated. It was not enough for Berg
to delete Wedekind's literary ruminations on the nature of
art. The composer had to take the responsibility for what
became a full reworking of the text for the sake of both
timing and singing.

Berg's second opera is, therefore, a significant literary
achievement, on the order of Arrigo Boito's Shakespeare-
based librettos for Verdi's *Falstaff* and *Otello,* even though
the music and the words are marvelously and inextricably
intertwined. Along the way, the composer purposely cut
the text in order to slant some of the characterizations to
fit his own tastes, making allowances also for the em-
phases the music itself would inevitably add. So Alwa,
Berg's onstage alter ego, is somewhat stronger in the
opera *Lulu* than he was in the play, and it is difficult but
possible to forgive Berg's Alwa his sins when the opera
makes it so clear that they have been made in the service
of beauty and art. The banker in Berg's Act III, Scene 1,
is much more broadly and clumsily drawn than he was
in Wedekind's thorough original, and the Countess
Geschwitz is neither as important nor as human in the
opera as she was in the play — perhaps by design, since
Berg did not feel any sympathy toward lesbianism, or,
just as likely, as a result of the trimming and slicing that
had to be done. The Lulu of the opera, however, is even
more provocative and enthralling than her speaking pro-
totype. Wedekind said, "In the description of Lulu, I attached importance to the way in which the words she
speaks paint the body of a woman. With each of her
remarks I asked myself if it served to make her young
and beautiful."

Such a young, beautiful woman suggested herself to opera. And in the process of setting Lulu to music, Berg enhanced her, made her all the more beautiful, dangerous, and mythic. *Lulu* is more old-fashioned than *Wozzeck,* despite its use of the twelve-tone techniques of composition. *Lulu* is every bit as much a singer's opera as *Il Trovatore;* it is filled with arias, duets, clearly demarcated set pieces, after which the audience may applaud — *must* react — just as they would applaud the lion tamer and the tightrope walker in the center ring. In describing the character of Wozzeck, it would not mean very much to say that he sings in a high baritone. But it is absolutely central to Lulu's personality that she is a high coloratura soprano. She must be able to soar to a high D and stay up there. She must be able to project the lithe purity of a child, for her tones have to float much as her spirit does, in an unreal world of dream and illusion.

Similarly, the Countess Geschwitz is a dramatic mezzo-soprano with a voice down in her practical, low-heeled shoes. Dr. Schoen is a *Heldenbariton,* a heroic baritone, mature and intelligent, able to rally his forces and strength and finally to overpower the supernatural force that is Lulu. Berg called Alwa a "young heroic tenor" in the score, perhaps flattering himself and the character with the "heroic," but still putting Schoen's son in his place in the hierarchy. The man who sings the roles of the animal trainer and Rodrigo should be a "heroic bass with *buffo,*" able to match Schoen and Alwa with his vocal ring, but parading around in a way the gentlemen would never try. None of the roles is easy. Every one of them is gratifying to the good voice, however; a superb vehicle for the artist who has mastered substantial musical and dramatic demands.

Berg had taken a procedural hint from Schoenberg,

who reported in 1931 that some of the text to his own
opera, *Moses und Aron,* had not been finally determined
until the music itself was being written. But some decision clearly had to be made far in advance. Berg wrote to
Webern in June 1928 that he was trying to deal with the
question of applying twelve-tone techniques to a full-
length opera, and had concluded that it would be to his
advantage to use as many tone rows as he found necessary to sustain the dramatic tension. Although such a
solution was unorthodox, it did not contradict Schoenberg's rules. And eventually Berg found a way to maintain the theoretical purity of construction with only one
row, while, at the same time, giving himself opportunities for variety. In the end, he did use a number of different rows and arrangements of chords, but all of
them — with one notable exception — derive directly (if
not always obviously) from the row assigned to Lulu herself. The one exception is the appearance of Wedekind's
own Lute Song in Act III, Scene 2, in tuneful tribute to
the playwright. It is an unexpected introduction of the
mundane, which has an effect as mysterious as any con-
jured by the more sophisticated sounds and techniques
that have gone before. The Lute Song leaves the impression that the outside world has become fully as strange
and as terrifying as the inner one, the world of the spirit,
and, indeed, that the distinctions between fantasy and reality have faded.

The basic row had to be Lulu's; she is the one from
whom the whole drama flows. Her line of pitches (B-flat,
D, E-flat, C, F, G, E, F-sharp, A, G-sharp, C-sharp, B)
is paraded by in full dress for the first time in the famous
song in which she fully identifies herself, according to the
score, "in the tempo of a pulse beat . . . in a determined
proud manner" in Act II. Then, by subdividing the

twelve notes of Lulu's row into four groups of three, Berg arrived at a quartet of chords to signify Lulu's portrait in the Pierrot costume, which plays a role in the opera quite as important as any of the living characters, and which, more than any of the people who are being carried down in Lulu's wake, symbolizes days that were and things as they might have been. Melodies derived from the various voices in these "portrait chords" stand for Lulu in her relationship to the painter and his work, her innocent beauty as well as her powers of destruction. These work neatly into singable, scalelike arcs.

By repeating Lulu's basic series and skipping first one note, then two, then three, and so on, Berg charted the row he would assign to Ludwig Schoen. Repeating the series again and again and pulling out every seventh pitch, the composer assigned a row to Alwa. The countess's basic set, similarly derived, was worked into a pentatonic system (based on the interval of the fifth), which harks back to the musical traditions of ancient Greece and the Isle of Lesbos. By filling out the countess's chords into clusters of tones, Berg characterized the rowdy harshness of Geschwitz's opposite, the athlete Rodrigo. A creeping, chromatic series full of half-steps and scored like chamber music would represent Schigolch, showing both the careful, rheumatoid way in which the old man moved and his highly suspect nature. No lesser character is ignored; every bit of the music — with the exception of Wedekind's song — derives from Lulu in a manner that can be drawn in intricate charts and also has both formal integrity and symbolic import.

But even this was not enough for Berg. The rows shape the individual segments, but they do not govern the final piecing together. That had to be done on a larger scale; the material had to be formed in such a way that it would be more directly apprehended by the listeners than would the eternal and eternally subtle repetitions of pitches.

And here Berg's solutions, derived through the greatest exertions of both imagination and experimentation, were nothing short of amazing. They combine with the text to create an aura that makes *Lulu* one of the striking musical and dramatic achievements of the twentieth century. *Wozzeck,* with its self-contained, almost independent scenes, could be built from self-sufficient forms — dances, inventions, a sonata-symphony. But *Lulu*'s working-out had to be different. Instead of "character pieces," the characters themselves had to be extended through the whole length of the drama, distinguishable and always changing, interrelating, working on one another until the final, gory dénouement, when only Schigolch, the thinly scored chromatic scale from which everything comes and to which everything in music — even *Lulu* — must return, remains. *Lulu* lived in its characters, so each of them, except the essential Lulu herself, took on a characteristic form, the significance of which depended on the role's importance in the drama. Only Lulu was chameleon enough to be part of all of them; only Lulu was strong enough to reign over each of them.

Doctor Schoen took as his signature the most important formal product of Western musical tradition, the sonata, which carries with it all the implications of history, breeding, cultivation, and also operates with a dynamic subtlety very much akin to Schoen's own. Like the good doctor, the sonata is expansive, and it develops, in stages, through much of the opera's first act, beginning partway into the second scene, when, as Schigolch leaves, Schoen turns to Lulu and says, "If I were your husband, this man wouldn't be allowed over the threshold." Lulu casually reminds him that it is all right to use the informal *du* when addressing her; they're alone, after all. And with the aid of the sonata's development, Schoen tries in vain to extricate himself from Lulu's web.

Berg told Webern about the sonata in a letter of July 23, 1931: "The finale of Act I . . . is a development and recapitulation of a sonata movement whose exposition and reprise have occurred much earlier. Now the difficulty . . . is to work the music, which is conditioned by musical laws, into the Wedekind text, which is determined by dialectic laws, make the two coincide and span over it the powerful arc of the action."

The sonata's development is precipitated by dramatic events: the death of the painter, Lulu's exerting her hold on Schoen, and the interference — or attempted interference — of the suitor, the prince. The themes, working like Wagnerian *Leitmotiven* for love and fate, but actually functioning in structurally crucial positions, tell just as much about Lulu's relationship with Schoen as the words do. At the same time, Berg's hierarchy of rhythms — again the use of the *Hauptrhythmus,* as in *Wozzeck* — insidiously suggests violence and destruction whenever it appears. The principal rhythm in *Lulu,* starting out with a dotted note and ending with two short punctuating slaps, begins to claim the ear at the first death (of Doctor Goll) and finally dominates so forcefully that, by the end, it is the pulse of the whole saga of denigration and decay.

Complex character that he is, Schoen is also treated to two other important, though shorter and less distinct, forms: He is an arioso (a style midway between recitative and aria) and a full-fledged, five-verse aria, both of which represent climactic slowings of the dramatic pace. As one might anticipate from their names, which are duly recog-

nized in the score, these are old-style set pieces, connected to the historic opera styles, in which the recitative
advances the action while the arias, ariosos, and so on
allow the characters more time for private introspection
and public vocal display (as in the works of Mozart and
Handel). Schoen's arioso, a monologue, comes near the
beginning of Act II; he and Lulu are married and, looking
around his heavily magnificent parlor, he muses, "So it
has come to this. The plague is here. Thirty years I've
labored and this is my life at home — the life I have
chosen . . . Has madness come and conquered my reason already? All filth — all filth."

Schoen's aria sets off Lulu's own coloratura *Lied* just
moments before she shoots him. The aria comes at the
wildest and most hopeless point in their relationship; his
verses are constantly separated and interrupted by the
various hangers-on who await Lulu's favors. "You
wretched thing, you were sent to drag me through the
gutter to the grave," he rails at his wife in a *tempo furioso*.
"Off with you, or by tomorrow I will be insane and my
own son will be lying murdered." Lulu suggests the possibility of divorce, but Schoen cannot and will not hear of
it: "The final insult! So tomorrow another man would
pursue his path of pleasures where I have shuddered from
horror to horror, with suicide to haunt me and you un-
scathed! Why should I divorce you? What does divorce
mean when two people in a lifetime have grown
together, leaving each a half-person?" Berg's music leaves
no doubt that Schoen is already aware of who that next
man would be. Someone else, in fact, has already begun
to take over in the music along that "path of pleasures,"
and the man is Schoen's own son, Alwa.

But Alwa, despite his dramatic musical conquest even
before his father's death, is a much simpler, shallower

character than the elder Schoen, and his characterization
in the opera is therefore based on an older, more straightforward musical form. Alwa is a rondo; the fact that he is
his father's son is well accounted for in built-in relationships between the two men's identifying rows and by
compatibilities in their respective forms, but the composer's relative youth and sexual eagerness give him a less
dramatic nature than his sire's. Alwa's theme music has a
minor-key flavor and a sweetness that make it especially
memorable in the opera's two large love sequences.
Alwa-Alban, like the rondo, keeps returning to the same
issue, Lulu's beauty. As Berg told Reich, "The artist sees
Lulu as she must be seen, so that one can understand
that — despite all the frightful things that come about
because of her — she is so beloved."

Alwa's large rondo carries through Act II, Scenes 1 and
2; its expanse is nearly as great as that of Schoen's sonata,
but the rondo does not give quite the same impression of
scope and breadth, and its building blocks tend to be
smaller. The official end of the rondo leads into one of
the opera's most important passages, Alwa's Hymn, a
parallel to Schoen's aria. Here the composer identifies
himself again, as if it had not been enough for him already to have said that an interesting opera could be written about Lulu while the orchestra played the opening bar
of *Wozzeck*. In the Hymn, Alwa-Alban brings in Hanna
Fuchs-Robettin with a map of her Lyric Suite; the musical movements mentioned in the text outline the sections
of the string quartet that was written for Hanna — the
grazioso ankles, the *cantabile* roundness, the *misterioso*
knees, and so on. And with this Hymn, Alwa has become excited to the point where he would follow Lulu
anywhere, even over the frontier. The harp's glissandos
suggest that somewhere there may be a heaven.

With Lulu reigning over the whole opera, and with

Alwa and Schoen having established their importance
with the dominating sonata and rondo, the interlude between Scenes 1 and 2 of Act II signals a recapitulation.
This is where Berg intended to place the silent film that
would show Lulu's path from arrest to escape. The idea
was intriguing but not practical. Too much action had to
be fitted to too little music, and, furthermore, the film
would have to be acted by the same people who were
doing the singing onstage, thereby necessitating a new
movie for each cast. The *ostinato* interlude is an expansion
of the *allegro misterioso* of the Lyric Suite. It is a rush to
replay everything that has gone before, and, at the midpoint, over an insistently repeating figure that harks back
to the chiming, low C-sharps of the piano's mysterious
entrance in the Chamber Concerto, the music turns on itself, goes into retrograde, and repeats, in the manner of a
palindrome. Lulu's luck has reversed and is running out.

The downhill slide after the midpoint of the interlude
parallels the rise in the first four scenes of the opera. In
Act II, Scene 2, Lulu is married to Alwa in the same
room with the same hangers-on as in Act II, Scene 1. Act
III, Scene 1, brings back the theatrical gaiety and frivolity
of Act I, Scene 3, in the dance hall, though in the later
scene there is nothing but the sad fate of shares in the
Jungfrau Railway to tie the utterly surreal action down to
earth, and Lulu must deal with the slave-trader, Casti-
Piani, without the upper hand she had over Schoen in
their letter scene. Act III, Scene 2, returns to all the
themes that were introduced as Lulu began her ascent, finally moving into the coda of Schoen's sonata as Jack the
Ripper comes in to claim another victim.

The secondary characters have been woven into the
whole with great individuality, but in the smoothest
ways possible. Without commanding forms that take
over the musical development, they appear either as part

of a larger unfolding or as brief commentaries. The countess is always accompanied or introduced by the Impressionistic pentatones; Schigolch is chamber music, intense and private.

Berg made sure that no one would miss the secrets he put into his second opera. Like *Wozzeck, Lulu* is painstakingly annotated, not just at the junctures of the larger structures (sonata, rondo), but down to the smallest details. Canons and variations are marked, as are the inflections of the voices in the segments of melodrama. With *Wozzeck,* Berg felt the need to act as the "ideal producer," as well as the composer. He did the same with *Lulu,* cramming the score with so many instructions, warnings, guidelines, and vivid descriptions that it would seem impossible for one production or performance of the opera to differ noticeably from any other. Fortunately or unfortunately, this is not the case. Some stage directors have seen fit to alter Berg's instructions — for example, by not having singers play two roles, as with Schoen and Jack the Ripper — thereby causing dramatic confusion.

The musical richness of *Lulu* is such that it is impossible to trace every reference and link. The most obvious ones — the quotation from *Wozzeck* when Alwa thinks about writing an opera on Lulu; the listing of the movements from the Lyric Suite — merely hint at a hoard of others, those found and others still waiting to be uncovered. The maze of musical connections is overwhelming. The structural implications of Berg's first opera were simple in relation to those incorporated into his second, where even the very existence of the twelve-tone methods of composition carries its own set of implications.

But does all this matter to someone spending a night at the theater?

Lulu is a sufficiently theatrical opera to carry an evening as sheer drama. From the moment the animal trainer begins to introduce the circus, the acts never stop parading by. As long as the audience can understand the words — and here, as in few other operas, it is imperative that the performance be in the vernacular or that the listener have prepared himself thoroughly — the compelling nature of the story guarantees excitement.

It is helpful, however, to know more. In the Prologue itself, which was the last part Berg wrote, the orchestra gives a quick insight into the characters of the circus by identifying them with animals: Lulu with the snake; Schoen with the tiger; the countess with the crocodile; Rodrigo with the bear; the marquis with the monkey; Schigolch with the vermin; Doctor Goll with the reptiles. The animal trainer himself takes Alwa's music — that is, Berg's own — leading the audience into the opera with virtuoso control. He begins to speak with bravura, then adjusts his pace to the rhythm of dancing and gambling from the Paris scene (III, 1), and begins to sing. As the themes from the opera gradually file by, he fills out his tones to full voice until he is singing a rich *cantabile* for Lulu — he is already in love with her. Then, like the interlude in Act II and, indeed, like the whole opera, the animal trainer does a turn-about and retreats into his speaking voice. The effect is dramatic; the force is also structural. Anyone who has not already familiarized himself with the themes of the individuals has no hope of learning them from this parade. But that is also not the point. The essential unity of the opera works on the subconscious of even the least tutored listener, much as Lulu worked on the souls of her victims. Without quite knowing why, though they sensed they were doomed, they could never leave or forget her.

Chapter 17

Touring

SUCCESS, that welcome companion, can also be distract-
ing. In the years of work on *Lulu,* Berg no longer
had to copy or arrange scores for Universal Edition; the
publishers were paying him a monthly stipend. Nor was
he working as unpaid secretary to Schoenberg; even the
teacher recognized that his student had gone beyond that
point. By now, Berg was one of the most acclaimed of
living composers, and his next opus was eagerly anticipated. The people who now had the power to separate
Berg from the piano where he composed were primarily
those who wanted to hear him talk about his music, or
who wanted to perform it; and, like most artists, Berg
was delighted to have a public whose requests he could
oblige.

In the summer of 1930, when his musical thoughts
were entirely with *Lulu,* he treated himself to something
he had coveted, a car of his own. He named the Ford the
"Blue Bird" and drove it with his characteristic combination of fussiness and gusto, keeping track of mileage and
routes on detailed charts, and dressing for the occasions
when he would take to the road.

In October 1930, Berg told Erich Kleiber, who had just returned from presenting his music in New York, that he had made headway with both the opera and the car: "I have brought *Lulu* a large step forward. My Ford, however, progresses faster and higher (sixty miles per hour and mountain roads up to six thousand feet!). But how high and wide will you have brought things in New York!!!"

Berg was in the comfortable position of being able to bargain in his own interests for the world première of *Lulu,* even though he was not in a position to say exactly when that event might take place. The composer who vividly remembered worrying that *Wozzeck* would never be behind the footlights had promised his incomplete second opera to Kleiber in Berlin, but then Leopold Stokowski entered the bidding, after leading the extremely successful first American performances of *Wozzeck* in Philadelphia and New York, in 1931. Berg felt no great urgency to make a choice. The opera was not close to being finished, and it was pleasant to have options.

Schoenberg, too, was being relatively gentle. Berg told Helene in September 1930 that he had received one of Schoenberg's "nicest letters," full of thanks and appreciation for a canon and poem Berg had sent as a birthday tribute and in honor of the fiftieth anniversary of the Frankfurt Opera House. The older man was especially pleased by Berg's musical and textual references in his four-voice canon to Schoenberg's opera *Von Heute auf Morgen,* which was first performed in Frankfurt in January 1930. But the canon was a modest gift compared to what was to come. For his sixtieth birthday, in 1934, Schoenberg would be receiving the dedication to all of *Lulu*.

While he was speeding with the Ford and *Lulu,* Berg

was also watching clouds gathering on the horizon. He watched the papers and followed the German elections, in which the Nazis became the second most powerful party in that country. Sensing something ominous in the air, Berg continued to insist that he was an *Austrian* composer, but he felt that this might soon be an unenviable position in Vienna, no matter how distinguished the tradition of the Austrian musical past.

In fact, he had never felt that he was appreciated in his native country, and he had to travel abroad to find the recognition that was important — if not, indeed, essential — to his sense of well-being. He did finally win the Arts Prize of the City of Vienna when the State Opera produced *Wozzeck,* but this was faint praise for an opera already well established on the international circuit; and this prize, like so many similar awards, came a decade too late to have any real effect on Berg's career. He was more pleased when, in January 1930, he was nominated to the Prussian Academy of the Arts. Webern wrote him a teasing letter about his "academic" successes, and, calling himself an "academician," Berg admitted that "it pleased me very much, especially on account of Vienna, that is, of Austria, which, as is well known, has virtually overloaded us for years with honors and appointments."

The last remark was, of course, facetious. It was in Germany in general, and in Berlin in particular, that Berg was most honored. He received overtures for a teaching job in Berlin but, despite Schoenberg's positive urging, Berg never expressed the required eagerness, fearing that the responsibilities of formal teaching and the time involved in moving to a new and foreign city would hinder his creative progress. Lacking an official affiliation, he kept in touch with colleagues who were not close personal friends by serving on juries, panels, and festival ad-

visory committees all around Europe — but not, of
course, in Vienna. He enjoyed the meetings. From the
sessions of the jury of the International Society for Contemporary Music in Zurich, in 1928, he wrote to Helene,
"The first session was in French spoken by Casella with
an Italian accent, by Volkmar Andreae with a Swiss, by
Dent with an English and by Jirak with a Czech accent."
Later that same year, the Society for German Music in
Duisburg prevailed on him to judge among fifty operas
submitted to its competition. This was the kind of honor
he found he could live without, and he told Schoenberg
that the process of checking through all the full scores,
vocal scores, and librettos had been "like cleaning a
sewer!"

He swore he would never judge again, but was lured,
without much reluctance, to serve on an ISCM panel in
Cambridge, England, early in 1931. The trip to a new
country via Ostend and the Channel appealed to him, and
it began with some unexpected excitement. Just west of
Linz, only a few hours out of Vienna, Berg left his fur
coat and bags in his compartment and walked to the
train's dining car for a cup of tea. The waiter made a
comment about being off to Paris; the dining car and the
front half of the train, it turned out, were going to
France, while the back half, including Berg's compartment and a newly added dining car, moved from Linz
through Passau to Ostend and England.

The composer was dumbstruck. "Can you imagine my
horror?" he asked Helene in a letter. "Without luggage,
ticket, passport, hat or coat, speeding on to Salzburg and
Paris." He found out that the actual point of branch-off
was at Wels; the train he was supposed to be on would be
making a brief halt there, but the Paris-bound train
would not. His best solution, according to the guard, was

to go on to Salzburg, then make arrangements to rejoin
his luggage in Passau, where it would have been removed
from the other train. Berg was in a state of "helpless
fury."

Then he plotted his course. It was worth the fine, he
decided, to do what was strictly forbidden and pull the
emergency cord, forcing the train to stop at Wels, where
he could wait for the right train. As he saw the station
approaching, he pulled "a whistle that lasted for ages; the
train braked and stopped . . . I got out proudly and
hurried to the station — behind me, the shocked train
people; coming toward me, the excited station people
. . . The train went on to the left, I paid the fine, and
soon my train showed up. I jumped on quickly (nobody
had missed me) and soon we went on to the right."

In a few minutes, Berg was happily resettled, amused
by the incident and even exhilarated by all the excitement
he had caused. But Helene was not amused. She had been
quite shocked at the thought of her husband's causing
such an uproar, but he continued to tell the story of
stopping the train, obviously relishing his own temerity.

All in all, the trip to England turned out to be one of
the most pleasant of his career. He found the crossing
from Ostend wonderful: "I dozed off in the fresh air, sitting in my coat on the open promenade deck, right on
the roaring sea . . . The sun is shining and in the distance
England's white chalk cliffs are gleaming."

He was to be a guest in "a genuine old English country
house," and was shepherded around by the ISCM's president, Edward Dent, a professor at Cambridge, "like a
kindly nanny." Cambridge, Berg decided, was "the odd-
est of towns," and though the food was occasionally
good and always plentiful, "the pheasant tastes exactly
like a turkey or a chicken," he concluded. But one of his

lasting impressions came from dinner in Trinity College hall, "among dons and undergraduates."

Always given to worrying, and not particularly fond of the inconveniences of travel, Berg tended to document the homely details of his journeys in his letters to his wife, and sometimes neglected the splendors. But the trip he made to Brussels, in February 1932, for performances of *Wozzeck* and the Chamber Concerto was particularly well reported in all its aspects. Once again, he was traveling without Helene and feeling somewhat sad and lonely. "Journeys for art mean nothing to me anymore," he wrote. "I would like to travel with you for pleasure as we're used to from our motoring." In fact, the Bergs never did travel extensively, not even on business, though he planned many trips in his imagination along the roads he saw from the windows of the train. On the way to Brussels, some of those roads appeared to be somewhat fuzzy, since Berg had broken his glasses. By this point in his life he was quite myopic, but was too vain to wear his glasses as often as he should have, and never left them on in front of the camera.

As the train crossed into Belgium about eighteen hours out of Vienna, Berg noticed the dense morning fog and made note of the dirt. "The countryside looks muddy and rather neglected, and in the towns everything is gray and shabby — in short, just the opposite of Germany." Arriving in Brussels in midafternoon, he was taken to a "modest but excellent" hotel near the theater, where, to his great delight, he discovered the range of the inexpensive French hors d'oeuvres. "Everything in Brussels reminds one of Paris: the indescribable mass of *brasseries,* cafés, cinemas, cabarets, the night life, the speeding taxis, and so on."

In light of the cheap and excellent food, the vitality of

the city, and the possibility of musical successes, Berg tried to persuade his wife to join him. Even though the first performance of *Wozzeck* would not be a "top event," and the king himself would not be in attendance, he wanted Helene to see the city and share his excitement. But she did not make the trip, either because she thought it would be too expensive or because she simply did not want to leave Vienna. Berg told her he felt as if it was all he could do to "complete my sentence of three more days" alone. *Wozzeck* had a "very great success," he reported to his wife in a telegram, and his series of diarylike missives ended curtly: "Thank you for your letter. I still can't see why you wouldn't come. I'd thought over my suggestion and the 'dream,' however short, would have been worth it. These are my last greetings from Brussels."

This *Wozzeck* trip, like all the others, was part of the business of the arts, a business full of conflicts and a necessary evil that could, if a composer was lucky, have some ameliorating side effects, such as new food and pleasant companionship. Very often, Berg had good luck. In a way, he was one of the last of a breed —world-famous *only* as a composer. Stravinsky was, too, though he was also pianist, conductor, and, with Robert Craft, eventually a writer. For his never having had to divide his interests and become a professor or a conductor, Berg had a handful of people to thank, most of all, Emil Hertzka at Universal. When Hertzka died, Berg spoke at the memorial service held in Vienna's small Musikverein hall on June 20, 1932. He talked of the accomplishments of Universal under Hertzka's guidance and traced the progress that had been made since the days when works by Bruckner, Mahler, and Schoenberg had been considered too radical for public performance. To some extent,

Berg was overstating the case; the works of Schoenberg had never reached the point of being considered "safe" in the same way as those of Bruckner or Mahler. But he did not exaggerate Hertzka's influence when he said that, in their concentration on the financial aspects of business, publishers often qualified as "enemies" of the arts, whereas Universal under Hertzka had been one of the great friends and supporters of the avant-garde of musicians. "Of the few friends that we living composers have," Berg concluded, "Hertzka was the greatest."

The friends were fewer and fewer. This kind of unsettled life, no matter how pleasant on some days, was limiting Berg's productivity. He had always managed to get most of his best musical work done during summers out of the city. But now, with fame calling him all over the Continent, Berg was turning peevish. And the political situation was looking worse and worse. Also, it was hitting home. The Bergs' financial situation was still secure, but not as certain as it had been, and there were signals to make them fear that it could worsen. So, in the summer of 1932, Helene sold her parents' estate at Trahuetten, and the couple began the search for a quiet place of their own in the country. They found a house in November of that year at Auen, on Lake Woerther, near Veldin. The previous owner had allowed the villa to fall into disrepair, so the Bergs could afford a larger place than they might otherwise have hoped to buy with the money they had to spend. Besides, to many prospective buyers, the house looked gloomy, surrounded as it was by dense clumps of trees that kept the sun from shining in. Hidden away in the forest, the new home was christened the Waldhaus (Forest House), and in April 1933 Helene went off to make it habitable while Berg and *Lulu* kept company in the city.

She faced all the predictable problems of unsatisfactory workmen, bad plumbing, and intolerably slow progress; and for almost two months, her husband sympathized in his letters with her problems and raged at the weather, the contractors, and the house itself. But by June, Alban and Helene were together in the refurbished home, insulated from the city, neighbors, and cold. As Berg reported to Webern, they were sure they had done the right thing. Berg was able to work again, and his thoughts were much more tranquil than they could possibly have been in Vienna. He wrote to Schoenberg, in December 1933:

> We are really still here in this wilderness, surrounded by snow and ice already for two months. Besides my work on *Lulu,* we are encumbered with all the small and petty worries of such a life, as for instance . . . which farmer sells the driest wood, or whether or not the pipes are going to freeze tonight, or whether we shall risk a little trip to Klagenfurt or Velden for the luxury of a warm bath, and so on . . . [Yet] I would rather be here than in Vienna, for only in this way can I find the concentration for composition. You will not be surprised that we describe our self-imposed exile as a "concentration camp."

With the Waldhaus comfortable even in winter, residence on Trauttmansdorffgasse became more the exception than the rule. Berg could work at peace in a house that he owned, and the pleasure he derived from being master of his own estate, however small, kept his mind away from the moral and political turbulence in the outer world. Since 1930, when the Nazis began their march to power through Germany, Berg had been increasingly concerned, predicting grimly that both he and Austria would fall to "complete ruin." He diligently followed the news, but the true urgency of the situation does not seem to have struck him until early in 1933, when Adolf Hitler became chancellor of Germany and raised the specter of the Anschluss, the unification of Austria and Germany, by treaty or by force. Berg, always reminding himself and whoever would listen that he was an Austrian composer, traveled to Munich, the city Hitler had named capital of the Nazi movement, on February 25, 1933, to be a judge at a convention of the Allgemeine Deutsche Musikverein, which fell at the same time as the Faschung, the loud and wild Mardi Gras festivities. He arrived only to find that a masked ball was taking place throughout his hotel, so he went for a beer to the nearby Café Luitpold, which was hardly any quieter. "One thing has become clear to me," he wrote to Helene. "We can never on any account ally ourselves with a people like this. True, they are a mixture of the North Germans and Austrians, but only a mixture of the disgusting traits of both races. They have none of the attractive qualities of the Berliners or the Viennese." Before he left the café, Berg was witness to a brawl between the doorman and a would-be customer. The establishment, Berg found out, was supposedly "Jewish," but "among all these thousands of people I haven't seen a single Jew — and more's the pity," he wrote to Helene.

By February 28, Berg had come to terms with even more political realities. "The Nazis have to be taken so much into account that even Schoenberg has dropped out, and also non-German names like Paul Pisk and Jelinek, who in different circumstances would certainly be honored. But please, keep this very much under your hat, and don't mention it to anybody," he warned Helene, as if he had discovered something of which no one else was aware.

Berg's spirits and his sense of humor were lifted, tem-

porarily, when he was a guest of honor at the Music
Congress held in conjunction with the first Maggio Mu-
sicale in Florence, late in April 1933. Austrian pride took
precedence as he wrote about Italian folk music to Helene:

> In Italy they are just discovering Richard Strauss. Not so
> surprising: a people whose primal instinct is for noise can't
> be as advanced musically as a people with primal instincts for
> melody or for rhythm. The most melodically-inclined people
> are the Austrians, whose primitive music (yodelling) is melo-
> dious. The people with the best rhythmic sense are the Rus-
> sians, or, perhaps, the Hungarians.
>
> You have only to hear a folk melody here. First condition,
> as loud as possible; second, rhythm; melody non-essential.
> Three or four notes are enough, taken up and down the
> scale.

When Berg returned to Vienna, the possibility of
teaching in Berlin arose once more, this time through the
recommendation of the composer Paul Hindemith. The
offer was never tendered officially, but Berg thought it
might actually come, since Schoenberg was no longer in
Berlin (having been dismissed by the Nazi Ministry of
Education). What Berg intended to do was to use Berlin's
offer as a lever to get a similar request from the Vienna
State Academy of Music. This also came to naught, however, and Berg was soon to find out just how far the
Nazis' influence had spread.

On May 17, 1933, he heard the official party line at the
opening ceremonies of a Brahms festival in Vienna, and
reported to Helene:

> Wilhelm Furtwaengler actually delivered the major address,
> which depressed me all day long. It was a Nazi-inspired
> speech on German music, which, he implied, had found its
> last representative in Brahms. Without mentioning any

names, he betrayed the whole of post-Brahmsian music, especially Mahler and the younger generation (like Hindemith). There was no reference to the Schoenberg circle as even existing.

It was horrible having to put up with all this and witness the frenzied enthusiasm of an idiotic audience. Idiotic not to realize how the Brahms choral songs which followed made nonsense of Furtwaengler's tendentious twaddle.

Berg did not object to Brahms, but he was angry and hurt that the cultural administrators of music would imply that nothing had happened in music since the turn of the century. The Nazis were doing their best to eradicate all traces of the Schoenberg circle, which was not particularly difficult since the school itself had dissolved, the students had separated, and Schoenberg was homeless. On July 6, Berg sent to Webern a letter he had received from Schoenberg, with the remark, "What a fate! Now at the age of almost sixty, expelled from the country where he could speak his mother tongue, homeless and uncertain where, and on what, to live." After months of dislocation and spiritual torment, in October 1933 Schoenberg moved to the United States. He stopped in New York and then settled in Los Angeles, where he joined a large and congenial group of fellow expatriates and taught first at the University of Southern California (which now houses the American Arnold Schoenberg Institute), then at the University of California at Los Angeles. Neither Berg nor Webern ever saw him again after he left for the United States. Schoenberg died in southern California in 1954, having outlived both of his most famous students.

The departure of the master was difficult for everyone. Webern, dreadfully poor and politically naïve, had affiliated himself with the Nazis for the purpose of getting

work. Berg, who was more than willing to prove his
Aryan ancestry with documents he always carried with
him, despaired at the persecution of his friends and colleagues, but never considered emigrating. At the Waldhaus, he was protected from the worst of the political
turmoil. He recognized that Schoenberg had had no
choice but to leave Germany and Austria forever; he and
Webern both worried about the fate of their mentor, if
not about the fate of the millions of other Jews who were
dislocated and suffering.

Through Reich's publication, 23, Berg tried to stage a
protest against the way Schoenberg had been ignored in
his own country (though he was welcomed as a celebrity
in New York), and against what he considered to be the
warped values in Austria "at a time when the Walters and
Hubermans are being celebrated and made into martyrs
. . . It is not enough that one knows . . . that Schoenberg is one of the hundreds of Jewish artists who have
fled to America. One has to make plain that what has
long been due has finally happened, because Schoenberg
is free."

It looked for a short time as if Hindemith would be in a
position to help Berg find a teaching position, but any
help the older composer could have offered would have
come too late. Within a matter of weeks after he met
Hindemith and his wife at the Brahms festival, Berg's
music was proscribed throughout Nazi Germany as decadent and degenerate. For a man who had just bought a
house and sunk thousands and thousands of schillings
into making it habitable, this meant ruin. At the beginning of 1933, Berg could have reasonably counted on a
steady or increasing income; by the middle of that year,
he was all but wiped out. Contracts for performances of
all of his works across Germany had to be canceled. The

value of the Austrian currency once again began to vacil-
late; then it sank precipitiously. Berg had already missed
the first deadline he had set for himself to finish *Lulu,* and
the 1932–1933 season had passed. Now it began to look
as if the opera might not be allowed onstage even if he
were to finish it, in the greatest haste.

One possibility was to sell the three volumes of the
manuscript score of *Wozzeck* for some quick cash. In his
letter of December 1933, written from the Waldhaus to
Schoenberg in America, Berg asked whether there might
be a purchaser for *Wozzeck* among his teacher's new ac-
quaintances. Shortly, the score had a safe new home in
the Library of Congress in Washington, D.C., thanks to
Carl Engel, director of the library's music division and a
long-time admirer of Schoenberg and his circle. It was
the first time Berg had sold one of his scores since the Society for Private Musical Performances had held its fund-
raising auction of waltz arrangements more than a decade
earlier. And even then, the buyer had seen that Berg's arrangement of Johann Strauss had been returned to its
young adapter.

Despite *Lulu*'s indefinite future, Berg plunged energetically ahead on the opera during the winter of 1933–1934,
his first at the Waldhaus, and seemed very satisfied with
his progress. He categorically refused to admit that *Lulu*
might not be performed. In the last week of February,
Helene went off for one of her cures, this time to luxuri-
ous Bad Gastein, near Salzburg; Berg wrote to her about
his work and about a broadcast he had happened to hear
on Radio Munich on February 22, 1934: "Another, rather
more pleasant *Gaufuehrer* spoke, with effusive friendliness, about the advantages of a reconciliation between
Austria and Germany. Not a single word of hate. Then
there was some music from the 'Fuehrer's native land';

very clever, for it was the real Austrian music . . . Our
own government seems to be remaining quite cool."

There was an undercurrent of anxiety, however, since
Berg noted in the same letter to Helene that Alma Mahler's home in Venice would be their choice for a "refuge,
in case we have to clear out of here — though I consider
that quite out of the question." The country air was filling him with energy, and he could also report to his wife
on the conditions of their country robins and titmice. A
nearby farmer had asked the illustrious new resident of
Auen to compose a four-line motto for a local choral society; Berg had no interest in socializing with his rural
neighbors, and, on February 24, he wrote facetiously to
Helene that he already had two lines: "Auen Village
sweet and kind/Can gladly look up my behind." To
pick up the mail and break his working routine, he drove
the car when the roads were clear and took the bus to
town on stormier days. His work went well, and on February 26 he wrote of a "quiet confidence — it really looks
as if everything will stay quiet, for the moment anyhow.
Mainly because of the Austrian-Italian-Hungarian alliance, which is growing firmer."

He wanted Helene to come home, but she stayed at the
spa until the third week in March. Meanwhile, the spring
thaw came, the problems posed by the musical setting for
the character of Countess Geschwitz were solved, and the
end of the opera was in sight. Erwin Stein had agreed to
make the piano score of *Lulu,* and though Berg considered allowing concert societies to schedule unstaged performances of the work, he still felt that the world première would somehow take place on the stage of a
German opera house, and that "friendly foreign countries," including England and America, would quickly
pick up the opera from there. He wanted to take a day or
two to drive to the spa to visit with his wife, but she did

not invite him, so he took the sun on the porch of the Waldhaus and went to the cinema in town. He was lonely, but his life had fallen into a rather pleasant routine.

A letter from Erich Kleiber put an end to Berg's solitary relaxation. Kleiber asked Berg to send him a final libretto for *Lulu* immediately, which presented many more difficulties than the conductor might have anticipated, since the libretto was not fully written. Berg bought some paper and got out the typewriter, knowing that even if he did manage to finish the estimated 150 pages of text in time to meet Kleiber's deadline, the libretto that was presented to the authorities in Berlin would be by no means the final one. The principal effect of Kleiber's request was to raise Berg's hopes and confirm his belief that he would see *Lulu* first performed in Germany, and that was enough to put him in good spirits despite the literary task before him.

At the end of March, Helene came home, spring arrived for good, and Berg's work went so rapidly that he could write important words to Webern on May 6, 1934: he had at last completed the first round of composition of *Lulu*. But the accomplishment had not brought the relief he had anticipated. Parts of Act III were still barely sketched in, and Berg had to face the prospect of going back and starting again from the beginning, to overhaul the huge work. "A project that stretches over years, and a musical development that cannot be quite completely surveyed right from the start forces one to look back over it, and there will be things that will have to be touched up," he wrote to Webern. He expected the revisions to take two or three weeks, and planned to start the instrumentation in June, with the prospect of finishing the rest of the polishing in time for *Lulu* to be presented in the fall.

Not only Berg, but Kleiber, too, was hoping for the

première of the opera in the 1934–1935 season. The conductor suggested that Berg make contact with the men who made the musical decisions in Nazi Germany, the Berlin Opera's general manager, Heinz Tietjen, and conductor, Furtwaengler, who now had the title of Staatsrat, or Official Councilor, on matters musical. Charged with fighting "cultural bolshevism" and "decadent modern art" of the type Berg composed, Furtwaengler either could not or would not accept *Lulu* for the German stage. Berg wrote to his "dear friend" Kleiber, on May 29, "The die is cast. I have just received a very charming letter from Furtwaengler which makes it plain that in view of the 'seriousness of the present situation' there is no question of the work's being accepted for performance in Germany. Although he knows (and 'one' knows) that I am a German composer and an Aryan, and also that Wedekind is a German and an Aryan."

Berg neither gave up nor expressed any anger, and in the same letter he told Kleiber that he had decided to herald the opera *Lulu* with a concert suite, a symphony lasting about twenty-five minutes, which would be published immediately by Universal. "Do you have the desire and the opportunity and the courage to do the first performance?" Berg asked.

Kleiber did, but he faced more difficulties than Berg expected, or even imagined. He had to fight for the *Lulu* Symphony just as he had fought for *Wozzeck,* and this time, the première of a work by Berg actually did mean the end of his tenure in Berlin. Berg finished the suite in July 1934, and the first performance took place on November 30 at a concert of the Berlin Staatskapelle in the old opera house Unter den Linden, where *Wozzeck* had had its première nine years earlier. Lilly Claus was the soprano soloist; Kleiber conducted.

Just as Marie represented *Wozzeck* in the Three Fragments from that opera, one character was singled out to represent Berg's second work for the theater on concert stages, and that character, of course, had to be Lulu. Whereas the Fragments concentrated exclusively on Marie, however, the *Lulu* excerpts surrounded the heroine with shades of her lovers. Like the opera from which they were drawn, the *Lulu* pieces are complexly populated, more complicated than their *Wozzeck* counterparts. Berg had been able to lift Marie out of *Wozzeck* with little effort, but Lulu would not be isolated, and the people around her depended on her too much to let her be taken out of their company.

Besides, the composer's primary concerns in arranging parts of *Lulu* for the concert hall were just as abstract as they were dramatic and practical. In a letter of June 9, 1934, he promised Kleiber "a Little Symphony from the opera *Lulu*," and though the resulting work has come to be known variously as the *Lulu* Suite, Five Symphonic Pieces from *Lulu,* and simply as the *Lulu* Symphony, its effect has been two-sided: it is both a tantalizing taste of the larger work, and an important, independent work for voice and orchestra.

Wanting to show off the different musical styles of the opera, Berg arranged the five segments *not* chronologically according to the progression of the drama, but so that they would work into a symphonic whole reminiscent of Mahler's Seventh Symphony. The five movements, which run almost thirty-five minutes (as opposed to the composer's original estimate of twenty-five) are (1) Alwa's rondo: andante and Hymn; (2) *ostinato:* allegro (the interlude film-music); (3) Lulu's Song: *comodo;* (4) variations on Wedekind's Lute Song from Act III; (5) adagio: *sostenuto — Lento — Grave,* the last eight-plus

minutes of music from the opera, beginning with Lulu's
death scream and continuing to the end. The Symphony
calls for only Lulu's coloratura *Lied* to be sung. In the interests of economy, the same singer can speak the words
of the countess that end the Symphony and the opera:
"Lulu — my angel — Let me see you again! — I am near
you — I shall stay near you — forever!" (Berg had cut
the last words Wedekind gave to the dying woman: "Oh,
damn, damn!")

Essentially, Berg did take the music of the *Lulu* Symphony from the larger opera score. But the very nature of
the source made more adaptations necessary than had
been the case at the time of the *Wozzeck* Fragments. Both
to serve their symphonic purposes and to enable them to
stand alone, the two outer movements — Alwa's rondo
and the countess's adagio — had to undergo significant
editing. The eight bars Berg stole from the Prologue to
represent Lulu at the very beginning of the Symphony act
as introduction. The orchestral version of Alwa's rondo
does away with the dramatic interjections that interrupt
him in the opera. The final adagio has been similarly
tightened; if anything, it is even more poignant in its
symphonic form than in the staged version.

How much of Berg's decision not to go to Berlin for
the première of the *Lulu* Symphony had to do with his
desire to avoid the physical exertion and excitement, and
how much had to do with his determination to stay out
of the way of attacks, both verbal and physical, is hard to
judge. At Kleiber's insistence, the authorities guaranteed
protection from any disturbances that might take place at
the concert itself, but they would make no promises that
riots would not boil up after the event, when every man
would have to fend for himself. In fact, the concert of
November 30, 1934, gave the Berliners who attended the

opportunity they had been waiting for: they objected to
the policies of the new regime by applauding Berg and
Kleiber. The enthusiasm was challenged by only one individual, who ran about yelling *"Heil Mozart!"* Kleiber
answered him coolly and with authority: "You have
made a mistake; this music is by Alban Berg."

The next day's newspapers ran scathing reviews of the
work, as could have been predicted, with complaints
directed at both the composer and the conductor. Kleiber
decided he would not stay to endure more abuse; he resigned his position only a few days later and left Germany early in 1935. But he had introduced the *Lulu* Symphony to the world. The work was performed numerous
times outside Germany in the following months, and
served Berg's purpose: it whetted audiences' appetites for
the complete opera. Indeed, for the next forty-five years,
the *Lulu* Symphony played an integral role in the story of
the *Lulu* opera, a role for which Berg had never intended
it.

Kleiber's having managed to push through the première of the *Lulu* Symphony renewed Berg's hope for a
première of the complete opera, if not in Berlin, then in
Munich or one of the other major German centers where
Wozzeck had already been established. Neither Furtwaengler's discouragement nor Kleiber's imminent departure could completely dash Berg's hopes, and the
composer's slow progress on the final stages of work on
his second opera can be understood as a kind of leisurely
wait for the moment when the phone would ring or a
telegram would arrive, announcing that permission had
been granted for the long-awaited première.

Berg had, or so he thought, won a lesser but similar
battle against Nazi influence shortly before the performance of the *Lulu* Symphony. For a year, his Lyric Suite

had been on the program for the September 1934 Biennale in Venice. But suddenly, just two months before the
scheduled event, Berg's music and name completely disappeared from the program. Not without some justification, the composer assumed that the Nazis were to
blame. On July 17, 1934, he wrote to his friend the composer Gian Francesco Malipiero saying that the prospect
of having such an honor bestowed on him at a major festival in Italy had made up at least to some extent for the
disturbances he suffered at home. "Imagine! Since the
Berlin Reichstag fire in the spring of 1933, not a single
note of mine has been heard in Germany, although I am
not a Jew. And in my own country, things are not much
different. For with the present tendency in Austria to glo-
rify the Jews as martyrs, I am hardly ever performed.
Therefore, the removal of my name from the Venice festival will be regarded as a kind of confirmation of the
measures taken against me in Germany."

Berg's petulant letter need never have been written.
The Lyric Suite had been removed from the program not
for political reasons, but because it broke one of the rules
of the Biennale. Any work played there had to be receiving either its world première or its first Italian performance, and the Kolisch Quartet had already toured Italy
with the Lyric Suite. The *Wozzeck* Fragments, which
Berg had offered as an alternative, had also been played,
in Rome. With explanations offered all around, then,
Berg was reinstated in the program with the first Italian
performance of *Der Wein,* conducted by Hermann Scherchen, with the soprano Hanna Schwarz. Both Alban and
Helene went to Italy for the performance, which went
well despite limited rehearsal time, the Nazi-influenced
press, and the disenchantment of the work even on the part
of Malipiero himself.

Berg uncharacteristically saw fit to respond formally to one of the German critics who had covered the festival:

Honored Herr Doctor, It is against my usual habit to react to a bad criticism; even against my conviction, for I cannot expect — I do not expect — my music to please everyone. I am making an exception in your case for the following reason: Your review of the music festival in Venice, printed in one or two dozen newspapers, contains the sentence: 'The music (of my aria *Der Wein*) circumvents utterly the content of the Stefan George/Baudelaire texts.' I found this sentence, in the same words, over and over again in other reviews that were different in other ways and even signed with other names, and so I was forced to conclude that thousands . . . of your readers have now accepted this statement as fact. Involuntarily, my interest in the originator of such a statement, presented as fact, was aroused. This may explain, honored Sir — naturally I do not take it amiss that you consider my aria, 'despite certain merits,' a 'monstrous' work — my polite request that you tell me in what ways my music circumvents the context of these texts . . . In answering this question perhaps you would consider me . . . not as the author of this music, and a subjectively interested party in whom you might incorrectly suspect the presence of a plaintive feeling of injustice, but as one of your many objective readers who is simply interested in a more explicit substantiation of the complete circum-composition that you claim. In the pleasant anticipation that you will not deny me the fulfillment of my request, I sign myself, with the highest respect . . .

To this icily polite, bitterly ironic letter there was, needless to say, no response. It is interesting, however, that Berg was sufficiently upset to take a critic to task on an issue that still seems to be a central weakness of *Der Wein,* which is, in turn, the weakest of his major works. After their trip to Venice, the Bergs returned to Vienna

and the flat on Trauttmansdorffgasse, and Alban went
back to work on the orchestration of *Lulu*. But in the
city, politics and persecution were all around him, and he
wrote to Malipiero on December 27, 1934, that, although
he had been born in Vienna and remained there for almost a half-century, "I am considered here, more than
ever, as not 'indigenous,' and am treated as I would be if
I were, for example, a Jew living in Germany . . . Indeed, I have it from the highest official quarter that the
production some years ago of my opera *Wozzeck* is now
being regarded as a 'desecration' of the Vienna State
Opera."

When, in January 1935, Schoenberg suggested a kind
of "spiritual defensive alliance" of Austrians, Berg responded enthusiastically: "You would never believe —
or, no — you do not have any notion how necessary
that is for us Austrians. Our art — which is not considered indigenous — and therefore our whole material existence is just as threatened here as in other places where
'cultural bolshevism' is being expressly persecuted." Berg
dreamed of taking the arts away from politics once again.
But with Schoenberg in America, with Webern not feeling particularly threatened, and with Berg ready to prove
his Aryan descent lest he invite trouble, the "spiritual alliance," whatever shape it might have taken, was never
formed. When the Austrian minister of education announced plans for the upcoming Vienna Festival Weeks,
only "truly Austrian" composers were to be represented,
not those composers who had made their reputations
abroad. Naturally, none of Berg's work was to be performed.

But the composer's fiftieth birthday, on February 9,
1935, was greeted with celebration, including a special
concert sponsored by the Society for New Music at 5:00

P.M. on the birthday itself, in the small hall of the Musikverein. Heinrich Jalowetz gave the welcoming speech; the
program included the Piano Sonata, three of the Seven
Early Songs, both settings of "Schliesse mir die Augen
beide," the Four Pieces for Clarinet and Piano, the first
Vienna performances of two segments from the *Lulu*
Symphony (in a four-hand piano arrangement, played by
Eduard Steuermann and Jakob Gimpel), and the Lyric
Suite, performed by the Galimir Quartet. Berg was not
impressed. On February 27, after he had visited with the
widow of Emil Hertzka in her home on the Kaasgraben,
he sent his hostess an old engraving with the following
descriptive note:

> On this picture you can see: (1) on the right, the shop where
> the seventh Beethoven symphony was published in 1812
> . . . A century later my Opus 1 was published in the same
> house. (2) On the top floor of the same house . . . this Opus
> 1 was first performed (by Director Hertzka's *Tonkuenstler*
> Society), and it was repeated in the same place . . . twenty-
> five years later for the occasion of my fiftieth birthday. (3)
> The house in the center, finally, is the house where, on Feb-
> ruary 9, 1885, I was born. And since, despite fifty years of
> living and working in my fatherland, I am still not consid-
> ered "indigenous," I have answered a questionnaire sent
> around by the *Echo* on the subject of Handel and Bach, who
> have just reached the age of 250, as follows: "What luck that
> Handel and Bach were born in the year 1685 and not two
> hundred years later! If they had been, there would have been
> a debate as to whether one was 'indigenous' to his fatherland,
> and the music of the other would have been considered 'cul-
> tural bolshevism.'

To let it be known that he was bitter and despairing,
Berg had a postcard printed of the engraving of the house
where he was born, much as he had had cards made up to

show the Waldhaus to his friends over a year earlier. He
mailed the picture of the big building on the Tuchlauben
with the following message: "I, who was born in this
house on February 9, 1885, had to learn that, after fifty
years which I spent in my native country without interruption, I am not a native composer."

Chapter 18

Last Days:
The Violin Concerto

IT WAS, PERHAPS, his depression more than his need for money that inspired Berg to abandon *Lulu* early in 1935 and accept the second commission of his career. Only *Der Wein* had previously been written tc order, and this work had functioned as a study for the second opera, which was already being planned, thus taking Berg on only a minor detour from his chosen path. But the Violin Concerto that was requested by the American violinist Louis Krasner had nothing to do with the operatic work Berg had laid out for himself at the beginning of what was to be the last year of his life.

Although friends had predicted that even the most generous of commissions would not separate Berg from *Lulu,* the composer accepted the violinist's challenge. Krasner, who had first been won over by Berg's Piano Sonata and was subsequently even more impressed by the Lyric Suite, was a champion of new music, and wanted a concerto that would follow the techniques of twelve-tone composition. At first, during their preliminary meetings in Vienna, Berg would not say a definite yes. But by March 28, when Krasner was back in America, Berg wrote to express pleasure that the violinist would return to Europe the coming summer, and added, "From May on, I will be on the Woerthersee (diagonally opposite Poertschach, where Brahms wrote his Violin Concerto) composing 'our' Violin Concerto." Berg looked forward to continued contact with Krasner, of whom he was already fond.

From the beginning, Berg would have been drawn to the project not only because the prospect of being represented by a major new work — especially before American audiences — appealed to him, but also because the dramatic implications of the concerto form stirred his imagination, just as they had done ten years earlier, when he wrote the Chamber Concerto, and, more recently, when he composed *Der Wein*.

As he began to concentrate on the violin and its possibilities, Berg made plans for an "absolute" concerto — pure music without a program in which the soloist would maintain his integrity as he did in the concertos of Beethoven and Brahms, without the frilly display allotted to fiddlers by lesser creators. But his ideas changed, then crystallized with the tragic death, on April 22, 1935, of Manon Gropius, the eighteen-year-old daughter of Alma Mahler and her second husband, the architect Walter Gropius. Beyond his friendship with her mother, Berg had been especially fond of Manon ("Mutzi"), and was stunned when the polio, which she had bravely and even cheerfully struggled with in 1934, spread and paralyzed her central nervous system, killing her. The Concerto for Louis Krasner became a requiem for Manon, dedicated both to the violinist and "To the Memory of an Angel."

The Violin Concerto was finished with a speed unprecedented in Berg's career. Reich recalled that the composer was at the Waldhaus working at a feverish pace only a few days after Manon died; on July 16 he was able to write to Krasner in America that the composition was finished. "I am more surprised at this than even you will be," Berg admitted. "I was keen on it as I have never been before in my life, and must add that the work gave me more and more joy. I hope — no, I have the confident belief — that I have succeeded."

Berg predicted that he would finish the instrumentation by August, and on the twelfth of that month the full score was completed. Krasner had seen no sketches, only the final product, in which he was taken aback to find how the various doodlings and idiomatic wanderings that he had improvised for Berg for hours on end had turned up in the work with both formal and melodic inevitability. At first, there was some talk between composer and violinist of making alterations to smooth out technical difficulties. But Krasner decided at the last moment to wait and practice before advising specific changes, and, in a few days, he found that the difficulties were surmountable. In the end, not a note was changed.

The most striking and the most famous element in the Violin Concerto is the well-known chorale *Es ist genug,* written by Johann Ahle and used by Bach in his Cantata Number 60, *O Ewigkeit, du Donnerwort.* Berg located it in the collection of *Sixty Chorale Melodies by Johann Sebastian Bach,* edited and selected by Herman Roth. It comes as a surprise, however, to realize that Berg did not work the chorale into the Concerto until only a few weeks before the work was completed. On June 8, 1935, Berg wrote to Reich, asking to borrow the full or vocal score of Bach's *St. Matthew Passion* and a collection of chorales, urging his friend and student to be discreet about Berg's plan to use a chorale in his work-in-progress. Reich sent the material by mail, and when he visited the composer at the Waldhaus just a week later, Berg pointed out with glee that the first four notes of the melody to *Es ist genug* (four ascending whole steps of the scale) perfectly matched the last four tones of the twelve-tone row on which the Violin Concerto had been built. On July 1, Berg had another request of his student; he had forgotten to write out the text of *Es ist genug* at the time he had copied out the melody, and wanted Reich to copy out the words for him. He planned to have the composition finished, he said, within two weeks.

This strange order of fast-moving events indicates how smoothly and almost fatalistically the composition of the Violin Concerto flowed. Before the chorale took its place as an essential part of the scheme, Berg operated from two principal elements: a twelve-tone row, and a lilting folk song from Carinthia. The row — the first to be used as a base in a solo concerto — is an amazing mass of congruities. The first nine notes trace the triads of G Minor, D Major, A Minor, and E Major, underlining the pitches sounded by the four open strings of the violin, G, D, A, and E. The ninth through twelfth pitches in the row (B, C-sharp, E-flat, and F) are the same as the first four pitches of the chorale melody, and, by chance or not, the ninth pitch is a B-natural (the German *H*) and the twelfth is an F — once again, H-F, Hanna Fuchs. This tone row, then, is obvious in both harmonic and melodic patterns. It takes neither hours of study nor even particularly intent concentration for the listener to hear the effects of the row's four triads (especially as the violinist "tunes up" on his open strings) and the chorale's natural place in the large scheme of the work.

The large scheme is powerful in itself. The Violin Concerto, originally envisioned as an abstract work without program, operates on two levels: the abstract intellectual one, and the very descriptive emotional one. The work is in two movements, each of which is itself divided into two parts, so the hearer counts four sections: slow, fast, fast, slow — with a break between the two fast ones. The Concerto begins with an almost reverent andante in three-part A-B-A design. The subsequent allegretto is a scherzo with two tacked-on trios, marked by the introduction of the folk tune, which gives the movement the nature of a gentle peasant dance.

Part II begins with an allegro in tripartite form that functions as a cadenza for the solo instrument; Berg asked that it be played "with improvisatory freedom." As the chorale tune builds up note by note, the fourth section of the Concerto starts off as an adagio. Like the second half of the first part of the work, this final segment divides into five sections: the chorale, two variations on it, reminiscences of the folk tune, and a coda in which both the nostalgic little song and the great chorale dissolve into the basic series from which the whole piece was built.

Whether the Concerto would have taken the same form had Manon Gropius lived is, of course, impossible to say — but could it have? That tragic event gave the work its emotional wealth, beginning with Berg's desire that the first half of the piece picture the young girl in life, and that the second half represent her death and transfiguration. The parallel to Strauss's tone poem is clear; though he had outgrown his youthful enthusiasm for the older composer's music, Berg still had special regard for *Death and Transfiguration,* and when, in March 1934, a critic from Geneva compared his Three Fragments from *Wozzeck* with Strauss's tone poem and pre-

ferred the Fragments, Berg was flattered — though he
was not in total agreement with the writer.

In this life-and-death musical drama, the violin represents the heroine throughout, dancing above the accompaniment of the orchestra in Part I, and battling, then
giving way to, the power of fate in Part II. Characteristically, Berg used a large orchestra sparingly, achieving
both a wide range of instrumental colors and a comfortable if not infallible balance between soloist and supporters.

The incorporation of the chorale makes musicologists
think at once of *Vor Deinen Thron tret' ich hiermit,* which
Bach dictated from his deathbed, and the organ chorale-
prelude *O Welt ich muss dich lassen,* which was Brahms's
last work. The structure of the Violin Concerto suggests
Mahler's last completed symphony, the Ninth; and passages also sound like tributes to *Das Lied von der Erde.* All
of these associations, as well as *Death and Transfiguration,*
have given the Violin Concerto a programmatic richness
beyond any that Berg could have planned. There is little
in the piece that is earthshaking in any technical sense; no
one who had followed Berg's work to this point could
have been surprised by the free uses of the twelve-note
row and the joyful exploitation of its tonal implications.
And the references to pre-existing melodic material, especially the folk tune, had been favorite devices since *Wozzeck,* more than twenty years earlier. The symmetrical
layouts of the movements, with numerological correspondences seeming to vibrate off the printed page, were
regular features of the composer's music. And the Con-
certo-as-tone-poem had been written by a composer who
was fond of telling musical stories, even though he did
not always reveal the details of his plots.

The idea of a chorale and variations had also shown up

in Berg's music as recently as *Lulu,* where *concertante* chorale variations set off the great conversation scenes, including, in Act III, the one between Lulu and Casti-Piani. Yet it is the chorale — *this* chorale — that gives the Violin Concerto its special quality. After the dances have ended, the chorale comes as a requiem. For Berg, like Mozart before him, had been writing his own requiem, in a fit of creativity that he himself did not fully understand.

In June 1935, when he was working on the middle of the Concerto, he had complained of being very tired, anxious, and asthmatic. But by the end of the second week in August, when he and Reich played through the finished work in its piano-duet form, the composer was eager to face the future. He was pleased with himself and looked forward first to finishing the instrumentation of *Lulu,* then to going on to a third string quartet, a piece of chamber music with piano, another symphony, something written especially for the radio, and, most interesting, a work for sound-film, of which he was a confirmed devotee. He also wanted to oversee the filming of *Wozzeck,* with special actors and singers, and thought he could do things in a film that had never been fully realized in the theater.

Only days after he finished work on the Violin Concerto, Berg began to be bothered by an abscess at the base of his spine. It resulted, he thought, from an insect sting; he had suffered, on occasion, from allergic reactions to bites and stings, and during the summer of 1932 at Trahuetten he had been attacked by a swarm of wasps and laid up for a full week. Now, baths and medicinal packs and doses of aspirin made him comfortable enough to return to work on *Lulu,* but he was annoyed that he had lost some working time, with the "frightfully painful

abscess that takes away all my pleasure." Still, he saw
enough improvement in his condition to conclude that
the worst had passed.

But the sore, which was probably a staphylococcal in-
fection, refused to go away. Berg was too uncomfortable
to attend the ISCM festival in Prague that September,
despite the lures of a scheduled performance of his *Lulu*
Symphony there and, of course, of the presence of Hanna
Fuchs. He stayed at the Waldhaus, working on the instrumentation of the opera, but he worried about both his
finances and his health. He calculated that he had money
to live on for about two more months, and after that,
nothing. He was "profoundly depressed," he told Reich,
and made plans to return to Vienna, where steps could be
taken to secure both income and medical treatment.

Helene went back to Vienna to prepare the apartment
on Trauttmansdorffgasse, and the letters her husband sent
her from the Waldhaus sounded almost cheerful at first. It
was the beginning of October, so the sun still hit the ve-
randa and the fall weather was inspiriting. Berg wrote of
a "friendly-dreamy-day" on which he sat in the sun and
took a bus ride to look at the shine on the lake. He was
also hopeful that Adorno or one of his other more successful students might come to his financial aid. The tradition continued, with Berg asking help from his senior
students in the same way Schoenberg had expected, and
received, aid from his. Berg wanted to find English
pupils and, perhaps, to sell the orchestral score of the
movements from the Lyric Suite. The original string-
quartet version, of course, was with Hanna Fuchs and
would never see the auction block. During the rural autumn, Berg would not have wanted to alarm his wife
with bad news about either his health or their finances;
his pleasure in the country life and in his surroundings
was genuine.

In the weeks that followed, Berg took long walks alone, tended to business (and feared he might have to sell the Waldhaus), listened to the radio, and made his usual trips to town for mail, coffee, and the newspapers. On one of his walks, he developed blisters on the bottoms of his feet. He thought that his shoes were merely rubbing the wrong way and that, in a few days, he would be able to go back to hiking. But on October 11, he had to write to Helene that the blisters were bad and his good humor was gone; he could no longer walk, and he was not charmed by what he called "Carinthian 'city' life."

Mr. and Mrs. Zoy, the caretakers at the Waldhaus, could help out a little, even if they were not stimulating companions, and Mrs. Zoy made the trips to the post office when Berg was not able to go himself. On October 12, he reported to Helene that he simply could not walk that far, but could sit at his desk, and hoped soon to be getting about normally.

I don't mind telling you that it has been pretty wretched. Last time I was in Klagenfurt it was so bad I could hardly get back from the cinema to the main square. Quickly to bed when I got home, the leg raised, and I put on an anti-phlogistic poultice. All day yesterday I was in bed, changing the dressings continually. Today I'm all right, keeping the leg down. Don't know exactly what the trouble was. Of the various blisters on both feet, all but one healed normally. There was just that one spot of inflammation right at the ball of the foot. It hurt like anything, and I thought another abscess was developing or something like that, and that in the end it would have to be lanced. Thank the Lord, nothing like it, and only the lesson: Never again go for a long walk!

Helene came to the Waldhaus to close up house, and together the couple went back to Vienna, on Tuesday, November 12, 1935. Though Berg believed the worst was over as far as the infections on his coccyx and the soles of his feet were concerned, he was still in pain, and even the huge doses of aspirin he had been prescribing for himself over the weeks would not keep his fever from rising occasionally, for no apparent reason.

From Vienna, on November 30, he wrote what was to be his last letter to Schoenberg, starting out with glowing reports of performances of the *Gurrelieder* and the George Songs, a song cycle by Schoenberg, and expressing pleasure with accounts of the warmth with which the *Lulu* Symphony was being met by foreign programmers. But, he continued,

> in spite of this all, things are not going well for me: badly in a financial way, because I cannot maintain my previous standard of living, including keeping up the Waldhaus (yet I cannot bring myself to sell the place where in two years I have done more work than in the previous ten); badly as regards my health, because for months I have been suffering from boils, and still have them, which explains my horizontal position! They began shortly after I finished the Violin Concerto, with an atrocious carbuncle resulting from an insect sting. This put an end to any possibility of an autumn period of recuperation, which I rather needed after the summer's hard work and the preceding *Lulu* years. Finally, things are bad morally, which won't astonish you, coming as it does from someone who suddenly discovers that he is not "indigenous" to his fatherland, and is consequently completely homeless. All of this is heightened by the fact that such things do not proceed without friction and profound human disappointments, and these persist.

Berg managed, with difficulty, to get from Hietzing into central Vienna for rehearsals and a performance of his *Lulu* Symphony on December 11; the Czech-born music publisher Ernst Roth saw him there, and reported that he looked pale and was obviously in pain. As Berg

described it, his legs made him feel as if he had a "toothache in the wrong place."

Aspirin and home remedies were obviously not helping, but, incredible as it seems, Alban and Helene insisted
on tending to the boils by lancing them with nail scissors
rather than seeking professional treatment. The pain got
worse and worse, until it was on the verge of becoming
unbearable. Then, on December 16, it suddenly vanished.
Evidence suggests that the abscess had broken inward and
that Berg's blood had been poisoned.

The next day, December 17, the composer was rushed
to a hospital (the Archduke Rudolf Hospital in Vienna's
III District). On the way, he remarked that he was already halfway to the famous Central Cemetery, with all
its graves of honor. At the hospital, he was operated on
and given a transfusion. The medical staff was, reportedly, second-rate, and no one on the staff could locate
the cause of his fever and his pain. Berg was strong
enough to want to thank the blood donor, who turned
out to be a young Viennese who could not have cared less
that his plasma had gone to a great musician. As the
donor left the room, Berg turned to Reich and said, "If
only I don't turn into a composer of operettas after this!"

A turn for the worse came on December 22, as his
heart began to give way. Berg realized the significance of
the new day: "Today is the twenty-third — it will be
decisive." Those who stood by him during his last hours
of life recalled his feeble attempts to conduct unheard
music, and his words, *"Ein Auftakt!!"* (An upbeat!!). He
died at about midnight, as December 23 became
Christmas Eve, 1935. Anna Mahler, the daughter of
Alma and Gustav, took the death mask.

The City of Vienna offered a grave of honor in the
small rural cemetery in Hietzing, just up the hill from the

house on Maxinggasse where Helene had grown up. It was cold and gray when Alban Berg was buried there, shortly after noon on December 28. The mourners included Ernst Krenek, who delivered the eulogy by the grave, Egon Wellesz, Stefan Zweig, former pupils, friends, and members of the family. Helene did not attend the funeral. She was grieving and distraught, plagued by the suspicion that better and faster medical attention might have saved her husband from death at the age of fifty.

Later, a plain wooden cross was erected to mark Berg's final resting place. Down at the end of a grassy path, surrounded by heavy marble memorials and Baroque vaults, in the company of so many corpses whose every earthly achievement has been chiseled into stone, the composer's grave is lyrically simple. It says only ALBAN BERG, 1885–1935.

Chapter 19

The Aftermath

ON THE DAY her husband was buried, Helene Berg received a message from Gerhart Hauptmann: "Deeply shaken, dear gracious lady, we press your hand. Why had so noble a man and master to take his leave so early? May Heaven give you strength in your great sorrow. In sincere admiration . . ."

In a special edition of the periodical *23*, dedicated to Berg's memory, on February 1, 1936, Reich wrote his "thanks, thousandfold thanks for every moment lived with us and for us, for every smile of his bright yet still so puzzling countenance, for every note of his inconceivably intense and inspired work!"

Schoenberg wrote to Webern on January 15, 1936, from Hollywood: "It is too terrible. One is gone from us who in any case were only three, and now we two alone have to bear this artistic isolation. And the saddest thing: the one of us who has had success, could have at least enjoyed it."

To Webern, who was equally upset, fell the assignment of conducting the first performance of the Violin Con-

certo, with Krasner as soloist, at the ISCM festival in
Barcelona on March 19, 1936. He had three rehearsals in
which to prepare the orchestra; he spent two of them
working on the very beginning of the Concerto, telling
the musicians, in his stumbling Spanish, all about Berg's
intentions. It was typical of Webern, and totally impractical. Before the third and final rehearsal, Webern withdrew, and Hermann Scherchen was once again called in
to save the performance. The incident was still troubling
Berg's friend two years later, when he wrote to Scherchen on New Year's Day, 1938: "To think that absolutely no one understood me! No one understood how I
felt so soon after Berg's death, and that I was simply not
up to the task of conducting the first performance of his
last work."

Webern did, however, conduct one of the English performances of the Violin Concerto, in a BBC concert in
May 1936, with Krasner as the soloist, as he was when
the new work was scheduled in the following months by
concert societies in Vienna (with Otto Klemperer conducting), Paris (under Charles Munch), Boston and New
York (both under Koussevitzky). Lush enough to gratify
twentieth-century symphonic tastes, and certainly
quicker and easier to assimilate than a full-length opera,
the Violin Concerto was quickly to become Berg's most
popular work — more favored, even, than *Wozzeck*.

And what of *Lulu?* The opera lay on the table in the
drawing room on Trauttmansdorffgasse, where Berg had
left it when he was rushed to the hospital. But not a
month passed between the bleak day of his funeral and
the beginning of a string of complications and irratio-
nalities that would keep his masterwork from being performed in its entirety for more than forty-three years.

The first move was probably made by Schoenberg,
who sent a letter of condolence to Helene from California

immediately after learning of Berg's death, and offered —
sincerely if somewhat casually — to finish whatever bits
and pieces of work remained to be done on the orchestration of *Lulu*. Schoenberg knew from Berg's letters that
the opera was virtually completed; he also knew his
former student and disciple well enough to assume that
the work would be clearly and precisely sketched and
diagrammed, with enough indications for an expert to
finish it off without any trouble.

Helene answered Schoenberg on January 14, 1936, saying that his offer had brought her a much-needed ray of
hope, and indicating that Schoenberg would be hearing
more from her or Universal Edition regarding the matter. Early in March, a hefty packet containing Berg's
sketches and the libretto went off to Schoenberg. He received the material, studied it, and sent it back, with a
polite but firm refusal; the task of finishing *Lulu,* he
wrote, would be harder and more time-consuming than
he had anticipated, and he could not undertake such a
project at that time. Among many, however, it became
known that Schoenberg was infuriated by Berg's por-
trayal of the Jewish banker, Puntschu, in Act III. Schoenberg may have been more sensitive than most to suggestions of anti-Semitism, but Puntschu is an unattractive
character who, if played with a thick accent and a weasely
bearing, can be brought down to the level of grotesque
caricature. Berg may have been counting on the banker
to help sell his opera to the Nazi authorities so that he
could realize his dream of giving *Lulu* a world première
in Germany. The composer used poor judgment and
probably acted opportunistically, but the portrait of
Puntschu is not in itself reason enough to label Berg anti-
Semitic. Schoenberg, of all people, should have known
that this was not the case.

Under the circumstances, Schoenberg did not allow

Helene Berg to know the full extent of his anger, but he
would have nothing more to do with *Lulu*. He took what
turned out to be the decisive step in keeping the opera
from being quickly completed by simply refusing to
work on it.

But, as Ernst Krenek has pointed out, aspects of
Schoenberg's decision are difficult to explain. Schoenberg
could have been in possession of what must have been
photostats of hundreds of pages of score, sketches, and
libretto for less than forty-eight hours in the spring of
1936 before he stated with conviction that the anti-Semitism did not come from Wedekind's original (which, indeed, it did not), and that Berg had added the offensive
words and accent of the banker, thinking they might help
him get the work produced in Nazi Germany. Had
Schoenberg really done such extensive homework, col-
lecting the Wedekind plays and preparing so painstakingly for *Lulu*'s arrival, the precise date of which he did
not know in advance? Or had someone informed him
beforehand of the anti-Semitic innuendoes? Krenek sus-
pects an informer had been at work. But who could that
have been? Certainly not Helene herself?

There were, naturally, others who could have finished
Lulu, among them Webern and Zemlinsky. Supposedly,
their names were on the first list of possible cooperators,
just beneath Schoenberg's, and they were approached by
Erwin Stein, representing Universal Edition. But both of
them declined — Webern because he probably felt he was
emotionally incapable, just as he had been unable to conduct the Violin Concerto; and Zemlinsky for reasons still
less clear. Stein, who was perhaps the next most likely
candidate, since he had prepared the piano-vocal score of
the complete opera under Berg's guidance, is said to have
been ready and enthusiastic to take on the project. But at

that point Universal Edition stepped in and put a halt to further negotiations; the publisher also stopped the printing of Stein's complete piano-vocal score after only a handful of copies had come off the presses. Like the full score, the short arrangement by Stein officially appeared only as a fragment, without Act III.

Over the years, other names entered the *Lulu* saga, among them those of the renowned composers Igor Stravinsky and Luigi Dallapiccola, both of whom expressed the opinion that the opera should be completed, and implied that they would be available to do the work. But no action was taken, and, with the passing of time, there grew a legend that it would be impossible to finish *Lulu,* that too much had been left undone, that only a genius could adapt to Berg's individual style to the extent where Act III would become a convincing climax to the whole opus — and, on the other hand, that any person capable of completing Berg's work would inevitably have a musical style of his own that would preclude his being faithful to the original composer's intentions. The arguments against completion tended to be conflicting. But if the purpose of those who repeated these arguments was to obscure the central issue, they succeeded. Instead of asking *why* the opera had never been finished, people started asking whether it ever *could* be. The answer was perhaps . . . someday.

But the fact was that *Lulu* was not a "fragment"; it was, rather, a virtually completed work. Unlike Mozart's Requiem, Puccini's *Turandot,* Mahler's Tenth Symphony, Weber's *Die drei Pintos* (which was finished by Mahler), and other works that had been completed by men other than those who began them, *Lulu* had no cause to become what is known as a "hyphen work," one created by two different composers. Berg's legacy included, in addi-

tion to Stein's complete piano-vocal score (incorporating
many of the composer's indications for orchestration),
the complete first draft in short score, the almost-
complete full score of Act III (which becomes sketchy at
bar 268 of Scene 1), the complete libretto, and the last
two sections of the *Lulu* Symphony, which use music
from the third act, fully orchestrated. The *Lulu* Symphony provided a fast and easy solution to the end of the
opera, since its final minutes had been lifted directly from
the Act III finale. The Symphony also provided models
for the sections immediately preceding, and gave many
indications of how Berg had intended to fill in the missing instrumental lines. Reich, who followed the progress
of the opera through Berg's last hours of work on it,
could write with assurance that except for very few bars,
Lulu was complete in short score, with all of the vocal
lines written in, "and the orchestral parts . . . notated
with skeleton instrumental indications, except for two or
three staves. The full score of Act III breaks off at bar
268, at the end of the second ensemble of the Society
scene. Bars 1120 through 1161 and 1268 through 1300 of
Act III were also orchestrated for the adagio of the *Lulu*
Symphony."

A few years later, H. F. Redlich added that the task of
orchestrating the end of the third act was facilitated by the
fact that it contained recapitulations and transpositions of
certain passages from Act I, Scene 2, and Act III, Scene 1.
The first significant stumbling block Redlich foresaw for
a future editor came at the re-entry of Countess Geschwitz (III, 2, bar 861 and following), "but even in that
section the continuity of the sketch in short score is unbroken," he wrote. "The passages for which no corre-
sponding models are to be found in the music of the
previous acts are in a minority compared with those

which are clearly based on reminiscences. The completion of Act III is therefore a distinct possibility . . .
which will have to be undertaken before Berg's finest and
most mature work can become part of the international
repertory of operatic masterpieces."

The situation was very strange. While there was no
doubt that only about 60 measures, in all, of *Lulu* had
been left so sketchy that they would have to be "composed" by someone other than Berg, and that filling in
the blanks in the 600 to 700 measures would be a chore
requiring sensitivity but no superhuman powers, *Lulu* became known, erroneously, as a fragment.

That is how Universal Edition published it, first with a
piano–vocal score in 1936 (Stein's work, but only Acts I
and II), and continuing in 1937 with the two completed
thirds of the full score. With the vocal score came a note
promising that the whole opera would be offered at a future date. One, two, three, and then four decades passed
without that promise being kept.

In the interim, however, *Lulu* was seen on the stage.
After postponements and much worry, the first performance of the two-act opera took place on June 2, 1937, in
the Stadttheater in Zurich, with Robert Denzler conducting, stage direction by Karl Schmidt-Bloss, and designs
by Roman Clemens. Nuri Hadzic was Lulu. Heinz
Rueckert directed the film that bridged the gap between
Scenes 1 and 2 of Act II, with no marked success; Rueckert provided proof that it is difficult if not impossible to
include all the visual images Berg wanted within the time
span of the music he provided. To make up for the absent
third act, the producer took the Zurich stage at the end of
Act II and offered a verbal synopsis of the drama's conclusion. Then the orchestra played parts four and five of
the *Lulu* Symphony, with the final murder episode acted

and sung in what the backdrop suggested was an attic room. Justifiably, the Swiss felt courageous; K. H. David wrote in the Zurich *Schweizerische Musikzeitung*, "It is a sign of the times that this work could be brought to performance only in Zurich. Yet it is in no way politically dangerous; it is an exceptional work on purely artistic grounds, to be hailed or condemned as such." Both the political situation and the accompanying cultural censorship, as well as the expectation of many people that the complete opera would soon be performed, perhaps within a matter of weeks or months, kept the first performance of the incomplete *Lulu* from receiving the volume of critical attention that had been lavished on *Wozzeck* twelve years earlier.

Another twelve years passed before *Lulu* was allowed to be heard again; on March 16, 1949, the ISCM and Austrian Radio cosponsored a concert performance of the "fragment" in Vienna. The major stage revival of the opera took place in Essen on March 7, 1953, when the second act was followed again by portions of the *Lulu* Symphony, with pantomime and text from the Wedekind drama to explain the action. Subsequent productions followed the lead of the Essen arrangement and combined sections of the Symphony with bits of Wedekind, leading up to the countess's last words, which could be presented directly from Berg. The solution was at least preferable to having the producer walk out before the audience to read the synopsis, but it could nevertheless be very confusing, and, obviously, it never gave listeners even the slightest idea of what Act III actually held in store. *Lulu* would not be forgotten. The American première, however, did not take place until 1963, when it was offered by the Santa Fe Opera; the Metropolitan Opera stayed away from the "modern" work until 1977. It is easy to understand why some producers preferred to wait until the opera could be performed in its entirety. *Lulu* had no ending, and it remained more a curiosity than a satisfying theatrical experience.

After the Zurich première, in 1937, Helene Berg wrote to Universal Edition to make it clear that she, for one, wanted to see *Lulu* finished and performed complete. Did she mean it? Schoenberg had already said he would not do the job, and Helene told some of her friends that she saw the refusal of her husband's mentor as a sign that the opera should be left as a fragment. And in those early months after Berg's death, Universal Edition was also exercising control over the fate of *Lulu*. It is perhaps understandable that a publishing house, facing the imminent fate of a Nazi takeover and war, would turn timid. Why should Universal have rushed to pour funds into having *Lulu* finished, printed, promoted, and produced, when the possibilities for a production were already limited, and would, in all likelihood, diminish even further?

It is clear, then, that the combination of Schoenberg's refusal to complete the work and Universal's reluctance to lavish more time and money on it made it necessary for Zurich to present *Lulu* as a fragment or not present it at all. At the time, no one could have known that a performance of the full work was not just a matter of months away and that a world war would intervene. *Lulu* was not on many people's minds during the late 1930s and the 1940s. So in 1953, Universal Edition could, with no objections from anyone, quietly reprint the opera's first two acts with the caveat, "The opera is to be performed as a fragment" and the recommendations that the two movements of the *Lulu* Symphony, taken and scored by Berg from Act III, be presented as the officially blessed ending.

But in 1953, the decision to keep *Lulu* incomplete was
Helene Berg's, not Universal's. The widow had changed
her mind; the score would not be finished as long as she
had any control over it. After Berg's death, Hildegard
Jone, the mystic and Symbolist poet and artist who was
an especially close friend of Webern and whose works
inspired all of that composer's late vocal compositions,
convinced Helene that she could still communicate with
her dead husband. It is not at all difficult to imagine
Helene's accepting this idea with curiosity, openness, and
eagerness. It is also not hard to believe that over the decades the gossip grew that whenever Helene was asked to
release Act III of *Lulu* or, for that matter, any of the other
sketches, compositions, and papers in her late husband's
estate, she would consult Alban, who, from his grave,
said no.

Helene stayed on in the apartment in Hietzing on
Trauttmansdorffgasse, representing and preserving what
she could of her former life. She had celebrated her fiftieth birthday on July 29, 1935, five months after her husband had marked his, during the time when he was hard
at work on the Violin Concerto. She was still a very attractive woman; she had worked to keep her figure and
her appealing, blond softness. She knew very little more
about music than she had on the day of her wedding, almost a quarter of a century earlier, but she had met many
of the people who worked in and controlled the music
world, and she had listened to their conversations. She
knew that, after all the tears had been shed and the mes-
sages of condolence had been answered, she had a power
she had never had before.

There is such a thing as a professional widow, and she
is no stranger to the world of the arts. She has spent
much of her life tending to the needs of her creative hus-

band, fetching his coffee, arranging travel plans, packing clothes, and shielding him from the rigors of everyday life so that he could devote himself to creating. She has come to believe that artists, somehow, are different from other, normal people; she, most distinctly, has been relegated to the world of the others. If she happens to be pretty, so much the better; she then makes an appropriate companion for those times when her husband wants to be seen. But a very small part of the creative artist's life is spent displaying himself; Alban Berg composed only thirteen significant works after his apprentice days, and two of those he did not live to hear performed. So over his fifty years there were only eleven gala world premières (not including the repeated *Wozzecks*), when he was the center of attention and could have paraded in with Helene smiling beside him. The rest of the time, when he said he was working, he was sequestered in his studio or in the drawing room on Trauttmansdorffgasse, writing music. To someone like Helene, this might have come to mean that he was spending days and nights on end sitting and banging out random notes on the piano, staring at the wall, and agonizing over the intangible, while she was alone.

But after Berg died, his widow became the sole representative of the composer's greatness and all that it signified. She did the negotiating with Universal Edition. She was the object of stares from curious onlookers in opera houses and concert halls. When the phone rang, it was for her. Instead of inquiring after the health of her husband or asking after her in the last sentences of their letters, the great and near-great asked her directly how she was feeling and what they could do to help. At the time of Berg's death, family funds had diminished, and they were to be reduced even further during the war. But the ever-thrifty widow never had to do without the necessities.

Helene Berg was not like her friend Alma Mahler. She had never had Alma's bold beauty, her ingenuity, her talent, or her money. Besides, Helene was already a good deal older than Alma had been when her first husband died. Though Viennese society expected Alma to consort with bohemians — and even waited for stories of her next conquest — those whom Helene wanted to count as friends expected her to live properly and quietly, surviving on the memory of her beloved Alban. So after Christmas, 1935, Helene took a job: that of keeping alive the memory of her dead husband. There were scandalmongers who said that Helene had young men friends around the house. If this was true, she kept it remarkably quiet.

On December 26, 1935, she phoned Hermann Watznauer to get the letters Berg had written to him in the years 1902 to 1904. She wanted to collect and preserve everything that might remind her and the world of her husband — down, it is said, to the cigarette butts he left in the ash trays when he was taken away from home for the last time. Books stayed on the shelves, music stayed on the piano, the letters he had written to her stayed in an old suitcase she kept under the bed. She planned to spend eight months of every year in Vienna and four at the Waldhaus, where the car was put up on blocks. Unlike Alban, Helene had no doubt that she could keep and maintain the Waldhaus. She still had some money from her inheritance, which her husband had been reluctant to make use of, and she trusted, with reason, that profits from performances of Berg's music would increase, sooner or later. Besides, the Waldhaus had been bought with money from the sale of the Nahowski home at Trahuetten, and even though the Bergs' house was not nearly as grand as Helene's family's country place had been, it was, by all rights, hers.

So Helene Berg set herself up in two museums, one in Hietzing and one in Carinthia. Instead of becoming living memorials to a great musician, these two residences were carefully frozen in time. The Bergs had lived well, if not lavishly, for nearly twenty-five years. Now, with Alban gone, Helene could practice all of her private frugalities, and the Berg estate grew in a relatively short period of time to the point where Helene was a millionaire. She refused to spend money on clothes or even on creature comforts. She skimped on fuel and lived in cold rooms, and even had the telephone taken out for a while, until members of the family convinced her that it was a necessity, not a luxury. She developed an antipathy toward all that was new, including not only noisy jet planes and cars, but the postwar improvements that became an integral part of modern life.

Surely, this had not been her original plan, not how she envisioned her future as she sat in the overstuffed chair in the silent apartment during those first few weeks after her husband had been buried. Then, she was actively interested in getting *Lulu* completed, knowing, despite her own lack of musical sophistication, that this would have been the masterpiece of a great career. Something, or someone, had changed her mind and caused her retreat.

In her attempts to locate and catalogue the valuable documents of her husband's career, Helene had come across a snapshot of a little girl. The photograph was about thirty years old, yellowed by time and wear, but the widow would have been able to spot the resemblance between her husband and his daughter. She immediately phoned Fritz Klein, the student of Berg who had been a friend and confidant, and ordered him to come at once.

But even before Klein arrived in Hietzing, Helene must have concluded that her husband had been a father and that he had carefully concealed that fact from her.

In the early 1970s, when Helene was approaching ninety and Berg's daughter was almost seventy, the composer's only child visited the Waldhaus. Charly's son, Erich Alban Berg, was there to meet his cousin; the widow was there, too. The details of the meeting have been conveniently forgotten, as has the daughter's name. All that is known is that she spent her life in the country, unconcerned with or ignorant of her father's fame and his art. The one reminder of her existence, the photograph, was kept by Erich Alban.

The next blow, assuming that it did indeed fall, would have been even heavier. It is probable that Helene Berg found out about the relationship between her husband and Hanna Fuchs-Robettin, although the circumstances of that revelation are still unknown. Alban had been careful to keep his correspondence out of Helene's range. He did not go to Prague without some kind of musical purpose. As much as he had wanted to be with Hanna, he had never reached the point where he was actually ready to make a break with Helene; for the sake of Fuchs and the children, Helene, and their reputations, the liaison had to be kept secret. But some people did know: Klein, Alma, Franz Werfel, and probably others. Helene had suspected, right after the two met, that there was some special relationship between Alban and Hanna. All she needed was a scribbled address, a forgotten letter, a picture, or even a vague reference in some musical sketch to confirm her suspicion.

It is hard to believe, in light of the many allusions Berg made to Hanna in his music, that there was no trace of her in his writing desk or in any of the other papers in the house. Yet even when Helene found evidence, she could not tell anyone that she knew — certainly not anyone outside her small immediate circle. Erich Alban Berg, who spent a good deal of time dealing with his aunt in both business and personal matters during the last years, is not sure whether Helene knew of her rival.

But if she did not know, what could have caused her to turn on *Lulu?* Helene had the power to stop the complete *Lulu,* and she did her best to do so. She had certain excuses, too. Some of her friends recall that she knew how important her husband's second opera was and would be, but others — the majority — say that she did not like or approve of the work. Her reservations were not on the same plane as those of Ernst Krenek, who finds *Lulu* too wordy and self-consciously literate; in 1978, Krenek had little hope that an appended Act III would give the work balance and proportion. Helene knew little and cared less about these aspects of the work; but she was concerned with the image presented to the world by the name Berg, and, in her opinion, *Lulu* was a tawdry story.

Even now, the Viennese are shocked (or pretend to be) that a nice man like Alban Berg could have written such a lurid opera. "If one writes *Lulu,* one isn't concerned only with ideal love," said the widow of a musician who knew the Bergs well. "No man who didn't love women could have written *Lulu,"* said another widow, remembering some comments her musician-husband had made decades before, and putting an accent on the plural, *women.* And as recently as July 9, 1961, after a trip home to Vienna from Oxford, where he was on the university faculty, Egon Wellesz wrote to the pianist Jean Reti:

> It is interesting to know how Helene Berg feels about *Lulu.* She adores the music but, I think, she finds Berg's death was dictated by fate so that he could not finish the last

act, which is too repulsive. And she does not allow to add
[sic] a spoken end to the opera, nor does she give permission
to score the sketches. I do understand so well that attitude.
Lulu was not born in Berg's creative mind, but in that of
Schoenberg, who lived in a world possessed by ghosts and
phantoms. This world is dangerously powerful; I experienced it at Vienna where abstract art flourishes, and Webern-
ite music.

Whatever prejudices may have contributed to this letter, Wellesz's reactions to *Lulu* were by no means unique.
The "ghosts and phantoms" were immediately associated
with Schoenberg because he was the one most commonly
known to be superstitious, and it was naturally assumed
that any of his students' beliefs in the supernatural had
come directly from the master. In fact, there is no reason
to assume that Schoenberg had anything at all to do with
the choice of *Lulu* as an operatic subject. Many Viennese — and not only those who would do almost anything to appear to be proper — were put off or frightened by the opera's subject matter. Equally detrimental to
Lulu's fate were the various negative reactions to the
music itself. Polnauer, for instance, is said to have advised Helene that Act III was weak on purely musical
grounds. Helene could say, with support from musicians,
that it was better that *Lulu* never be performed, that it
was something that the public needed to be shielded
from, and that it was not a work of consistently good
quality.

The widow lived quietly through World War II and
into the prosperous years that followed, tending her
museum-homes and her gardens, with caged birds in
Hietzing and wild birds whom she befriended at the
Waldhaus to keep her company. She had some domestic
help, and she kept in touch with old friends. She listened

to music, especially to works of Mahler, Mozart, and Bruckner, on the phonograph and on the radio, and she had a television set. She went to concerts until she was well into her eighties. She talked to people who were interested in finding out more about her husband and his music, and was especially eager to meet and help young students. It was, she felt, her job and her duty. But when she heard Webern's early works, she decided that those of her husband which were not already published should remain unknown; they lacked his mark of genius, she thought. She became known, in one observer's words, as a "monumental character." It is not clear whether his accent was on the word "monumental" or on "character."

Helene was in touch with the surviving members of the Berg family. During the war, one of them, either Hermann or Charly, suggested that she write to Baldur von Schirach, Hitler's deputy in Vienna, reminding him that her dead husband had been certified as an Aryan, and appealing to him to lift the nine-year-old proscription on Berg's music. She replied to her brother-in-law on New Year's Day, 1942, from the Waldhaus, where she had spent the holidays, rejecting his suggestion:

> Alban Berg's art belongs to the eternal beauties of the divine and spiritual world. I could never bring myself to do anything not in accord with his beliefs: this man of utter integrity who never compromised in artistic matters. It would seem to me only a profanation to have him "taken up" by people who are completely alien to his works, and must remain so.
>
> Alban can wait with confidence until this Hell on earth has ceased to rage. His time will come — a better time, I am convinced . . . My life's sole purpose is to watch over his legacy and preserve its purity. What else is left for me in this world estranged from God!

Her relations with her husband's relatives were only superficially cordial. As Erich Alban Berg put it, "She wanted to be the only Berg." In 1950, Helene celebrated her sixty-fifth birthday, and shortly afterward she decided to turn some of Alban's manuscripts and papers over to the National Library in Vienna for safekeeping. The material was not in order, and both Universal Edition and the directors of the library had no choice but to go along with the widow's wishes and not make available to the public the great bulk of the precious material they had under lock and key. Helene was particularly adamant on one issue: no one should be allowed to touch, let alone to work on, *Lulu*.

In the postwar boom of the 1950s, royalties were accumulating and being paid at a prodigious rate. Every time a work by Berg was performed, half of the royalties went to Universal Edition and half to Helene, except in the cases of *Wozzeck* and *Lulu,* the fees for which were also shared with the estates of the playwrights. Helene asked for little help when it came to tending to finances, but she finally hired an accountant after her taxes were audited. In the late 1950s, she began to plan a foundation, which would occupy her through much of the rest of her life.

Helene contended that Berg had wanted to aid young composers, and had dreamed of turning the Waldhaus into a subsidized musical retreat, where young musicians could go to study or compose music, free from the distractions and cares of daily urban life. Like so many ideas of Helene's later years, this one harked back to the prewar days of the 1920s and 1930s, to the country houses of her married life, and to her husband's determination to make his way as a composer without ties to any other parts of the music world. But the Waldhaus was not physically suited to such a purpose. It was too small, too dark, and too gloomy. So, on the tactful advice of her few remaining advisers, Helene made the possible establishment of such a retreat only one of several provisions when she established the Alban Berg Foundation, which was duly registered with the City of Vienna on July 19, 1968. Whether the idea for such a foundation could actually have been traced back to its namesake, it has put the interest and dividends from several million dollars back into the service of twentieth-century music in general, and the memory of Alban Berg in particular. Performers, composers, and musicologists may apply for grants in aid. Preference goes to Viennese and Austrians. Helene turned over the funds from her account in a Zurich bank and half of the income she would be receiving from future performances of her late husband's music, and she retained full veto power over a five- to nine-person board of directors and a three-person executive committee, all appointed by her. Ultimately, the foundation assumed ownership of both the Waldhaus and the building at Trauttmansdorffgasse 27, where Helene continued to live until her death. Maintaining and restoring these properties for use as museums or retreats became a principal foundation effort.

Although Helene may not have realized it, by forming the foundation she had laid the basis for future conflict. The board of the foundation had to be made up of those who were, at the least, very concerned with the music of Berg, his circle, and his followers; preferably, it would consist of people who, as composers, directors of libraries, conductors, and performers (including representatives of Viennese orchestras that programmed works of Berg) were involved with Berg's music. Naturally, not everyone who thought that he should be on the board

was asked to participate. Inevitably, word went out that
the foundation had been "stacked" — by the lawyers, by
Helene herself, or by power-hungry confidants. No one,
possibly not even the widow herself, was completely satisfied with the way the foundation was being run. The
most sympathetic observers concluded that very little had
been accomplished beyond clearing up the tax questions
and saving the Waldhaus. Those who were unsympathe-
tic felt that the board members had lost touch with Berg
and were simply serving themselves. Except on such
matters as providing financial incentive to young groups,
such as the Alban Berg String Quartet from Vienna,
which was obviously good public relations, battles raged
within the foundation, where the presentation of a united
front was not only desirable, but increasingly urgent.

At the time she drew up the provisions for the foundation, with the guidance of her attorneys, Helene may
have sensed that the future could bring trouble. In 1963,
backed by his fine reputation as a major scholar of serial
music, especially that of Alban Berg, George Perle had
been allowed two weeks to study the cache of manuscripts for the complete *Lulu* in the vaults of Universal
Edition. Someone must have hoped that the American
professor would be quiet about the readiness of the material for performance, or else tell the world that *Lulu* was
indeed incomplete and far from being ready for presentation.

But Perle said something very different, and he said it
loudly enough to alert the music world, which had put
Lulu into the back of its collective mind. There was
something odd, Perle knew, and he went beyond saying
that what Berg had left for Act III was more than a sketch
and that the work was almost ready for performance. He
said that the opera's final act was crucial to the dramatic

development and that, without it, the world was being
denied appreciation of the work. Since Perle had made his
move on the suggestion of Stravinsky and his associate,
Robert Craft, the professor reported to them shortly after
he finished his study of *Lulu,* addressing his letter to
Craft: "In the concluding scene Lulu has become dear to
one in the way that Desdemona is in Act IV of *Otello*
. . . The scene has a pathos beyond anything that I know
in opera." No matter how intriguing and colorful audiences had found Lulu in the opera's first two acts, no one
who had seen the truncated version would ever have referred to her as "dear."

Nevertheless, Universal Edition had the score and
could not do a thing with it. Helene said no, calling on
Alban's voice to back her up. The *Lulu* question had
grown in her mind to such proportions that she hated the
heroine, was jealous of her, and felt that if Act III were
released and Alwa, the opera's representation of her husband, were allowed to die onstage, then the spirit of
Alban Berg would die, too.

What Universal Edition could do, however, was make
sure that the complete *Lulu* would be ready to go onstage
the moment Helene Berg died. To this end, and completely without the widow's knowledge or approval, the
publisher assigned the composer, conductor, and musicologist Friedrich Cerha to fill in the missing notes. Universal evidently acted at approximately the same time, perhaps even somewhat before, Perle saw *Lulu.* According
to Viennese archivists and librarians, the opera had been
complete for more than fifteen years before it could be
publicly performed in its three-act entirety.

Meanwhile, after a goodly number of entreaties from a
Munich publisher (the Albert Langen Georg Mueller Verlag), Helene reluctantly agreed to compile a selection of

the letters she had received from her husband over the
years, on the understanding that the volume would not
be released until after her death. Acting in what most
people say was a highly unprofessional manner, and serving her own interests more than those of history, Helene
pulled the suitcase of letters out from under the bed and
began to dictate to a secretary the sections she deemed interesting or important. She worked on this task while
Perle worked on *Lulu*. But unlike Universal Edition,
where, while she lived, the widow's wishes were honored despite offers of bribes and convoluted plots to
make off with *Lulu*, Mueller Verlag had no legal obliga-
tion to delay publication, and offered the volume immediately. The collection of letters was released in 1964,
edited by the critic Franz Willnauer, who was in the awkward position of never having seen any of the original
sources, and thus having not the vaguest idea whether
Berg's words were Berg's, or whether they were the widow's belated ideas of what he might have said.

Among the 569 letters or parts of letters in the first edition, Erich Alban Berg found several that, in his opinion,
defamed the character of his father, Charly Berg. These
letters had to do with the administration and the ledgers
of the Berghof. The nephew sued, and the matter went to
trial. Willnauer, whose position had been untenable from
the start, testified that the widow had incorporated those
particular letters in order to tell the world how badly
Alban had been treated by his family. The court ruled
against the inclusion of the material in question, Willnauer paid a nominal fine, and the offending passages
were artlessly blacked out of the printed copies of the
book. Copies with the marked deletions quickly became
collectors' items. Helene took advantage of the situation
to do some further censoring of her own, so the German

edition of Berg's *Letters to His Wife* was chopped back in size and published without index, footnotes, or commentary.

For the English edition, translated and edited by Bernard Grun and published in London by Faber and Faber in 1971, annotations were provided, along with a polite explanation of the shrinkage; the cuts had allegedly been made to avoid repetition and to spare the reader the boredom of the details of family life. Four hundred and eighty-eight items remained.

Helene had not been able to stop publication of the letters, but all was not lost. She would see that *Lulu* was tied up for good, specifying in her will that the complete opera was never to be performed. She lived out the final years of her life in relative serenity, even when arthritis did not let her get around much anymore. As she approached her ninetieth birthday, in 1975, she made sure that her husband's archives would be equitably divided between the Austrian National Library and the Library of the City of Vienna, moving more and more papers out of her living quarters and into the eager hands of archivists. She had to spend some time in a wheel chair, but was still alert, attractive, and dedicated to her cause. When callers came and brought her flowers, she had them put on the piano as a gift for Alban.

By 1976, Helene Berg's physical decline became more marked, and she seemed distracted, tending to repeat herself and finding it harder and harder to adjust to new people and things around her. Her infirmity troubled her greatly: "Why doesn't the good Lord take me?" she asked Wolfgang Ploderer, one of the original members of the foundation board and son of the composer Rudolf Ploderer. She felt relatively strong during the first part of the summer of 1976, even though she decided to stay in

Vienna instead of moving out to the Waldhaus, as had been her custom. In August, she took a turn for the worse, and died at home, in the care of a nurse, on August 30, 1976.

Instantly, the *Lulu* issue was raised with renewed urgency. The Metropolitan Opera had planned its first production of the opera for March 18, 1977, and though the company went ahead with the then-standard two-act version (with the traditional parts of the Symphony tacked on the end), music director James Levine told the *New York Times* two months after Helene's death that he and his colleagues were "perfectly prepared (a) to finish it; (b) to copy it; and (c) to teach it to our principals." London's Royal Opera House would have been equally obliging, had fate so decreed.

The Vienna State Opera would also have welcomed the honor of producing the first complete *Lulu*. But as Stefan G. Harpner, one of the directors at Universal Edition, told the *New York Times,* "The devious methods of expression of any opera director in Vienna would not make it possible for him to express any desire directly." Since so many directors were expressing their desires very directly, Vienna's chances were nil.

Yet even before Helene Berg's will was probated, while the widow was, as Harpner put it, "hardly cold in her grave," a mysterious front runner emerged. The soprano Teresa Stratas, who had been the Metropolitan Opera's first choice to sing the title role, had bowed out, possibly because another company had offered her the chance to sing the first performance of the complete work. Pierre Boulez, whose music is also published by Universal and who was then the music director of the New York Philharmonic, was reported to have put the finishing touches on Berg's score already. Someone, it was said, had been led into the back room at Universal, witnessed the ceremonious unlocking of the vault, and been allowed to hold — but not to scrutinize — the complete *Lulu,* with notes filled in in what was supposedly Boulez's hand.

The front runner turned out to be the Paris Opera, represented by Boulez and its general director, Rolf Liebermann, another composer represented by Universal Edition. Having admitted that he had approached Helene Berg on the subject of presenting the complete *Lulu* as early as the mid-1950s, Liebermann finally announced that the long-anticipated second première of *Lulu* would take place on February 24, 1979, in Paris, with Boulez conducting, Miss Stratas as Lulu, and Yvonne Minton as the Countess Geschwitz, and direction by Patrice Chereau. Not long afterward, John Crosby, the founder and general manager of the Santa Fe Opera summer festival, made it known that the American première of the three-act version had been set for his 1979 season, in a production based on the sketches created by Rudolf Heinrich for the 1963 American première of the truncated version. Crosby also made it abundantly clear that the Metropolitan Opera never had had a real chance to introduce the three-act *Lulu* to America, and New York would have to wait to revive its 1977 production until the 1979–1980 season (with Stratas in the title role). While negotiating for rights to the two-act *Lulu* more than fifteen years earlier, Crosby had secured an agreement with the publisher that his festival would also be the first in the United States to stage the whole opera, at whatever time it should become available. Although Alfred Kalmus, the man with whom Crosby had been in contact at Universal, had died in the interim, a number of letters, cables, and memoranda were enough to prove to Kalmus's suc-

cessors that Crosby had long since won the American
race for the complete *Lulu*.

But which complete *Lulu?* Although Helene Berg's
will had specified that the work was not to be completed,
her order would not have withstood a test in the courts,
especially with Universal Edition ready and eager to deliver the complete score. No one believed that it had
taken Cerha years of work to prepare Act III for performance, but by spreading the "fifteen-year" rumor, Universal had lessened the danger of having to wage a legal
battle, since Helene's will had been written well after
Cerha began (and probably after he finished) his assignment. It was to Universal's benefit and to the benefit of
the Berg estate to release Act III. Indeed, the release
would be little more than a formality, since copies of the
last act as Berg left it and of the complete short score had
been circulating for some time in the musical un-
derground.

Some of the old-guard members of the foundation's
board of directors, however, still felt that the opera
should never be finished, because of its musical weak-
nesses, its immorality, or because they had become convinced that, in light of the difficult job facing an editor,
the work should remain just as the composer left it. In
addition, a number of composers resented Universal's
having chosen Cerha to prepare the work; among the
many people involved, Boulez was one of the very few
who were satisfied with the publisher's decision, and he
had no intention of undertaking the challenges posed by
Lulu's score. One composer explained that it was humi-
liating for Universal to have entrusted Cerha, a relatively
little known composer published by the house, with such
an important task. The irony was that Berg himself had
spent years doing similar staff and free-lance work for

Universal, and would probably have approved with understanding and enthusiasm.

The central figure in the final *Lulu* battles in Vienna was Gottfried von Einem, probably the city's most revered composer in the mid-1970s. Von Einem was adamantly opposed to letting the world meet *Lulu* in the Cerha version. Because he was a member of the board of directors of the foundation, von Einem's opinion counted.

As announcements were made, with no references to possible changes of plans, however, the chance of a battle diminished. With Universal Edition in command, and with the foundation obliged to do what was best for Berg's music and its finances, no individual was going to take credit or blame for perpetuating a musical cover-up. Furthermore, it was not worth the bother. The prevailing copyright laws made it necessary to wait only until 1985 before *Lulu* became public domain. Even the moral arguments, which so many Viennese still posed, were beginning to sound silly and stale.

The question that no one could answer was the final and crucial one: What path best served the interests of Berg's music? And the interesting corollary was not whether *Lulu* should have been finished, which was by now academic, but why the composer himself never got to the point where he could close the cover on the large manuscript books and say, once and for all, that *Lulu* was complete.

The case can be made that Berg did indeed have time to finish all of *Lulu*, even allowing for poor health, distractions, and time spent on the Violin Concerto, and that it was only his own lack of enthusiasm that was keeping him from putting down the last few notes. Practical-minded people will point out that, with no prospects of the opera's being performed during the years when his works were proscribed throughout Germany, there was certainly no hurry. But Berg always kept alive the hope that *Lulu* would be performed in Germany. And if he had really begun to lose interest in *Lulu* so late in the work's progress, would his instincts not have been to finish it quickly, rather than to linger over the all-but-completed score?

It could be that Lulu and her circle had become too sordid and distressing even for Berg, and that the two sides of his personality had entered into moral conflict. Was the man who wanted nothing more than to be the respectable, good-looking, honored *grand seigneur* struggling with another part of himself, the part that loved a woman other than his wife and had been ineluctably drawn to the amoral heroine of Wedekind's drama?

Or perhaps Berg feared that, in finishing *Lulu,* he would also be bringing to a close the time when he could move freely in his heroine's dark and dreamlike world, and would have to return to the realities of Vienna, the hypocrisy that surrounded him, the political turmoil, the loss of economic, moral, and social stability. It took courage for Alban Berg to write *Lulu.* Maybe, in the last days of his life, he was just beginning to realize how much.

Epilogue

THERE IS an old dictum that modern audiences are fifty years behind the music of their time, that even a masterwork of the twentieth century must wait five decades before it is accepted into the repertory. In many cases, the rule has applied: Mahler, Schoenberg, Webern, Varèse, Bartók, Ives, Janáček, and even, to some extent, Stravinsky, had to endure one or two generations of apathy or derision before their works were understood, and could be judged on strictly aesthetic grounds and heard without prejudice.

But the dictum never pertained to Alban Berg. If it had, we should just be discovering *Wozzeck* in the mid-1970s. Schoenberg wrote to Webern, right after Berg died, that Berg was the one of the three of them to have known success in his lifetime, the one who knew the warm feeling of acceptance and acclaim. If Berg had lived longer and written more, he could, perhaps, have known the kind of celebrity that belonged in the mid-twentieth century solely to the Stravinsky who wrote *Le Sacre du printemps* and *The Firebird*.

Between 1908, the year of the Piano Sonata, Opus 1, and 1935, the year of the Violin Concerto, *Lulu,* and his death, Berg wrote only thirteen works. If we add the Three Fragments from *Wozzeck,* the orchestration of the three middle movements of the Lyric Suite, and the *Lulu* Symphony, the total reaches sixteen.

In one respect, the numbers tell us very little; Pietro Mascagni is remembered only for his *Cavalleria Rusticana,* and Georges Bizet needed nothing other than *Carmen* to secure his place in history. Yet it is important to understand why Berg left us fewer works than he might have, and why he was so sensitive about what he felt to be his own lagging productivity that he decided to stop using opus numbers after he finished *Wozzeck,* Opus 7. He was a slow and painstaking worker, and he died at the relatively early age of fifty. More significant, however, is the fact that he lived and composed at the beginning of an era when writing music no longer means filling in the blanks, and when there are no longer formulas to be followed.

Haydn could write 104 symphonies, Mozart could write 25 piano concertos, Bach could write more than 250 cantatas, and Donizetti more than 80 operas, because each could apply his originality or genius to prescribed forms. Berg had no such advantage.

He could no longer end a movement or a piece with the traditional dominant–to–tonic cadence, because there was no longer a dominant or a tonic, so each time he had to search for new solutions to problems that had been solved for composers for more than two hundred years of history. Similarly, when Berg wrote a sonata, he had to deal with the old form as if it were brand new, since its old structures had been torn down. Hardest of all was the question of how to deal with opera in an age when such lavish forms of entertainment were no longer paid for by princes or kings, and when producers were discovering that their economic survival depended on the melodies of Puccini and Verdi, and not on the experiments of the avant-garde.

Yet Berg did more than solve the problems of cadences and sonatas; he assured his immortality in the extravagant, treacherous world of opera. Had he not written *Wozzeck* and *Lulu*, he would be remembered for the Lyric Suite, the Violin Concerto, and the Chamber Concerto, but his contributions to the art would probably be thought of as minor or incidental. He would be remembered as a composer of a few emotional instrumental works, and would probably have to be judged as someone who had never fulfilled his promise.

It is impossible to think of Berg as the composer of only these instrumental pieces, however, because it was his dramatic genius that marked the operas and informed the rest of his works. Listening to all of the music, one cannot help feeling that, practical considerations aside, the operas were the works that Berg had to write, and that everything else led up to or reflected them. Even forty years after his death, the name Alban Berg does not always spark recognition; the name *Wozzeck* almost always does, and once *Lulu* enters the repertory and loses its stigma as a fragmented curiosity, that name will be recognized, too. Some opera producers still think of *Wozzeck* and *Lulu* as modern works to be feared; yet audiences' reactions to these theatrical tours de force have proved — and will continue to prove — that genius does not need tonality or an old-fashioned love story in order to be able to communicate in the theater.

The very fact that Berg's primary achievements were in the unreal world of opera gives a clue to the reason

that Berg so promptly achieved fame and even a degree
of popularity for which his friends and colleagues could
never hope. Berg never wanted, or felt obliged, to forget
his heritage. Beyond that, he knew how to combine sincerely inspired nostalgia with fully contemporary idioms.
It can be argued that Berg was principally a modernist
and that his major contributions were in the realms of
musical advances; it can also be maintained that he was a
conservative, a sentimentalist, someone who bowed to
the new while paying homage to the old.

But neither extreme gives the full picture of the composer or his work. What Berg could do that eluded his
contemporaries and even many of his successors was find
a way to move forward without wrenching free of the
past. He kept the continuity, made his own mark without
breaking the chain that was so important not only to the
proud and reactionary Viennese, but to listeners all over
the world. Throughout the history of Western music, the
composers of greatest genius and greatest popular appeal
have seemed to come at the end of an era (Bach and Beethoven are only two); those who are considered to be important but whose music is relatively rarely heard were
the explorers who broke with the past (Schoenberg is
one; Monteverdi another). Berg worked at a time when a
break from tradition was necessary and unavoidable. But
he was a man of the theater, and he knew that communication depended on links and references. As a result,
he can be remembered for both his intellectual accomplishments and his musical ones; the combination is
more unusual than it would seem.

The question of influence is a harder one to deal with at
a time when musical heroes are the conductors and performers who present the music of Schubert, Beethoven,
Mahler, and Liszt, and when creators are splintered into

factions with little hope of having their music heard by anywhere near the number of people who witnessed *Wozzeck* in the first three years of its existence. The techniques of twelve-tone composition served their purpose and went out of fashion decades ago, only to be replaced by a variety of techniques, both human and electronic, none of which has become sufficiently pervasive to have played a dominant role in the contemporary development of the art. Schoenberg and his students in the New Viennese School did break through the bounds of an old aesthetic, but they did not leave in its place a new one that could survive in a rapidly changing society.

As an individual, Berg taught his own lesson. He proved that the past did not need to be denied, and he showed that opera was not dead. He did not leave a school or a theory book, but he brought music drama into the twentieth century. The mantle of the art form we call opera was handed from Monteverdi to Gluck to Mozart; to Rossini, Donizetti, and Bellini; to Wagner; to Verdi and Puccini and finally to Alban Berg. No younger composer has yet taken the mantle from Berg's shoulders, and until that time comes, twentieth-century opera will continue to be defined by *Wozzeck* and *Lulu*.

A Critical Discography
Select Bibliography
Notes
Index

A Critical Discography

This selective and subjective discography is drawn from recordings that are both available and well made. In instances where no recording is recommended (for instance, the Piano Sonata), interested listeners would be well advised to check among new releases, since a number of record companies have Berg's music either on their schedules or already on tape but not yet available.

Seven Early Songs: Heather Harper, soprano; BBC Symphony Orchestra, Pierre Boulez conducting; Columbia. Though out of print, this record can still be found in some stores, and is worth searching for.

Piano Sonata, Op. 1: No recommended recording.

Four Songs, Op. 2: Dietrich Fischer-Dieskau, baritone; Aribert Reimann, piano; Deutsche Grammophon. Again, some searching may be necessary before this recording is found, but it is fully worth the effort. The alternative is Heather Harper's performance on Angel, also excellent. Miss Harper includes the two settings of "Schliesse mir die Augen beide."

String Quartet, Op. 3: Two very fine performances of this work are available, one by the Alban Berg Quartet on Telefunken, and one by the LaSalle Quartet on Deutsche Grammophon.

Altenberg Songs, Op. 4: Compromise is essential here. One may select either the very fine singing of Bethany Beardslee (with Robert Craft conducting on Columbia) or the expert conducting of Pierre Boulez (with Halina Lukomska, also on Columbia).

Four Pieces for Clarinet and Piano, Op. 5: Expertly performed by clarinetist Richard Stolzman and pianist Peter Serkin, on the Orion label.

Three Orchestral Pieces, Op. 6: Conductor Boulez and the BBC Symphony offer an energetic and accurate performance on the Columbia recording, which also includes the Altenberg Songs and the Chamber Concerto. The four-record Schoenberg-Berg-Webern set performed by the Berlin Philharmonic and conductor Herbert von Karajan on Deutsche Grammophon is more expensive, but the rewards are proportionally greater. In addition to Berg's Opus 6 and the composer's arrangement of three movements from the Lyric Suite for string orchestra, the Karajan-DG package includes three works by Schoenberg (*Pelleas und Melisande, Verklaerte Nacht,* and the Variations for Orchestra, Opus 31), and four by Webern (Passacaglia, Opus 1; Five Movements, Opus 5; Six Pieces for Orchestra, Opus 6; Symphony, Opus 21).

Wozzeck: The Deutsche Grammophon recording with Karl Boehm conducting is preferable to the Columbia set with Boulez, but it is good to be able to make the choice between two high-quality performances.

Chamber Concerto: Again, the Boulez–BBC Symphony disc on Columbia can be recommended (which is fortunate, since it is also the only recording currently in wide distribution). The soloists are pianist Daniel Barenboim and violinist Sachko Gawriloff.

Lyric Suite: Both the Alban Berg Quartet and the LaSalle Quartet pair the Lyric Suite with the Op. 3 String Quartet (on the Telefunken and Deutsche Grammophon labels, respectively). The Karajan–Berlin Philharmonic four-record set of music from the New Viennese School includes the three central movements of the Lyric Suite in Berg's orchestration for strings.

Der Wein: No recording currently available.

Violin Concerto: Among several good recordings, the performance by violinist Arthur Grumiaux, with Igor Markevitch
conducting the Concertgebouw Orchestra, is outstanding
(on Philips).

Lulu: Here again, Karl Boehm's version on Deutsche Grammophon is preferable to the out-of-print Angel recording
conducted by Leopold Ludwig. The renaissance of interest in
Lulu in its entirety, however, promises new recorded treatments of the work.

PUBLISHER'S NOTE

Some of the author's recommended recordings may not be readily
available in Great Britain. The following additional recordings are available at the time of going to press:

Piano Sonata, Op. 1: Fellegi (Hungaroton/Selecta); Barenboim
(Deutsche Grammophon)

String Quartet, Op. 3: Kohon Quartet (Decca)

Altenberg Songs, Op. 4: London Symphony Orchestra, conducted by
Abbado (Deutsche Grammophon)

Four Pieces for Clarinet and Piano, Op. 5: de Peyer and Crowson
(Solstice/Rediffusion); Pay and Barenboim (Deutsche Grammophon)

Three Orchestral Pieces, Op. 6: LSO, conducted by Abbado (Deutsche
Grammophon)

Chamber Concerto: Prague Chamber Ensemble, conducted by Pesek
(Pinnacle/Supraphon); Budapest Chamber Ensemble, conducted
by Mihaly (Hungaroton/Selecta); InterContemporain Ensemble,
conducted by Boulez (Deutsche Grammophon)

Lyric Suite: Ramor Quartet (Decca/Turnabout); New York Philharmonic, conducted by Boulez (CBS)

Der Wein: New York Philharmonic, conducted by Boulez (CBS)

Violin Concerto: Czech Philharmonic Orchestra, soloist Suk, conducted by Ancerl (Pinnacle/Supraphon); BBC Symphony Orchestra, soloist Menuhin, conducted by Boulez (EMI/HMV)

Lulu: Vienna Philharmonic, conducted by Dohnanyi (Decca)

Select Bibliography

Adorno, Theodor W. *Berg, Der Meister des kleinsten Uebergangs.* Vienna, 1968.

Berg, Erich Alban. *Alban Berg: Leben und Werk in Daten und Bildern.* Frankfurt, 1976.

Berg, Helene, ed. *Alban Berg: Letters to His Wife.* English edition translated and annotated by Bernard Grun. London, 1971.

Blaukopf, Kurt. *Mahler, A Documentary Study.* London, 1976.

Buechner, Georg. *Complete Plays and Prose.* Translated, with an introduction, by Carl Richard Mueller. New York, 1963.

Carner, Mosco. *Alban Berg: The Man and The Work.* London, 1975.

Champigneulle, Bernard. *Art Nouveau.* Translated by Benita Eisler. Paris, 1972.

Comini, Alessandra. *Gustav Klimt.* New York, 1975.

Friedell, Egon. *A Cultural History of the Modern Age.* Translated by Charles Francis Atkinson. New York, 1954.

Hilmar, Ernst. *Wozzeck von Alban Berg.* Vienna, 1975.

Hilmar, Rosemary. *Alban Berg: Leben und Wirken in Wien bus zu seinen ersten Erfolgen als Komponist.* Vienna, 1978.

Iggers, Wilma A. *Karl Kraus: A Viennese Critic of the Twentieth Century.* The Hague, 1967.

Janik, Allan, and Stephen Toulmin. *Wittgenstein's Vienna.* New York, 1973.

Kolneder, Walter. *Anton Webern: An Introduction to His Works.* Translated by Humphrey Searle. Berkeley, 1968.

Kraus, Karl. *Literatur und Luege.* Vienna, 1929.

Krellmann, Hanspeter. *Webern.* Hamburg, 1975.

Leibowitz, René. *Schoenberg and His School.* Translated by Dika Newlin. New York, 1949.

Mahler Werfel, Alma. *And the Bridge Is Love.* Translated in collaboration with E. B. Ashton. New York, 1958.

Redlich, Hans Ferdinand. *Alban Berg: The Man and His Music.* New York, 1957.

Reich, Willi. *The Life and Work of Alban Berg.* Translated by Cornelius Cardew. London, 1965.

———. *Schoenberg: A Critical Biography.* Translated by Leo Black. London, 1971.

Roth, Ernst. *The Business of Music.* London, 1969.

Scherleiss, Volker. *Alban Berg.* Hamburg, 1975.

Schnitzler, Arthur. *My Youth in Vienna.* Translated by Catherine Hutter. New York, 1970.

Selz, Peter. *German Expressionist Painting.* Berkeley, 1957.

Stein, Erwin, ed. *Arnold Schoenberg: Briefe.* Mainz, 1958.

Strobl, Alice. *Gustav Klimt.* Translated by Inga Hamilton. New York, 1976.

Webern, Anton. *The Path to the New Music.* Edited by Willi Reich; translated by Leo Black. Bryn Mawr, Pennsylvania, 1963.

Wedekind, Frank. *The Lulu Plays.* Translated, with an introduction, by Carl Richard Mueller. Greenwich, Connecticut, 1967.

Wellesz, Egon. *Arnold Schoenberg: The Formative Years.* London, 1971.

The Newsletter of the International Alban Berg Society is published under the auspices of the doctorate program in music of the City University of New York, 33 West 42nd Street, New York, New York, 10036.

The music of Alban Berg is published by Universal Edition, Vienna.

Notes

Translations are by the author unless otherwise noted.

CHAPTER I

page

4 studying religion, German: Further details of Berg's school-
ing are given in Rosemary Hilmar, *Alan Berg: Leben und
Wirken in Wien bis zu seinen ersten Erfolgen als Komponist*
(Vienna, 1978); Appendix 2, pp. 168 ff.

6 "Certain facility . . . talent": H. F. Redlich, *Alban Berg: The
Man and His Music* (New York, 1957), p. 225.

6–7 "My dear Hermann . . . for ever": Quoted in Willi Reich,
The Life and Work of Alban Berg, trans. Cornelius Cardew
(London, 1965); see also the manuscript of Hermann
Watznauer's biography of the composer (1929) in the Library
of the City of Vienna.

10 Bach's suites: complete information printed in R. Hilmar,
Alban Berg, Appendix 3, pp. 173 ff.

11 "Heiliger Himmel": The first page of this manuscript is
reprinted in Erich Alban Berg, *Alban Berg: Leben und Werk in
Daten und Bildern* (Frankfurt, 1976), p. 77.

12 ff. Frida Semler's full account of her summers at the Berghof
was printed in the Newsletter of the International Alban
Berg Society, December 1968.

15 "my living ideal": Letter to Watznauer, August 1, 1904, Pierpont Morgan Library, New York.

17 "I'm too dull . . . Finding nothing": Reich, *Berg,* pp. 15–16.

CHAPTER 2

22 "breaking through . . . aesthetic": From Schoenberg's notes to the program of January 14, 1910; quoted in Willi Reich, *Schoenberg, A Critical Biography,* trans. Leo Black (London, 1971), p. 49.

22–23 "His was a . . . his own creation": Egon Wellesz: *Arnold Schoenberg: The Formative Years* (London, 1971), p. xv.

23 "even music . . . used to": Letter to Watznauer, July 16, 1903, Pierpont Morgan Library.

23–24 "a little child . . . heroes": Letter to Watznauer, August 1, 1904, Pierpont Morgan Library.

25–26 "In the girls' . . . October": *Neue Musikalischen Presse,* October 8, 1904.

26 Berg's list of song titles is reproduced in Erich Alban Berg, *Alban Berg,* p. 90.

26–27 "In the condition . . . orchestration": *Arnold Schoenberg: Briefe,* ed. Erwin Stein (Mainz, 1958), p. 8.

27 "In art . . . imitation": Wellesz, *Arnold Schoenberg,* p. 45.

28 A complete accounting of the property inherited by Johanna Berg can be found in R. Hilmar, *Alban Berg,* pp. 19–20.

29 "Friend and . . . other": Hanspeter Krellmann, *Webern* (Hamburg, 1975), p. 18.

31 "represents . . . music": René Leibowitz, *Schoenberg and His School,* trans. Dika Newlin (New York, 1949), p. 251.

32 "The atmosphere . . . of the hall": Wellesz, *Arnold Schoenberg,* p. xi.

32–33 "The scene . . . hall first": *Arbeiter-Zeitung,* January 2, 1909.

35 "Now, next autumn . . . good": Letter to Frida Semler, July 1907, Library of Congress; also quoted in Reich, *Berg,* p. 21.

35 "the really new . . . modern works": Reich, *Berg,* p. 22.

37–38 "When Alban . . . great man": Original in Arnold Schoenberg Institute, University of Southern California, Los Angeles; also quoted in Redlich, *Alban Berg,* p. 245.

38–40 "Two things . . . his composing": Original in Arnold Schoenberg Institute, Los Angeles; also quoted in R. Hilmar, *Alban Berg*, p. 40.

CHAPTER 3

44 "I hope . . . glory": Letter to Watznauer, October 18, 1906, Pierpont Morgan Library.

44 "She looked . . . battles": Erich Alban Berg, *Alban Berg*, p. 19.

45 Altenberg's "H.N." is reproduced in Erich Alban Berg, *Alban Berg*, p. 121.

47 "For twenty-eight . . . eternity": Helene Berg ed., *Alban Berg: Letters to his Wife*, trans. and annotated Bernard Grun (London, 1971, hereafter referred to as *Letters*), p. 11.

47 "With your . . . D Minor": *Letters*, p. 19.

47–48 Isn't it . . . of love": Ibid.

48 "Well . . . letter": *Letters*, p. 20.

56 "out of . . . benefit": Letter to Frida Semler, July 1907, Library of Congress.

59 "After a long . . . Monday evening": *Illustrierte Wiener Extrablatt*, April 26, 1911.

CHAPTER 4

61 "Somebody had . . . job": *Musikblaetter des Anbruch*, commemorative issue celebrating Schoenberg's fiftieth birthday, Vienna, September 1924.

65 "feverish . . . necessity": Anton Webern, *The Path to the New Music*, ed. Willi Reich, trans. Leo Black (Bryn Mawr, Pennsylvania, 1963), p. 47.

66 "It is really . . . dead": Webern, *Path*, p. 47.

66 "that at present . . . music": Webern, *Path*, p. 37.

68 "a proving ground . . . thorough school": Quoted in Allan Janik and Stephen Toulmin, *Wittgenstein's Vienna* (New York, 1973), p. 67.

69 "There is no . . . purpose": Wilma A. Iggers, *Karl Kraus: A Viennese Critic of the Twentieth Century* (The Hague, 1967), p. 110.

70 "Adolf Loos . . . an urn": Quoted in Janik and Toulmin,

Wittgenstein's Vienna, p. 89.

70 "I command . . . independent": Quoted in Janik and Toulmin, *Wittgenstein's Vienna*, p. 102.
71 "things became . . . hands": *Letters*, p. 29.
72 "He was . . . studio": Alma Mahler Werfel, *And the Bridge Is Love*, trans. with E. B. Ashton (New York, 1958), p. 12.

CHAPTER 5

74 "But the man . . . culture": Alessandra Comini, *Gustav Klimt* (New York, 1975), p. 6.
78 "happy family . . . brandy": *Letters*, p. 39.
78 "hidden, romantic . . . sweetness": *Letters*, p. 42.
79 "I can see . . . perfection": *Letters*, p. 63.
79 "empty delusion . . . Americans": *Letters*, p. 85.
84–85 "It is true . . . engaged to her": *Letters*, p. 106 ff.
86 "almost . . . pieces": Undated letter, Library of City of Vienna.
87 "The idiom . . . Berg": *Illustrierte Wiener Extrablatt*, April 26, 1911.
87 "four fair-haired . . . musicians": *Letters*, p. 324.
87 "artistically . . . prize": *Letters*, p. 325.
91 "My dearest . . . Amen": *Letters*, p. 123.
92 "No one . . . work": Reich, *Berg*, p. 34

CHAPTER 6

97 "absolutely . . . play": R. Hilmar, *Alban Berg*, p. 111.
97 "sixty-six . . . strings)": R. Hilmar, *Alban Berg*, p. 64.
98 "a loose . . . form": R. Hilmar, *Alban Berg*, p. 66.
99 "Speak . . . that": R. Hilmar, *Alban Berg*, p. 73–74.
99 "for having . . . success": Undated letter to Schoenberg, Library of Congress.
99 "coming to grief . . . life": Reproduced in Erich Alban Berg, *Alban Berg*, p. 131.
100 "genius . . . sterility": Reprinted in its entirety in Reich, *Berg*, p. 36.
100 "How despondent . . . Mahler": Redlich, *Berg*, p. 231.
102 "Go ahead . . . orchestra": R. Hilmar, *Alban Berg*, p. 93.

105 "unique . . . sentimentality": From the notes to the Columbia recording.

106 "obvious . . . awkward": R. Hilmar, *Alban Berg*, p. 93.

107 "dangerous . . . fresh": R. Hilmar, *Alban Berg*, p. 95.

108–109 "Anton Webern . . . hissing": *Die Zeit*, April 2, 1913.

109 "I laughed . . . depression": Wellesz, *Schoenberg*, p. 35.

109 "The master . . . with me": Reich, *Schoenberg*, p. 73.

CHAPTER 7

110 "The whole . . . away": Reich, *Berg*, p. 41.

110 "I haven't . . . circumstances": *Letters*, p. 159.

115 "As for the . . . other day": *Letters*, p. 160

116 "I only know . . . of nature": Letter to Schoenberg, July 20, 1914, Library of Congress; quoted in Mosco Carner, *Alban Berg, The Man and The Work* (London, 1975), p. 27.

116 "But I must . . . serious beauty": Reich, *Berg*, p. 41.

118 "If what . . . always remain so": Letter to Schoenberg, November 1915, Library of Congress.

118 "made . . . life": Letter to Schoenberg, June 8, 1914, Library of Congress.

118 "lots of important . . . inside me": *Letters*, p. 158.

119 "giving lessons . . . own thinking": Ibid.

119 "Now my work . . . about it": *Letters*, p. 161.

119 "very tender . . . put together": *Letters*, pp. 162–63.

120 "You know . . . completely healed": *Letters*, p. 163.

120 "paternal . . . wrong with it": Redlich, *Berg*, p. 68.

121 "projects . . . two and a half years": Letter to Schoenberg, November 1915, Library of Congress.

122 "I have to ask . . . last compositions": Redlich, *Berg*, p. 67.

124 "I don't need . . . *Pastoral*": Volker Scherliess, *Alban Berg* (Hamburg, 1975), p. 58.

126 "more complicated . . . before": Ibid.

127 "a performance . . . rehearsals": Reich, *Berg*, p. 114

127 "The Præludium . . . march itself": Quotes in Reich, *Berg*, p. 115.

CHAPTER 8

128 "So, war . . . amazed": R. Hilmar, *Alban Berg*, p. 113. (The year is misprinted in Mrs. Hilmar's book; it should be 1914.)

128–129 "Even here . . . to report": Letter to J. Polnauer, August 1, 1914, Library of City of Vienna.
129 "I must . . . longer": R. Hilmar, *Alban Berg*, p. 113.
129 "shameful . . . events": Letter to Schoenberg, August 24, 1914, Library of Congress.
129 "even . . . war": Letter to Schoenberg, September 8, 1914, Library of Congress.
129 "Can I . . . morning": *Letters*, p. 165.
130 "I breathed . . . at all": Ibid.
130 "will give . . . power": Letter to Schoenberg, December 15, 1914, Library of Congress.
130–131 "I sometimes . . . spirit is": *Letters*, p. 170.
131 "I couldn't . . . two weeks": *Letters*, p. 177.
131–132 "Life *outside* . . . form": Letter to Schoenberg, January 1, 1915, Library of Congress.
132 "The way . . . public favor": *Ostdeutsche Rundschau*, May 1, 1915.
134 "a not . . . phase": Letter to Schoenberg, June 20, 1915, Library of Congress.
134 "like everybody . . . the rest": *Letters*, p. 178.
134 "going down . . . glutton": *Letters*, p. 179.
135 "a constant . . . superiors": *Letters*, p. 184.
135 "This is Hell . . . clothes on": *Letters*, p. 185.
136 "The beds . . . get over": Ibid.
136 "marching . . . and so on": *Letters*, p. 187.
136–137 "bronchial . . . duties": *Letters*, p. 189.
137 "Report at . . . straight": R. Hilmar, *Berg*, p. 120.
138 "It has been . . . sitting up": *Der Wiener Tag*, December 25, 1936. Reprint of letter to G. Kassowity, December 25, 1915.
138 "more than enough . . . regular": *Letters*, p. 192.
140 "You are very . . . as I": Newsletter of the International Alban Berg Society, January 1971.

CHAPTER 9

142–145 Quotes taken from the score and from the libretto provided with the Columbia recording, Pierre Boulez conducting; trans. Eric Blackall and Vida Harford.
146 "Peace . . . perjured judge": *Georg Buechner: Complete Plays and Prose,* trans. and ed. Carl Richard Mueller (New York, 1963), p. 169.

147 "the word *must* . . . this thought": Mueller, *Buechner,* p. xiii.
147–148 "The dramatic poet . . . for Schiller": Mueller, *Buechner,* p. xviii.
149 "I demand . . . beauty": Mueller, *Buechner,* p. 150.
153 "because . . . do it": Ernst Hilmar, *Wozzeck von Alban Berg* (Vienna, 1975), p. 10.
155 "to render . . . extra-musical": Quoted in full in Reich, *Berg,* p. 63.
157 "There is a . . . occurred to me": *Letters,* p. 229.
157 "polyphonic. . . groaning": R. Hilmar, *Alban Berg,* p. 119.
158 "already . . . planning": E. Hilmar, *Wozzeck,* p. 20.
158 "I fill . . . crucial scenes": Letter to Webern, August 19, 1918, Library of City of Vienna.
161 "I was always . . . for the theater": Letter from Schoenberg to Emil Hertzka, October 24, 1921, Universal Edition.

CHAPTER 10

164 Chart in Reich, *Berg,* p. 121.
170 "a symphony . . . voice": Leibowitz, *Schoenberg,* p. 168.
174 "He kept on . . . feel annoyed": *Letters,* p. 306.
174 "Schoenberg . . . Chamber Concerto": *Letters,* p. 315.
177 "one of the . . . him myself": *Letters,* p. 317.
178 "all went well . . . the press": Letter to Webern, June 17, 1924, Library of City of Vienna.
182 "the whole orchestra . . . rehearsal": *Neues Wiener Journal,* February 14, 1926.
182 "under the . . . Kleiber": *Letters,* p. 344.
183 "Be glad . . . manage it": *Letters,* p. 347.
183 "terrific . . . fantastic": *Letters,* p. 349.
184 "tortured . . . orgy": From *Wozzeck und die Musikkritic* (Vienna: Universal Edition, 1926).
185–186 "The best thing . . . disappeared": Letter to Schoenberg, November 10, 1926, Library of Congress.
186 "colossal successes . . . calls": *Musikblaetter des Anbruch,* vol. VIII, no. 1, 1926.
186 "Aaron Berg . . . Berlin": E. Hilmar, *Wozzeck,* p. 54.
187 "tumultuous success": *Letters,* p. 360.
187 "the fairy tales . . . for all": Letter from Schuler to Hertzka, March 14, 1929, Universal Edition.

187 "a wonder": Letter to Watznauer, March 5, 1921, Pierpont Morgan Library.

188 "the unexpected . . . this Wozzeck": *Abendzeitung*, June 19–20, 1957.

188–189 "You know . . . everything": Letter from H. Jalowetz to Berg, March 1934, Universal Edition.

CHAPTER 11

190 "starving . . . first course": *Letters*, p. 224.

191 "Schoenberg . . . good calibre": *Letters*, p. 225.

195 "checking . . . tenents, etc": *Letters*, p. 250.

196 "today was . . . of the Berghof": *Letters*, p. 251.

196 "Here I am . . . in the war": Reich, *Berg*, p. 51.

197 "It has always . . . cannot take it": Letter to Schoenberg, January 15, 1920, Library of Congress.

198–199 "she could live . . . myself for it": *Letters*, p. 262.

199 "I think . . . in the summer": Reich, *Berg*, p. 51.

200–201 "Believe me . . . of existence": Reich, *Berg*, p. 52.

CHAPTER 12

204 "all the secrets . . . works": *Letters*, p. 310.

209 "at long last . . . come of it": Letter to Schoenberg, July 12, 1923, Library of Congress.

209 "forgive . . . elephantiasis": Ibid.

210 "pretend to . . . will come": *Letters*, p. 333.

210 "Tell the doctor . . . clean little soul": *Letters*, p. 335.

211 "psychoanalysis . . . cure": Quoted in Janik and Toulmin, *Wittgenstein's Vienna*, p. 75.

211–212 "a little memorial . . . in threes": *Pult und Taktstock*, February 1925.

214 "on the one hand . . . of an hour": Ibid.

216 "If in this . . . for once": Ibid.

218 "Berg's . . . work": From the notes to the Columbia recording.

CHAPTER 13

222 "If only . . . like love": *Letters*, p. 154.

223 "I'm sure . . . enjoy life": *Letters*, p. 70.

224 "committed . . . act": Carner, *Alban Berg,* p. 19.

226–227 "the musical . . . simple life": *Letters,* p. 337.

227 "the most . . . world": *Letters,* p. 341.

227–228 "The taxi . . . same of you": Ibid.

228 "Mopinka . . . charms": *Letters,* p. 342.

229–230 "Not a day . . . with you in thought": *New York Times,* March 27, 1977.

231 "the artist . . . life": Reich, *Berg,* p. 34.

231 "a latent opera": Theodor Adorno, *Berg, Der Meister des kleinsten Uebergangs* (Vienna, 1968), p. 110.

232 "literally . . . drama": Newsletter of the International Alban Berg Society, June 1977.

236 ff. Perle's complete analysis appeared in the Newsletter of the International Alban Berg Society, June 1977.

245 "Slowly I am . . . into limbo": Newsletter of the International Alban Berg Society, January 1971.

245–246 "That's why . . . free style": Newsletter of the International Alban Berg Society, January 1971.

246 Maegaard's article was translated by Joan Allen Smith and Mark DeVoto and reprinted in the Newsletter of the International Alban Berg Society, January 1975.

248 "This fear . . . at my side": *Letters,* p. 112.

250 "The twenty-five . . . years (1900–1925)": *Die Musik,* February 1930.

250 "the words . . . composition": Redlich, *Berg,* p. 131.

CHAPTER 14

255 "For God's . . . eternal rest": Frank Wedekind, *The Lulu Plays,* trans. and ed. Carl Richard Mueller (Greenwich, Connecticut, 1967), p. 26.

255 "What is there . . . spirituality": Ibid.

258 ff. From the libretto printed in the score by Universal Edition, with reference to Arthur Jacobs's English translation on the libretto to the EMI/Angel recording of the opera.

265–266 *"Eine Seele . . .* as he pleases": *Die Fackel,* June 9, 1905, and July 1925; also in Karl Kraus, *Literatur und Luege* (Vienna, 1929), and in Reich, *Berg,* p. 157 ff.

267 "a spiritually . . . instinctive": Carner, *Berg,* p. 198.

267 "The curse of . . . instincts": Frank Wedekind, *Pandora's Box*, Act I, Scene 1.

CHAPTER 15

269 "real theater . . . think": Letter to Schoenberg, January 10, 1927, Library of Congress.

270–271 "completely natural . . . circles": *Letters*, p. 366.

273–274 "Theirs were . . . a pistol": Egon Friedell, *A Cultural History of the Modern Age*, trans. Charles Francis Atkinson (New York, 1954), vol. III, pp. 299–300.

274 "My early black . . . and pain": Peter Selz, *German Expressionist Painting* (Berkeley, 1957), p. 165.

282 "had composed . . . right": *Letters*, p. 380.

282 "one big *ossia*": Adorno, *Berg*, p. 122.

CHAPTER 16

284 "I hope . . . in me": Letter to Schoenberg, May 18, 1930, Library of Congress.

284 "hand in hand . . . a long time . . . the inversion": Letter to Schoenberg, August 7, 1930, Library of Congress.

287 "In the description . . . and beautiful": Carner, *Berg*, p. 201.

292 "In the finale . . . of the action": Scherliess, *Berg*, p. 120.

294 "The artist . . . so beloved": Reich, *Berg*, p. 168.

CHAPTER 17

299 "I have . . . New York": Reich, *Berg*, p. 80.

300 "it pleased . . . appointments": Redlich, *Berg*, p. 238.

301 "The first . . . Czech accent": *Letters*, p. 361.

301 "like . . . sewer": Letter to Schoenberg, November 6, 1928, Library of Congress.

301–302 "Can you . . . on the right": *Letters*, p. 374.

302 "I dozed off . . . gleaming": *Letters*, p. 375.

302 "a genuine . . . undergraduates": *Letters*, p. 376–77.

303 "Journeys for art . . . motoring": *Letters*, p. 383.

303 "The countryside . . . and so on": *Letters*, pp. 384–85.

304 "complete . . . from Brussels": *Letters*, pp. 391–92.

305 "Of the few . . . greatest": The entire speech is reprinted in Reich, *Berg*, pp. 84 ff.
306 "We are . . . concentration camp": Letter to Schoenberg, December 9, 1933, Library of Congress.
307 "One thing . . . the pity": *Letters*, p. 398.
307 "The Nazis . . . to anybody": *Letters*, p. 400.
308 "In Italy . . . the scale": *Letters*, p. 407.
308–309 "Wilhelm Furtwaengler . . . twaddle": *Letters*, p. 413.
309 "What a fate . . . to live": Redlich, *Berg*, p. 239.
310 "at a time . . . is free": Reich, *Berg*, p. 91.
311–312 "Another, more . . . quite cool": *Letters*, p. 415.
312 "refuge . . . behind": *Letters*, p. 416.
312 "quiet confidence . . . firmer": *Letters*, p. 418.
313 "A project . . . touched up": Reich, *Berg*, pp. 92–93.
314 "the die . . . performance": Scherliess, *Berg*, p. 114.
315 "a little . . . Lulu": Scherliess, *Berg*, p. 115.
317 "*Heil* . . . Berg": Recounted by Reich, who represented Berg at the première.
318 "Imagine . . . Germany": Carner, *Berg*, p. 68.
319 "Honored . . . respect": Reprinted in Reich, *Berg*, p. 96.
320 "I am . . . opera": Carner, *Berg*, p. 70.
320 "You would . . . persecuted": Reich, *Berg*, p. 98.
321 "On this picture . . . bolshevism": Letter to Frau Hertzka, February 27, 1935, Universal Edition; also Reich, *Berg*, p. 99.
322 "I, who . . . composer": Library of the City of Vienna.

CHAPTER 18

324 "From May . . . Concerto": Reich, *Berg*, p. 99.
325 "I am more . . . succeeded": Letter to Louis Krasner, July 16, 1935, Library of Congress.
329–330 "frightfully . . . pleasure": Reich, *Berg*, p. 101.
330 "profoundly depressed": On November 4, 1935, Reich, *Berg*, p. 103.
330 "friendly . . . day": *Letters*, p. 429.
331 "Carinthian . . . life": *Letters*, p. 432.
331 "I don't . . . walk": *Letters*, p. 433.
332 "in spite . . . persist": Letter to Schoenberg, November 30, 1935, Library of Congress.

333 "toothache . . . place": Ernst Roth, *The Business of Music* (London, 1969), p. 150.

333 "If only . . . upbeat": Reich, *Berg*, p. 104.

CHAPTER 19

335 "Deeply . . . admiration": *Letters*, p. 436.

335 "thanks . . . work": *23*, February 1, 1936.

335 "It is too . . . enjoyed it": E. Hilmar, ed., *Arnold Schoenberg Gedenkausstellung* (Vienna, 1974), p. 61.

336 "To think . . . last work": *Die Reihe*, vol. 2, 1955.

340 "and the orchestral . . . Symphony": Reich, *Berg*, p. 176.

340–341 "but even . . . masterpieces": Redlich, *Berg*, p. 202.

342 "It is a . . . as such": *Schweizerische Musikzeitung*, July 1937.

349–350 "It is interesting . . . Webern-ite music": Austrian National Library.

351 "Alban Berg's . . . from God": *Letters*, p. 437.

355 "In the concluding . . . in opera": Newsletter of the International Alban Berg Society, December 1976.

358 "perfectly prepared . . . grave": *New York Times*, October 31, 1976.

Index

No 339 Ber (Mon)